TOLEDO

TREASURES AND TRADITIONS

TOLEDO

TREASURES AND TRADITIONS

INTRODUCTION BY
JAMIE FARR

ART DIRECTION BY
KAREN GEARY

SPONSORED BY THE
TOLEDO AREA
CHAMBER OF COMMERCE

URBAN
TAPESTRY
SERIES
TOWERY
PUBLISHING, INC.

CONTENTS

by Jamie Farr

Tony Bennett may have left his heart in San Francisco. Frank Sinatra may have found Chicago his kind of town, and he may have made it in New York, New York, as well.

But I found my soul in Toledo, and I wouldn't trade it for either of their discoveries.

I don't remember the exact hour, or the day, or the month, or even the year that I fell in love with this irresistible city by the Maumee River. By the way, Maumee is an American Indian name. I don't know what the word means, and I don't know which tribe named the river. However, since I am Lebanese, I was hoping the tribe would have had good relationships with the Lebanese. Actually, Lebanese sounds Indian. Instead of bows and arrows being shot at you, we would have shot shishes and kabobs.

I also fell in love with humor in Toledo, and with acting, and with people. I give Toledo great credit for this. Maybe you have to have a sense of humor to live in Toledo. After all, this is a city that gets picked on all the time. It's like a punch line for every joke about American cities: ". . . but at least we're not in *Toledo!*" You supply the joke; that's the sort of punch line I'm talking about.

This is really unfair, because Toledo is a great little city, with all sorts of wonderful amenities that just blow people away when they come here for the first time. Sure, Toledo has taken quite a few hits, but it has been voted more than once as an All-America City. Those of us who know the city just smile about all of this, because we know something the rest of the country doesn't: that Toledo is really a terrific place to work, or to raise a family, or to visit on vacation. ➤

Greetings from

8

was born in 1934 in Toledo, and spent most of my childhood and teen years living in the North End—the end of town where the streets are named after either the Great Lakes or trees. In the years I spent growing up, I lived on Erie, Superior, and Michigan. That takes care of the lakes. We also lived on Magnolia and Mulberry. So much for the trees. With the one exception on Magnolia Street, all of the houses we lived in were duplexes, and most of the time we had the upstairs. I always felt sorry for the renters below us, especially when my mother made me take accordion lessons from Trick Brothers in downtown Toledo. I always wanted to give the downstairs neighbors free earplugs and a music "depreciation" book.

My mother was born in Cedar Rapids, and at the age of 17, she met my father, who had just emigrated with his brother from Lebanon. After a short and arranged courtship—thanks to my grandfather—they were married and moved to Sioux City. In 1924, my sister was born, and shortly thereafter, my family decided to move to greener pastures—that's right: Toledo.

It was a blue-collar town, no doubt about it, with lots of big industry in automotive products and heavy machinery. It offered—and still does—a good mix of midwestern simplicity and eastern sophistication. Back in the 1930s, though, what I experienced wasn't what you'd call sophisticated. There were gravel playgrounds in the school yards in our neighborhood, but most of the kids played in the alleys instead.

My sister attended the Stickney grade school on (wouldn't you know it?) Stickney Avenue. However, I attended LaGrange Elementary. It was just across from the Erie Thomas Pie Company, a company that produced all kinds of delicious pies in various sizes. Their headliners: the regular, large size, and a smaller, 10-cent version, with apple, cherry, rhubarb, and various berry fruits. During the spring months, because of a lack of air-conditioning, to stay cool our school left the windows open for circulation, and we could smell those wonderful aromas coming from the pie company. They had a greater ability to instill temptation in us than anything the devil offered at the time.

That pie company is no longer in existence, but I swear the aromas are still there. ➤

Budapest
RESTAURANT
PARKING ONLY

In addition to the pie company, LaGrange Street had a number of other interesting establishments on it. There was the LaGrange Street Pool Hall, where you could rack up balls and rack up debts very quickly, if you were not a good player or if you didn't cheat. Then there was the Band Box, a nightspot where you could dance, drink, or even die if you didn't know how to street fight. And sometimes even knowing how to street fight wouldn't stop someone from dying. The lucky ones walked out with broken bones and broken relationships; the others were carried out feet first.

Not far away from the Band Box was the J and J Sweet Shop, a fancy name for the local beer joint owned by Bobby Jacobs, who happened to be comedian Danny Thomas' cousin. You could be guaranteed a fight on the weekend, with someone invariably being tossed through the front plate-glass window. On Monday mornings, it seemed like there was always a wooden board covering the damage.

If a double-feature movie and serial and short subjects were your interest, there was the Mystic neighborhood theater, right next door to the North End Fire Station. The firemen got in for nothing. When a fire call came, the firemen in the theater were alerted by alarms that the Mystic had installed inside the auditorium as a courtesy. Many a movie was interrupted by the clanging of those in-house alarms. One time, the theater itself caught fire, which meant that the alarm in the theater went off, and the firemen dutifully ran next door to the firehouse, only to put on their helmets and grab their hoses so they could run back inside the theater to douse the fire. It would have made a good episode in a Keystone Kops serial.

Across the street was Hanf's Drug Store, a great place for phosphates, sodas, and ice-cream sundaes at the fountain counter. Above Hanf's Drug Store was a hall that was used for dances. Because our neighborhood was composed of many ethnic groups, there were all types of dances going on: Polish, Greek, Arabic, Jewish, Italian, German, Hungarian. I don't recall any Chinese or Japanese, but those are the only two I can think of that didn't rent that hall. Toledo is still like this—a city with lots of different ethnic groups, lots of what we today call diversity. ➤

TOLEDO

There were big-time nightclubs in Toledo, of course, but I was too young to get into most of them, so I never went to any of them—and that's the truth! Kasee's Night Club was like the ones you see in 1940s Warner Brothers black-and-white movies—all polished chrome and draped tablecloths and shiny, marble dance floors. Kin Wa Low's was a Chinese eatery with good entertainment; both the food and the show were usually good. The Ace of Clubs was a nightspot owned by Danny Thomas' brother, Bill Jacobs.

There were, thankfully, plenty of North End places that did admit young people. There was the Friendly Center Community Center, the Boys Club, the Swing Inn Canteen (great for get-togethers after football games on Friday night), and the Riverside Park Shelter. All were great spots to meet with friends, and by and large, they offset the rough and tough establishments where the grown-ups and older youths hung out.

Riverside Park is, today, near and dear to me for several reasons, one of them obvious. Not only did I used to play there as a kid, but it was also the place where I went to sit on a swing and watch the river on the evening before I left for California to pursue my dream as an actor. And today, it's a great honor to know that this park has been renamed Jamie Farr Park. I can only hope that others will enjoy it as much as I have.

There's always been plenty to do in Toledo. Again, this is contrary to national opinion, which somehow maintains that we roll up the sidewalks at sundown. This may have been true for a brief time, but it's not that way any longer.

Mention Toledo to any Toledoan, and immediately their chest swells with pride for our city treasures. The Toledo Museum of Art, for instance, is one of the finest in the Midwest. It has been offering exhibitions and a very fine permanent collection since 1901. The museum—as locals have come to call it—just put up a new wing that's very, very modern, and that complements the

Jamie Farr
Park
Toledo, Ohio

This park is dedicated to Jamie Farr, Actor and Comedian, born and raised in North Toledo, graduate of Woodward High School, star of stage, screen and television who brought joy to millions of people around the world and who always remembered his home town. "May I and this park always serve you well and make you proud. May Jamie Farr Park be always safe for children to play in, families to congregate in, lovers to walk in and most importantly, for dreamers to dream in."

June 1999

older building very well. When I was a child, there was a big exhibit at the museum called *Toledo Tomorrow* that showed what Toledo was going to look like in the future. I don't recall the details, but I'd swear that Toledo today is pretty much what that *Toledo Tomorrow* exhibit said it ought to look like.

Then, there's the Toledo Zoo, started in 1900. The zoo is one of the finest in the country, with everything from cuddly koalas to prehistoric-looking rhinos, and some 600 other species as well. In all, there are about 4,000 permanent animal residents at the zoo. As a sign of just how well respected the zoo is, when the pandas came from China in 1988, the Detroit Zoo didn't get them, but the Toledo Zoo did.

In addition to those two stellar attractions, you've got one of my favorite all-time pastimes: the Toledo Mud Hens minor-league baseball team. In what promises to be the finest minor-league ballpark in the country, hands down, our downtown stadium will ensure that the Mud Hens tradition is kept alive for decades to come. The stadium is state-of-the-art, offering all the modern amenities without giving up any of the old-time elements that make baseball so special.

I'm happy to see downtown making such a comeback, because I've got all sorts of special memories associated with this part of Toledo. Like most American cities, downtown Toledo sort of sagged a little in the 1970s, but recent developments have made it stronger and better than ever.

Summit Street, the street that runs down by the Maumee River, had a great number of open markets, which sold the best fish, meats, poultry, vegetables, fruits, fresh flowers, and canned goods. Summit Street was also the home of Tiedtke's, the best general store I have ever seen. Whatever you needed, Tiedtke's had it: food, clothes, tires, tools, hardware, appliances, you name it. The store was the forerunner of Costco and Sam's Club, but in addition to its low prices, it was famous for having the largest piece of cheese I have ever seen—sitting on a counter at the front of the store. The salespeople would cut off hunks of it

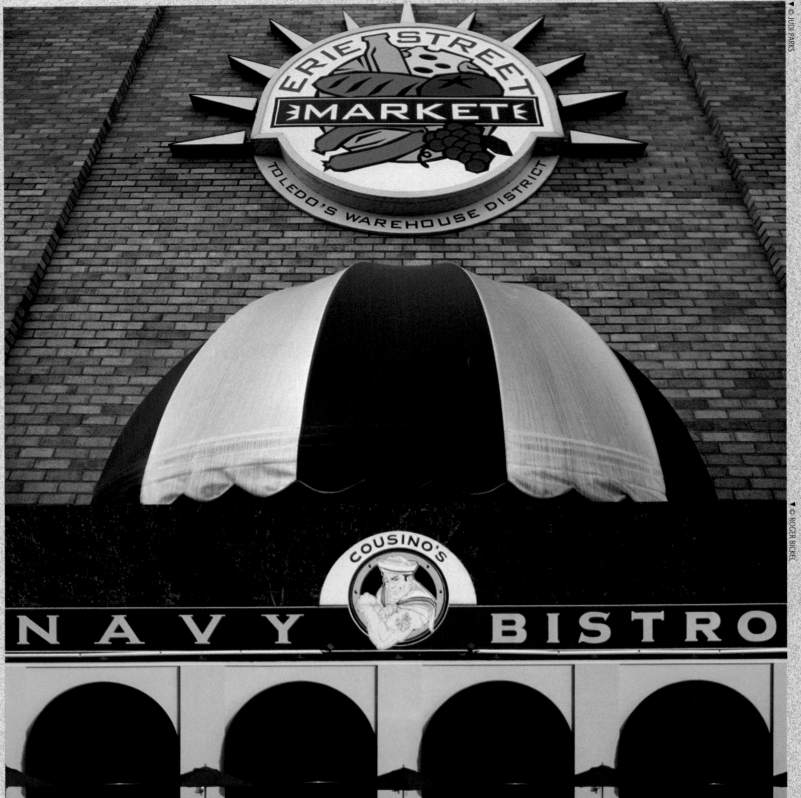

ERIE STREET MARKET

TOLEDO'S WAREHOUSE DISTRICT

COUSINO'S

NAVY BISTRO

and sell it to customers. The store seemed enormous—several stories tall—and it was always packed with people. I can still recall the salivating aroma of freshly brewed coffee permeating the entire store. The cry was always "Meet me at Tiedtke's." Alas, the cry is now gone, because Tiedtke's is gone.

Today, there's Erie Street Market down there, a big, central marketplace that we didn't have when I was growing up. It's sort of replaced all the many smaller, open-air markets that once flourished in the area.

In addition to shopping, there were always good eating places in the heart of downtown: Williams Cafeteria, a fun place to have lunch before you went off to the movies; Eppes Essen, a great Jewish deli, with a long counter and booths and the most wonderful kosher smells in northwest Ohio; and then there was my favorite—Tony Packo's—for those delicious hot dogs with chili and hot peppers and pickles. My mouth is watering now, just remembering them.

And who could forget one of the favorite meeting—and eating—places for the young and old, Chili Mac's. For a quarter, you could get the greasiest chili (or, some said, the chilliest grease) served on a mound of spaghetti and lined with the stalest soda crackers anywhere. You'd leave the joint with the worst heartburn—but with the best taste and the best bargain in town. It always reminded me of one of Will Rogers' lines: about how chili was the world's most economical food because you can eat it once and enjoy it for three days. Sadly, Chili Mac's went the way of Tiedtke's, and is now but a memory.

But, there are now many, many other eating places—all creating indelible memories like these—for those who are fortunate enough to patronize them. Everyone's got their favorite, and to try to list even a few would hurt feelings and cause fights because of all the great ones I'd have to leave out. Let's just say that downtown Toledo isn't hurting for great places to go out and have dinner to suit just about anybody's taste. And now, across the river from Summit Street, there are even more great restaurants, with transportation to and from them by boat. ➤

That one street—Summit Street—is now home to all sorts of new and refurbished establishments that take full advantage of the river. The SeaGate Convention Centre has spurred a lot of development, with new hotels and office buildings springing—sometimes soaring—up around it. And, with the restaurants and shopping and nightspots that actually stay open past sunset, the whole area is flourishing and full of people into the late-night hours.

The performing arts are thriving as well. Toledo once had several great movie theaters downtown—they were tabernacles, shrines, cathedrals to watch films in. The motifs then were Egyptian, Gothic, Grecian, and Awesome. Unfortunately, most of those gorgeous buildings were torn down to make way for progress—like parking lots.

Fortunately, we still have the Valentine Theatre, which dates back to the 1890s, and which has been refurbished and turned into quite a venue. The Valentine Theatre is now home to such organizations as the Toledo Symphony, Toledo Opera, Toledo Repertory Company, and Toledo Ballet. These are terrific troupes, and they're blessed to have such a lovely, lovely venue to call home, just as the city is blessed to have them.

Industry has always been important to Toledo. Good old American blue-collar traditions, the work ethic, family values—all have been mainstays of Toledo's culture. Some of our famous industry names have been Toledo Scale, DeVilbiss Vaporizers, Champion Spark Plug, and Auto-lite Products. But, no more. Industry was hit hard in Toledo, and the city is no longer known strictly as a blue-collar, manufacturing community.

There are still a number of industrial businesses that are thriving. The former Willys-Overland Jeep Company, now DaimlerChrysler; Dana Corporation; Owens Corning; Owens-Illinois, Inc.; Libbey Glass Inc.; and Ford Motor Company—these are just a few of the businesses that still make Toledo something of an industrial center.

But the economy, like the population, has become diversified, meaning that service industries, agriculture, finance, even tourism are strong sectors. ➤

COURTESY OF JAMIE FARR KROGER CLASSIC

And, of course, there's recreation. It may not be the top money earner among local business sectors, but it's the richest one in my heart. In addition to all sorts of parks and playgrounds and nearby camping facilities, Toledo features some of the best golf courses in the country—perhaps in the world—and I'm proud to be able to host my annual LPGA tournament right here, in my hometown, where the golf is unparalleled.

The golf course at Inverness is listed as one of the top 100 courses in the world. Decades ago, it was the first golf course to allow the professional touring players to use its locker room; at the time, the clubs didn't let the touring pros use the locker rooms because they were considered gypsies or vagrants or something, and the clubs thought they'd come in and mess up the fine locker rooms that were reserved for members only. Inverness is so highly regarded that it customarily hosts the prestigious PGA Championship every few years.

And then, there's the Highland Meadows Golf Club, which is also close to my heart, since it's the place where we host the Jamie Farr Kroger Classic LPGA tournament each summer. This tournament, which I've been honored to host since 1984, has so far distributed more than $3.5 million to 50 local children's charities.

This, of course, humbles me and honors me and makes me grateful to be a part of the whole thing. But there's one other emotion that I have surrounding the golf tournament that not many people know about: I get a great kick each year out of inviting all these people—from all over the world—to my hometown, to Toledo, to play golf. I know the ones who haven't been here probably have this slightly horrified reaction—Toledo?—when I tell them where the tournament's going to be held. After all, they've heard all the jokes, and like you, they probably know all the punch lines by heart.

And then, the golfers come here and they can't believe what a great place Toledo turns out to be. It defies all of the jokes, all of the expectations that they have. They can't believe the friendliness and cooperation of the people here, or the beauty of the area, or the spirit of the city. And the last thing they say to me, when the tournament is over, is that they can't wait to come back next year.

And that, for me, is the best punch line in the world. ★

Greetings FROM
TOLEDO
OHIO
Amphitheatre
Walbridge Park

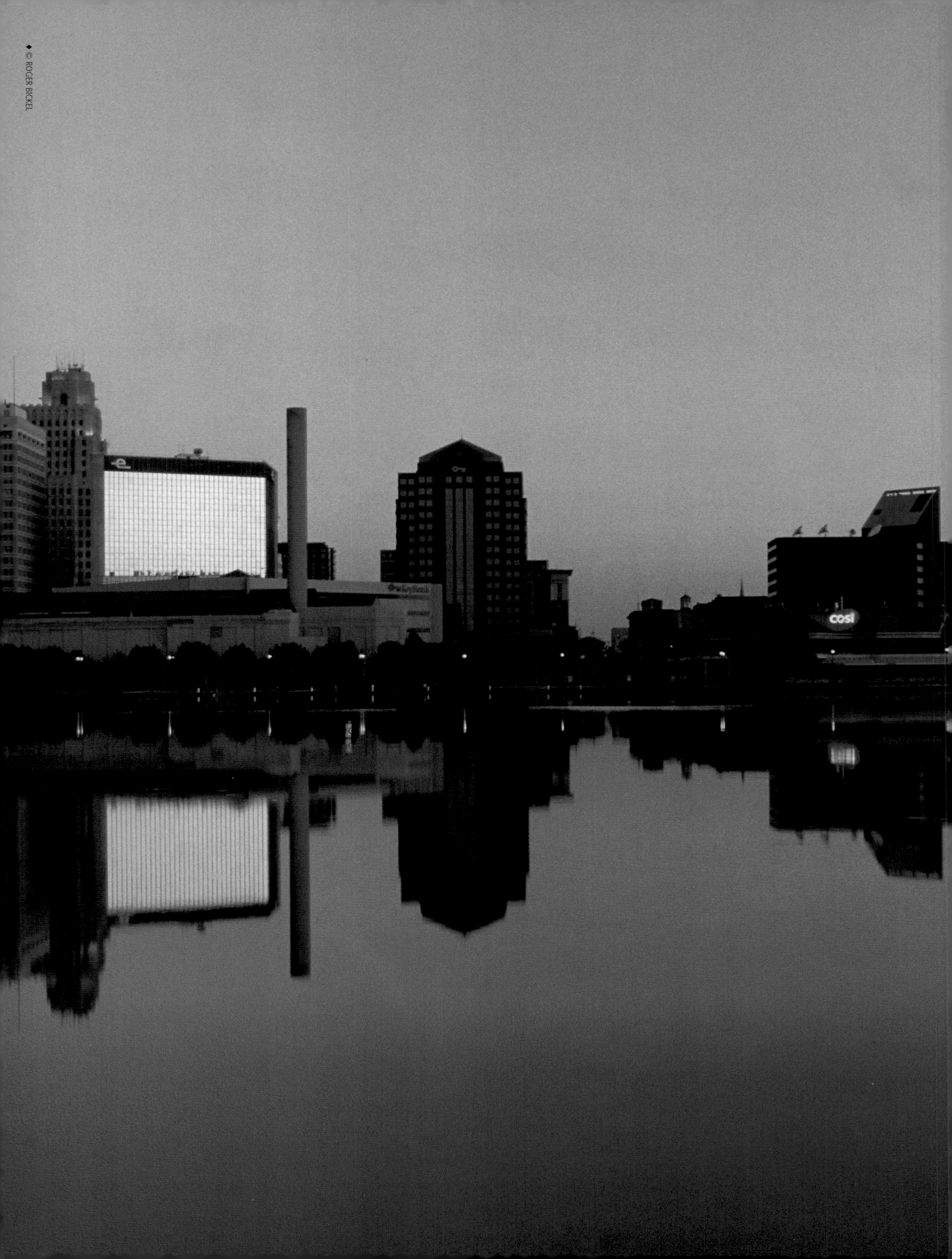

◆ © ROGER BICKEL

NESTLED ON THE SHORES OF Lake Erie and bisected by the Maumee River, the city of Toledo reflects its population's diversity and spirit.

THESE ARE THE PEOPLE IN YOUR neighborhood: A sense of warm, welcoming friendliness pervades Toledo's communities, home to approximately 320,000 Ohioans.

RIBBIT: POISED FOR SUCCESS, Toledo blends its sense of humor with its sense of enterprise. Local artist Steve Muncey (ABOVE, ON RIGHT) created the prototype hopper (ON LEFT) for the city's *It's Reigning Frogs* exhibit, held in summer 2001. Covered with colored glass, the sculpture represented the city at a public art exhibit at Lincoln Park Zoo in Chicago. Toledo's creative atmosphere has attracted many businesses to sectors like historic Fort Industry Square (OPPOSITE, PAGES 30 AND 31), helping local enterprises leapfrog over the competition.

FORT INDUSTRY SQUARE

COSi
Science
Center
← BUS

ONE
WAY
←

EXCEPT

TOLEDO ISN'T JUST BLOWING smoke when it honors its storied history. In nearby Perrysburg stands Fort Meigs, which was built in 1813 to help defend the Northwest against the invading British armies. Each Sep-tember, the fort—one of the largest wooden walled fortifications in the United States—hosts reenactments of that famous battle, in addition to many other historical events held throughout the year.

BRONZE, GRANITE, AND MARBLE commemorate Ohio's military heroes. A tribute to Commodore Oliver Hazard Perry, who gained a victory over the British at the Battle of Lake Erie in 1813, the Perry Monument (LEFT) in Perrysburg is a bronze re-creation of a marble statue sculpted by William Walcutt in 1860. The original is now housed at Put-in-Bay. Erected in 1929, the Battle of Fallen Timbers Monument (OPPOSITE) marks the legacy of General "Mad" Anthony Wayne.

TOLEDO

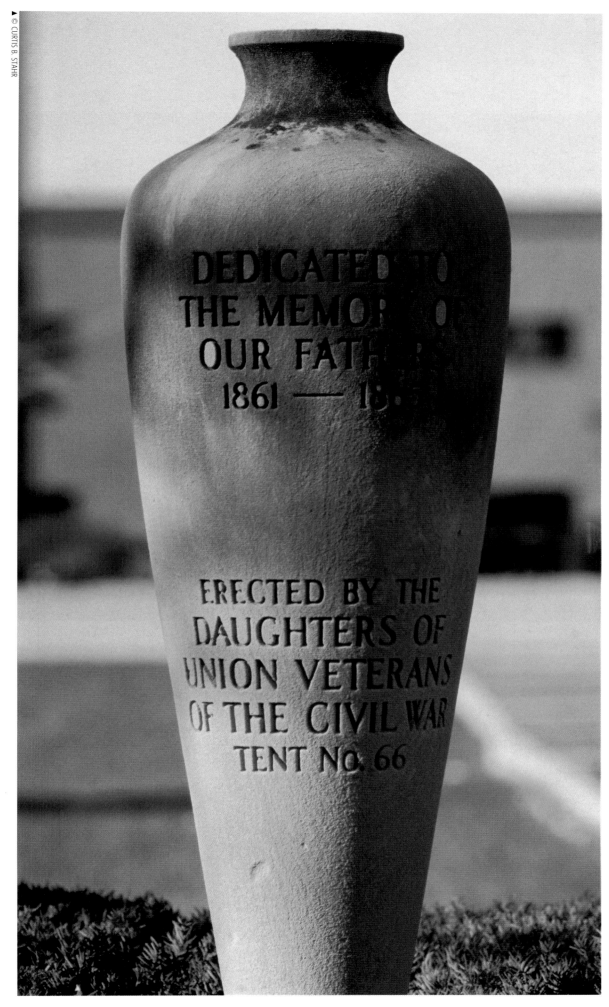

DEDICATED TO
THE MEMORY OF
OUR FATHERS
1861 — 18

ERECTED BY THE
DAUGHTERS OF
UNION VETERANS
OF THE CIVIL WAR
TENT No. 66

REMINDERS OF TOLEDO'S participation in the Civil War abound throughout the region, from the Civil War Urn (LEFT) in the city's Civic Center Plaza to the granite-and-stone soldier's monument standing more than 18 feet high (OPPOSITE) in Hood Park in Perrysburg.

RESIDENTIAL FLOURISHES AND fine architectural details lend style and splendor to Toledo's historic Old West End district. One of the largest neighborhoods of late Victorian, Edwardian, and Arts and Crafts houses in the United States, the Old West End contains the former residences of many of the city's most prominent politicians and businessmen.

THANKS TO THE CITY'S PRESER-vation efforts, many of Toledo's historic buildings have found new life as restaurants and inns. Serving up American fare in a unique atmosphere, the Linck Inn (LEFT) is located in the former Commercial Building, which was constructed in 1836 and today stands as the oldest commercial structure in Maumee. In the Old West End neighborhood, several residences have been transformed into moneymakers: The Old West Inn (OPPOSITE TOP) is a bed-and-breakfast, and the Mansion View Inn (OPPOSITE BOTTOM) opens its doors for conferences and other special events.

Lucas County Courthouse

700 Adams Street

TOLEDO SALUTES ITS LOCAL, state, and national heritage in proud displays of the Ohio and U.S. flags. A monument outside the Lucas County Courthouse (OPPOSITE)–listed on the National Register of Historic Places since 1973–pays tribute to native son William McKinley, who served his country as two-term governor of Ohio and two-term president.

LOCATED A SHORT DRIVE FROM Toledo in Fremont, Ohio, the Hayes Presidential Center commemorates the legacy of the 19th president of the United States, Rutherford B. Hayes. The center, which is situated on Hayes' expansive Spiegel Grove estate, encompasses the Hayes Library (ABOVE), the first presidential library in the country; a museum housing some 13,000 historical artifacts; and the president's residence (OPPOSITE), where he died in 1893. Another historic residence, the Wolcott House (PAGE 46)—originally built in 1827 and now a part of the Wolcott Museum Complex—gives visitors a glimpse of life during the 19th century.

WHETHER THEIR INTERESTS are horticultural or merely cultural, visitors to the Toledo Botanical Gardens (PAGES 47-49) will encounter a great deal to feed their fascinations. In addition to landscapes sculpted with a wide variety of plants and flowers, the garden houses the Peter Navarre Log Cabin (OPPOSITE), which contains the Pioneer Life exhibit.

G ETTIN' HITCHED GOES A LONG
way in the Toledo lexicon.
From the quaint confines
of local businesses to the bonds
of holy matrimony, togetherness
casts a long shadow.

SPRAWLING OVER MORE THAN 17 acres just outside Elmore, Ohio, Schedel Arboretum and Gardens explodes in a palette of natural colors. The attraction—containing countless species of plants, as well as waterfalls and lakes that are home to fish and waterfowl—is owned and operated by the nonprofit Joseph J. and Marie P. Schedel Foundation.

EAT YOUR VEGGIES: THE TOLEDO Farmers' Market, established in 1832, sells a cornucopia of produce, meats, and flowers, all grown by farmers around the region.

56

FARMLAND COVERS TENS OF thousands of green acres across Lucas County, yielding crops of produce and herds of livestock. While the area's cattle industry remains small, many farmers are working to beef up their production.

TOLEDO'S HOSPITALS AND PHYSI-
cians stand ready to respond
quickly and efficiently to
emergencies around the area.
A major tool in this crusade, St.
Vincent Mercy Medical Center's
Life Flight service enlists a small
fleet of state-of-the-art Dauphin
helicopters to transport patients
to medical facilities throughout
Ohio and Michigan.

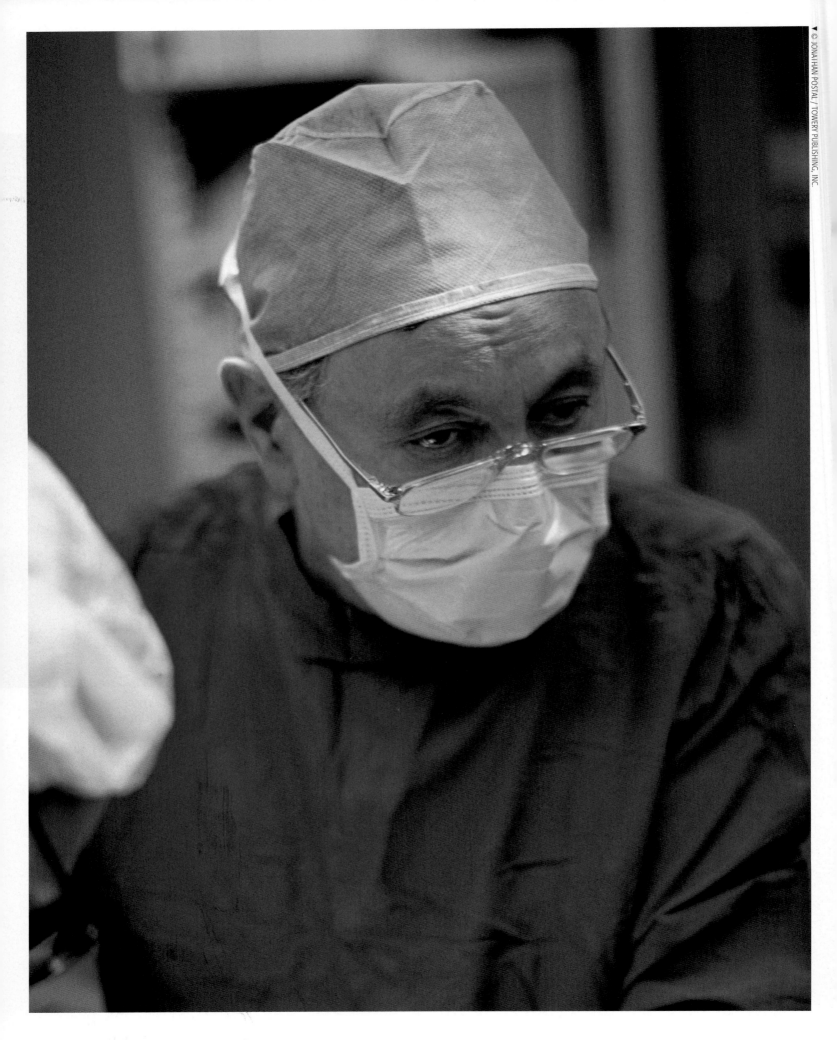

TOLEDOANS ARE IN GOOD HANDS at the city's numerous hospitals and medical centers, which provide an array of top-notch services and facilities.

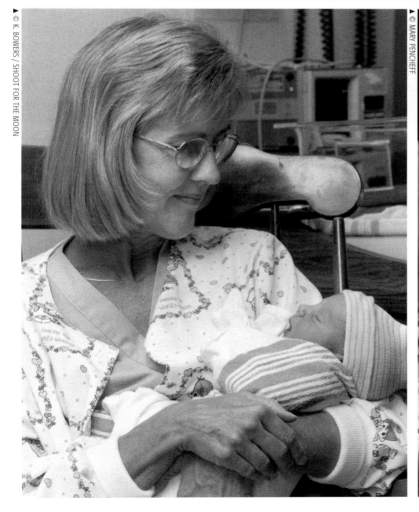

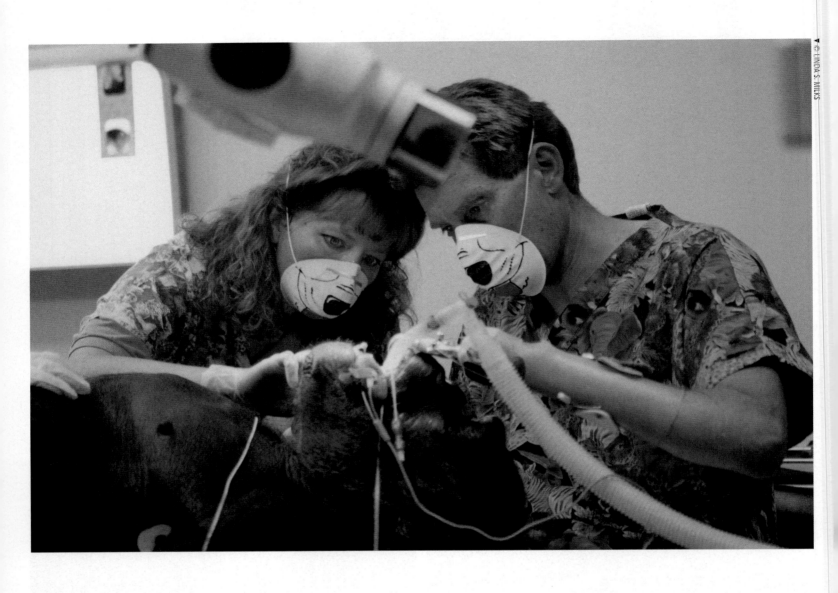

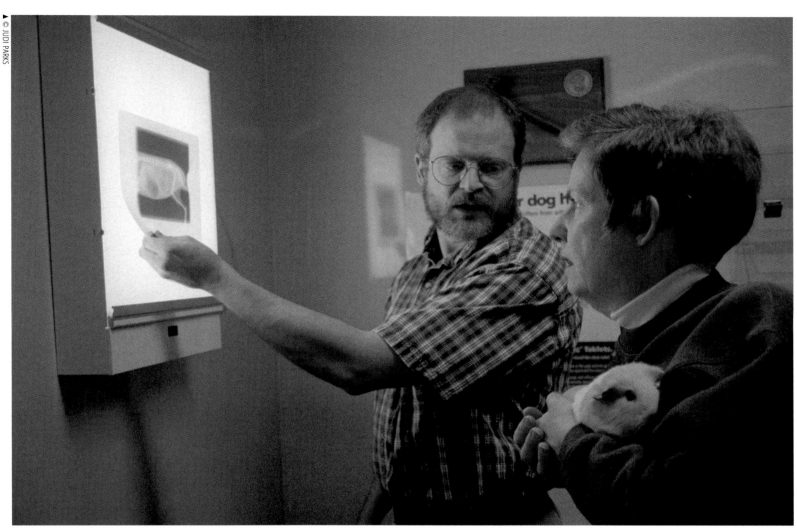

ATTENTIVE MEDICAL CARE IN Toledo extends well beyond the human race. At Countryside Animal Hospital in Sylvania, David Drake, DVM (ABOVE, ON LEFT), works to keep area creatures in tip-top shape. Specially trained keepers at the Toledo Zoo make sure animals such as Elaine the gorilla get regular medical and dental check-ups (OPPOSITE).

PURPLE PASSION: WHEN RESI-
dents want to treat them-
selves royally, they pick up
a pastry at one of Toledo's many
fine bakeries or spring for a make-
over at any of the beauty parlors
in the area, including the Willow
Creek Salon, owned and operated
by Mary Anne Johnson (OPPOSITE,
ON RIGHT).

WITH A LOT OF CLASS AND an excellent national reputation, the University of Toledo provides rigorous academic courses in an engaging social atmosphere. The institution, which enrolls more than 20,000 students on several campuses, offers some 200 student organizations and more than 150 degree programs in eight colleges.

TOLEDO

WORKING WITH LOCAL organizations and businesses, Toledo's universities and colleges—including the Medical College of Ohio (OPPOSITE BOTTOM) and Owens Community College (OPPOSITE, TOP LEFT)—graduate highly skilled students into the regional workforce. Located just a few miles south of Toledo, Bowling Green State University (ABOVE) enrolls more than 19,000 students in its undergraduate, graduate, and doctoral programs.

WORKING TO GIVE CHIL-
dren many opportuni-
ties to learn and play,
the Toledo-Lucas County Public
Library (LEFT) and the Toledo Public
Schools system (OPPOSITE) offer
protective, provident environments
where young imaginations can
flourish.

72

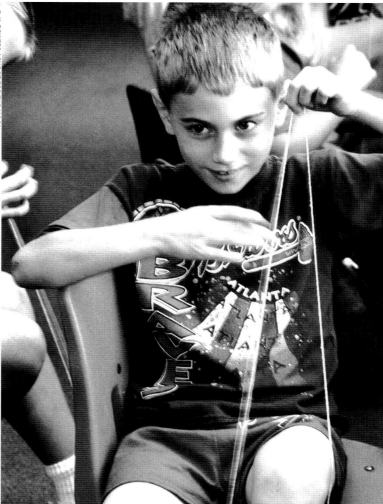

MAKE A JOYFUL NOISE: AREA students experiment with makeshift instruments in area classrooms (ABOVE). Through outreach programs like Community Music Lessons, mem- bers of the Toledo Symphony give children a chance to attend concerts and to create music of their own (OPPOSITE AND PAGES 74 AND 75).

WITH A FLAIR FOR THE innovative and the ingenious, Toledo encourages curiosity at a young age. When she was 10 years old, Becky Schroeder-Perry (RIGHT) received her first patent for a clipboard that allows people to write in the dark, making her the youngest female inventor in the world. Today, with 14 domestic and five international patents, she continues to work with phosphorescent materials and encourages creativity in children through school programs for gifted and talented students.

LOCATED IN THE HEART OF downtown Toledo, COSI— the Center of Science and Industry—wows kids and adults alike with its interactive exhibits. The High Wire Cycle helps children reach new heights—20 feet, to be exact—and learn about equilibrium and gravity as they pedal across an inch-thick wire that stretches the length of the atrium.

WITH EIGHT DIFFERENT Learning Worlds— including Whiz Bang Engineering, MindZone, Water Works, and Life Force—COSI will put a smile on every child's face as it reveals strange and amazing new discoveries through a number of special exhibits and events.

82

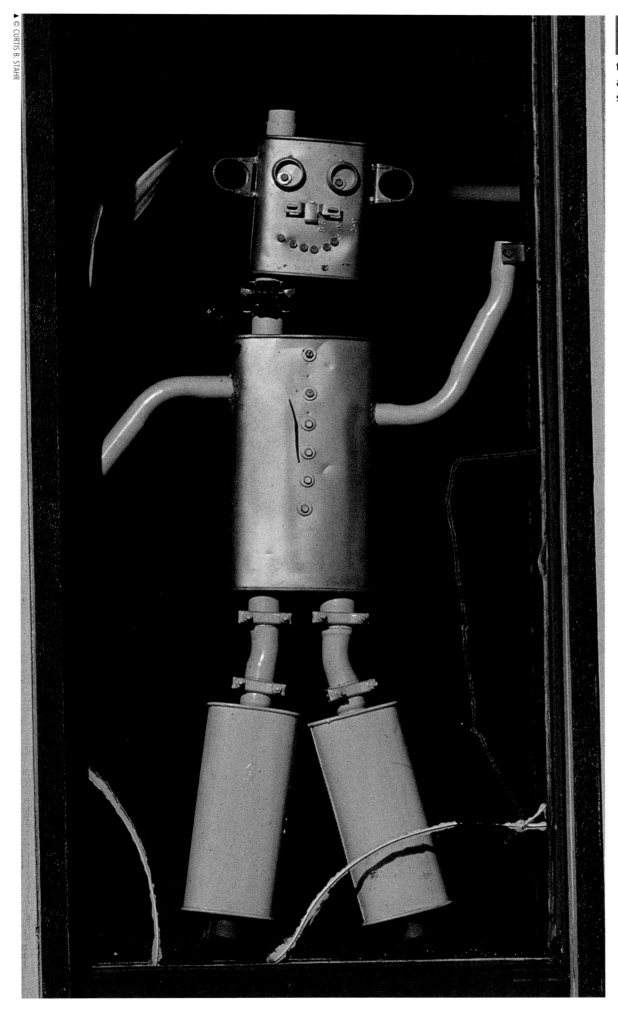

NHABITING ADVERTISEMENTS AND public spaces, Toledomatons thrive throughout the city and take steps to greet passersby with a friendly wave or a nuts-and-bolts smile.

© ERIC WUNROW

ZOOM AND VROOM: FOR THE excitement of professional auto racing, fans can motor over to events at the Toledo Speedway or trek a little further to attend races at venues like the Mid-Ohio Sports Car Course (ABOVE AND OPPOSITE) in Lexington.

THE PAST AND THE FUTURE OF automotive innovations merge in Toledo, former production site of some 20,000 Jeepster recreational vehicles (OPPOSITE BOTTOM), now considered classic antiques. The new Jeep Liberty (OPPOSITE TOP) started rolling off the assembly line at the equally new—and highly mechanized—Toledo North Assembly Plant in May 2001. The $1 billion facility will produce right- and left-hand drive Liberty models for some 90 countries.

S PARKING SUCCESS IN THE CITY'S industries—which include plastics, glass, and primary and fabricated metal products— Toledo's dedicated labor force consists of highly trained, highly skilled workers. A major scene of commercial activity, the Toledo-Lucas County Port Authority (PAGES 90 AND 91) helps bolster the city's reputation as a transportation hub.

WILLIS B. BOYER

ERIE PRODUCTS

WILLIS B. BOYER
THE CLEVELAND-CLIFFS STEAMSHIP

EACH YEAR ALONG THE MAUMEE River, more than 800 lake and overseas vessels transport a variety of cargo—such as coal, grain, iron ore, and petroleum products—to and from the Port of Toledo (ABOVE AND PAGES 92 AND 93). Commemorating the city's legacy as a shipping center is the 617-foot S.S. *Willis B. Boyer* (OPPOSITE), which is moored at International Park and houses artifacts and exhibits maintained by the Western Lake Erie Historical Society.

FROM SHIP TO SHORE, A LITTLE flexibility goes a long way. A parade-balloon replica of Smokey the Bear (ABOVE) probably could have benefited from a bit of engineering expertise incorporated into the Martin Luther King Jr. Memorial Bridge (OPPOSITE), which opens up for tall vessels along the Maumee River.

■N THE SWIM OF THINGS: THE Toledo Zoo offers unique, underwater views of many of its animals. Hippopotamuses take a rest in freshwater pools at the Hippoquarium (TOP), while the Arctic Encounter (OPPOSITE)—the largest exhibit in the zoo's history—features a 1,600-square-foot pool where polar bears paddle along in search of fish.

ESTABLISHED IN 1900, THE Toledo Zoo showcases more than 700 types of animals in their natural habitats, ranking it fourth in the nation for number of species. Each year, more than 850,000 members of the human species visit the park to view their animal counterparts.

TALENT OF ELEPHANTINE PROportions: The Toledo Zoo is full of creative creatures. Helping animals at the zoo feel right at home, local artist Forest LaPlante (ABOVE) painted the habitat backdrops with foliage and scenery.

MUSIC SOOTHES THE SAVAGE beasts at the Toledo Zoo—and attracts lots of humans, too. On Sunday evenings during the summer, the Toledo Concert Band, under the direction of conductor Samuel Szor, delights crowds of music lovers from around the region with its free Music Under the Stars concert series at the zoo's amphitheater.

THE ROUSING AROMA OF RACKS of ribs beckons thousands of area families to Toledo's Promenade Park for the annual Northwest Ohio Rib-Off. A trad-ition since 1987, the event features nearly 20 area and national restaurants competing for the Golden Rib Award.

MAUMEE DEAREST: THE Maumee River has had a profound impact on Toledo's history, culture, and economy, but many locals—whether by beak or bait—still troll the waters for a simple meal.

S THE SUN RISES BEHIND Toledo's skyline, residents begin the day with a scenic commute. While some get to work by car or bus, others travel via commuter planes departing from Toledo Express Airport (ABOVE).

GOOD TO THE LAST DROP: As they drink their morning coffee, Toledoans tune in to 92.5 KISS-FM for *The Breakfast Club* with Denny Schaffer (OPPOSITE). Nicknamed the Big Dog of Toledo Radio, Schaffer is one of the top-rated radio personalities in the region.

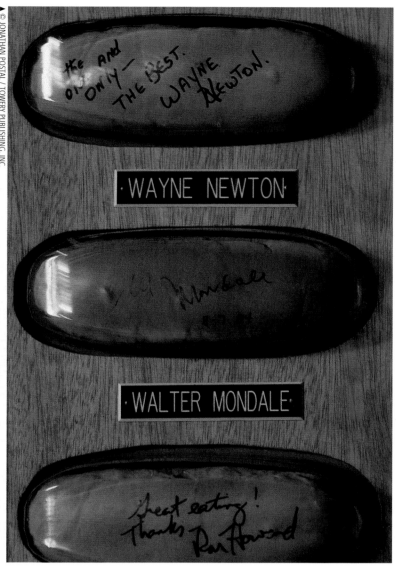

MADE FAMOUS BY JAMIE Farr on *M*A*S*H*, Tony Packo's Café has served up tasty Hungarian cuisine—including its specialty, the Hungarian hot dog—since its founding in 1932. The restaurant, owned and operated by a second generation of Packos—including Tony Packo Jr. (OPPOSITE, ON LEFT)—has some nice buns: For some 30 years, the eatery has collected hot dog rolls signed by celebrities and politicians passing through Toledo.

116

TOLEDO

▼ © JONATHAN POSTAL / TOWERY PUBLISHING, INC.

TOLEDO SERVES UP A FULL MENU of fine restaurants, including Fifi's, founded in 1980 by Fifi Berry (RIGHT); the riverfront Cousino's Navy Bistro, which features the culinary innovations of Executive Chef Chris Bates (LEFT); and Georgio's Café International, run by Chef George Kamilaris and Chris Kamilaris (OPPOSITE, FROM LEFT).

At Put-in-Bay on South Bass Island, the Round House Bar (top) draws beers and crowds at its site in a building dating back to 1873, and the Beer Barrel Saloon (bottom) boasts the longest permanent bar in the world: Measuring just less than 406 feet long, it accommodates 160 bar stools and 56 beer taps. After a late night at either establishment, carousers can head back to Toledo and a warm cup of coffee at the White Tower 24-Hour Restaurant (opposite).

N 1997, MICKEY FINN (TOP) revitalized a historic block of buildings and the city's nightlife with the opening of Mickey Finn's Pub, the only authentic Irish pub in Toledo. Today, the bar hosts a number of local music legends, including John "Blues" Baker (BOTTOM) and Patrick Lewandowski (OPPOSITE).

NO STRUCTURE IS SAFE WHEN two of Toledo's most popular bands take the stage. Playing rhythm and blues with energy and soul, the Home-wreckers (ABOVE) regularly bring the house down at Steven Jay's. Touring the region, Johnny Reed and the House Rockers (OPPOSITE) blow through Toledo and raise the roof at Mickey Finn's Pub.

AT THE HOP: The city's night-life bustles with activity as residents descend on establishments like Club Bijou, located along Frogtown Alley. Jeramie Cavallaro (OPPOSITE), owner of Center Stage Entertainment, a professional DJ service, keeps things jumping in Toledo, spinning records in clubs and bars around town.

TOLEDO

ALL THAT JAZZ: TOLEDO TAKES note of its storied musical history and those who have contributed to the city's rich culture. During the 1950s, Ohio native Jon Hendricks (LEFT) helped develop a style of singing called Vocalese, which influenced such artists as Tony Bennett and Bobby McFerrin. Today, the music legend continues to influence younger generations as a professor of jazz history at the University of Toledo. A local celebrity who has brought jazz to the city since 1963, Rusty Monroe (OPPOSITE, FOREGROUND) runs Rusty's Jazz Café on Tedrow Road—which Mayor Carty Fink-beiner rechristened "Jazz Avenue" in her honor—and gives musicians like veteran saxophone player Gene Parker (OPPOSITE, BACK-GROUND) a place to practice and perform.

AT THE VALENTINE THEATRE, all Toledo's a stage: The 900-seat venue features musical and dramatic performances by the Toledo Ballet, Toledo Opera, and Toledo Repertoire Company. In May 2000, the theater dedicated a sculpture garden (TOP) featuring work by Anne and Patrick Poirer.

SEA GATE CENTRE

BUILT IN 1987, THE SeaGate Convention Centre has helped revitalize downtown Toledo and spur the city's tourism economy. With 75,000 square feet of meeting space, the facility hosts a full calendar of sporting events, concerts, and family-oriented performances, as well as meetings and conventions.

BARRE NONE: ONE OF THE MOST prestigious cultural organizations in the region, the Toledo Ballet Association (OPPOSITE AND BOTTOM LEFT)—under the direction of Artistic Director Nigel Burgoine (TOP)—performs a large repertoire that includes *The Nutcracker* and *Alice in Wonderland* at the Valentine Theatre. Emphasizing education and Christian music, the Cassandra Ballet of Toledo (BOTTOM RIGHT) stages spring productions featuring dancers of all ages.

PERFORMANCES BY IMAGENES
Mexicanas, a local ballet
folklorico, swirl with color
and culture, as members move
audiences throughout Ohio with
folk dances from various regions
of Mexico.

S TAYING IN TUNE WITH ITS regional audiences and offering a string of classical and pop performances throughout the year, the Toledo Symphony has earned international renown. With the help of local supporters like Lucas County Commissioner Sandy Isenberg (TOP, ON LEFT), the organization has brought such legendary musicians as Itzhak Perlman (TOP, ON RIGHT), Yo-Yo Ma (MIDDLE), and Mstislov Rostapovich (BOTTOM) to Toledo.

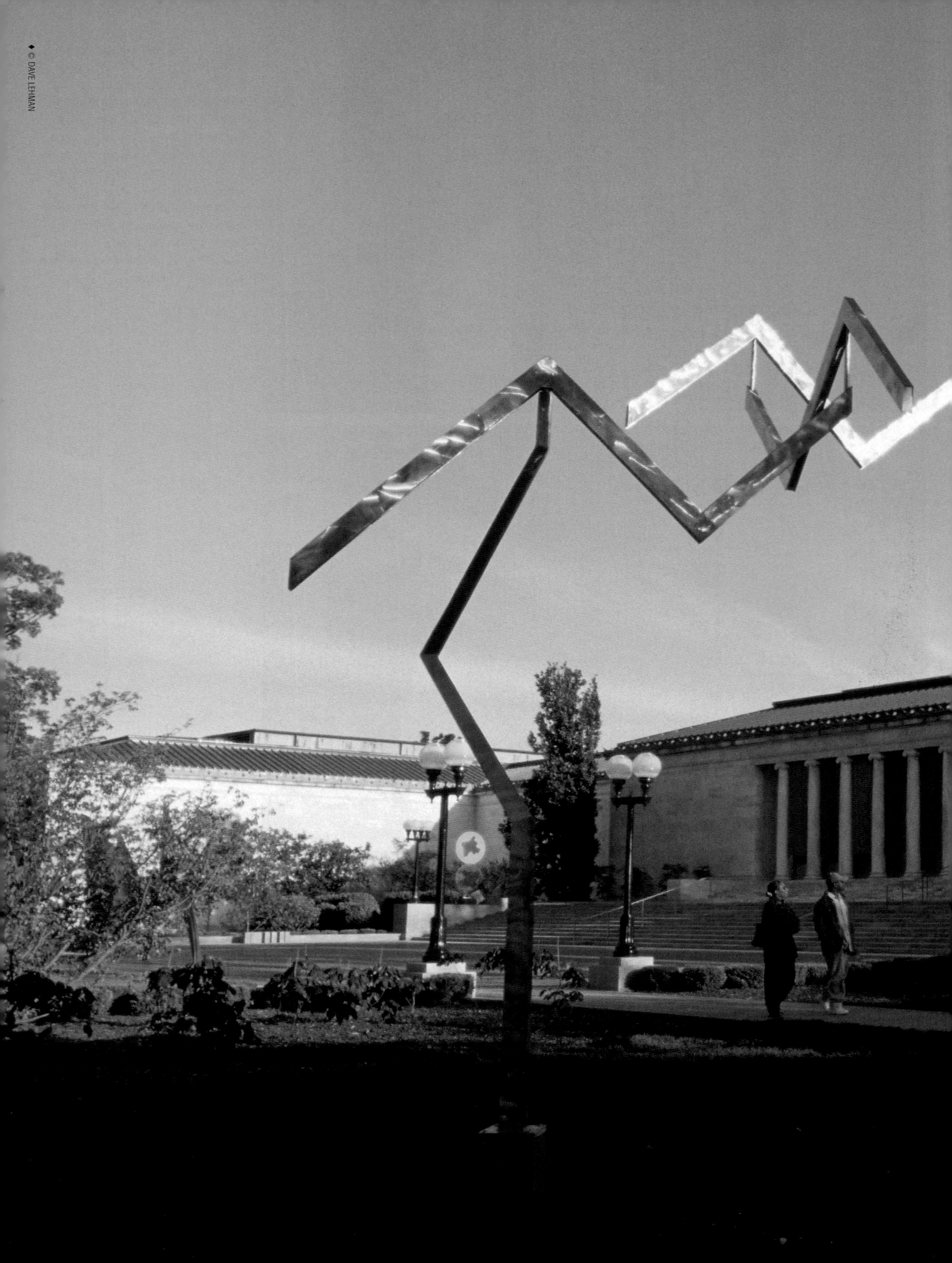

ESTABLISHED IN 1901 BY BUSI-nessman Edward Drummond Libbey and his wife, Florence, the Toledo Museum of Art (PAGES 140 AND 141) in the Old West End district has become one of the top art institutions in the country. The museum, under the leadership of Director Roger M. Berkowitz (ABOVE), has amassed an impressive 30,000-piece collection that represents many cultures and periods and includes a piece by Peter Paul Rubens (OPPOSITE).

144

PROMOTING CREATIVITY AND good hand-eye coordination, the Toledo Museum of Art offers a variety of educational opportunities that allow budding artists to study works by Edgar Degas and Vincent van Gogh (TOP LEFT AND BOTTOM RIGHT). At the Common Space Center for Creativity (OPPOSITE), children can create their own masterpieces in studio art classes sponsored by the Arts Council Lake Erie West.

ESIGNED BY INTERNATIONALLY
renowned architect Frank
Gehry and dedicated in
1992, the Center for the Visual Arts
is a work of art in its own right.
Adjacent to the Toledo Museum
of Art, the center houses the University of Toledo art department
and features workshops and gallery space for student and faculty
shows.

WHIMSY AND IMAGINATION rule the local arts scene. Michael Elliot McWhorter (ABOVE) forms fanciful sculptures from Plexiglas, while twins Michael and Mark Kersey (OPPOSITE) prove that two heads are better than one: Known together as Mr. Atomic, they create paintings and sculptures that explode with bright colors and imaginative shapes.

GLASS ACT: BRIAN LONSWAY (RIGHT) makes blown and molded glass pieces at his studio in Waterville, and occasionally takes his oven—which he built himself—to art fairs around the region to demonstrate his trade. Based locally since 1888, Libbey Glass Inc. (OPPOSITE) is now the top producer of glass tableware in North America, and Owens Corning (PAGES 152 AND 153), an offshoot of Owens-Illinois, Inc. and Corning Glass, has become a global manufacturer of fiberglass products.

unset casts an eerie iridescence over Lake Erie, as the glowing sun outshines the Davis-Besse Nuclear Power Station in both brightness and power.

WHETHER SPEEDING ALONG its surface on a recreational boat or sitting among the driftwood on its shore, Toledoans consider Lake Erie a local treasure for its natural beauty as well as its resources.

EGRETS, I'VE HAD A FEW: HERONS, great egrets, and other birds of a feather flock together above the banks and piers along Lake Erie, searching for blue skies and handouts from visitors.

160

S TANDING MORE THAN 60 FEET tall on the tip of Marblehead Peninsula, Marblehead Light (LEFT) has shone the way since 1822, making it the oldest active lighthouse on the Great Lakes. Rising high above Put-in-Bay, Perry's Victory & International Peace Memorial (OPPOSITE) was erected in 1915 to mark its namesake's triumph over the British navy during the War of 1812 and to commemorate the resulting treaties that brought peace between the United States, Britain, and Canada.

COME HULL OR HIGH WATER: Forsaking fiberglass, many sailors favor the feel of wood for their boats. Each year, more than 30 wooden vessels compete in the Great Lakes Wooden Sailboat Regatta, held at the Battery Park Marina in Sandusky, Ohio, since 1983.

SOUTH BASS ISLAND PROVIDES a peaceful place to get away from it all. In addition to numerous historical attractions and shopping venues, the island also offers quiet spots for camping and calm Lake Erie waters for boating.

© ROD BERRY

AN AREA RICH IN NATURAL resources as well as recreational opportunities, Maumee Bay State Park covers more than 1,450 acres of forest, prairie land, wetlands, and shoreline. The park, which allows boating on its 57-acre inland lake as well as on Lake Erie, also maintains a picturesque golf course, the state-of-the-art Trautman Nature Center, and the Quilter Lodge (OPPOSITE TOP), which features some 120 guest rooms.

T R E A S U R E S   A N D   T R A D I T I O N S   **167**

LOCATED AT INTERNATIONAL PARK, The Beach Volleyball Complex is a haven for local setters and spikers, with a number of sand courts and several highly competitive leagues. Each year, the park hosts the Pollyball tournament, a fund-raiser benefitting the Victory Center, which helps families of cancer patients.

TOLEDOANS TRAVELING THE Maumee River have numerous choices in locomotion. While many propel themselves with small engines or motors, members of the Toledo Rowing Club (ABOVE) strong-arm their way around.

TOLEDO

Not an Entrance

TOLEDO'S STAIRS AND WALKWAYS often become obstacle courses for the city's young adventure-seekers, while professional daredevils like Matt Garreau (OPPOSITE) defy gravity at skate parks around the region.

THE EYES HAVE IT: AGILITY, strength, coordination—and sometimes a dazzling smile—are just a few of the qualities that make for great hockey players. Young aspirants to the sport find role models in the Toledo Storm, the city's East Coast Hockey League team.

ICY WEATHER DOESN'T PREVENT Toledoans from enjoying a day in the park. Skating professionally since 1981, Laurie Haener Buckley (THIS PAGE) teaches figure skating to children at Ottawa Park, while others brave the chilly winter to go ice sailing on frozen lakes.

178

WHETHER BOWLING OR boxing, Toledoans knock 'em all down with style and muscle to spare. In addition to running his own pro shop, Don Genalo (LEFT) has become a local bowling legend with six national tour titles in the Professional Bowlers Association. Twice a junior middleweight world champion, Bronco McKart (OPPO-SITE) trains at the International Boxing Club on Front Street.

O NCE A WEEK, TOLEDO'S Secor Lanes becomes music row as local fiddle players, banjo pickers, and mandolin strummers meet at the bowling alley to strike a few bluegrass chords.

F ROM LOUD COSTUMES TO EVEN louder cheering, Toledo sports fans display their support for local teams in a variety of styles. And whatever sport strikes their fancy, children will no doubt find athletes to look up to.

BASEBALL FANS FLOCK TO NED Skeldon Stadium to root for the AAA Toledo Mud Hens and their mascot Muddy. A formidable presence in the International League and an affiliate of the Detroit Tigers, the team opens a new, state-of-the-art ballpark near the SeaGate Convention Centre downtown in April 2002.

FOUNDED BY JUDD SILVERMAN in 1984 and hosted by native son Jamie Farr (OPPOSITE), the annual Jamie Farr Kroger Classic tournament draws more than 100 top-ranked Ladies Professional Golf Association players—including 2001 champion Se Ri Pak (LEFT)—to take a swing at the Highland Meadows Golf Club. The July event attracts thousands of golf enthusiasts and, over the years, has benefited more than 50 local children's charities.

BUILDING AND RENOVATING homes for families in need, Maumee Valley Habitat for Humanity is staffed by a dedicated crew of local volunteers, all under the supervision of David Belknap (OPPOSITE, BACKGROUND).

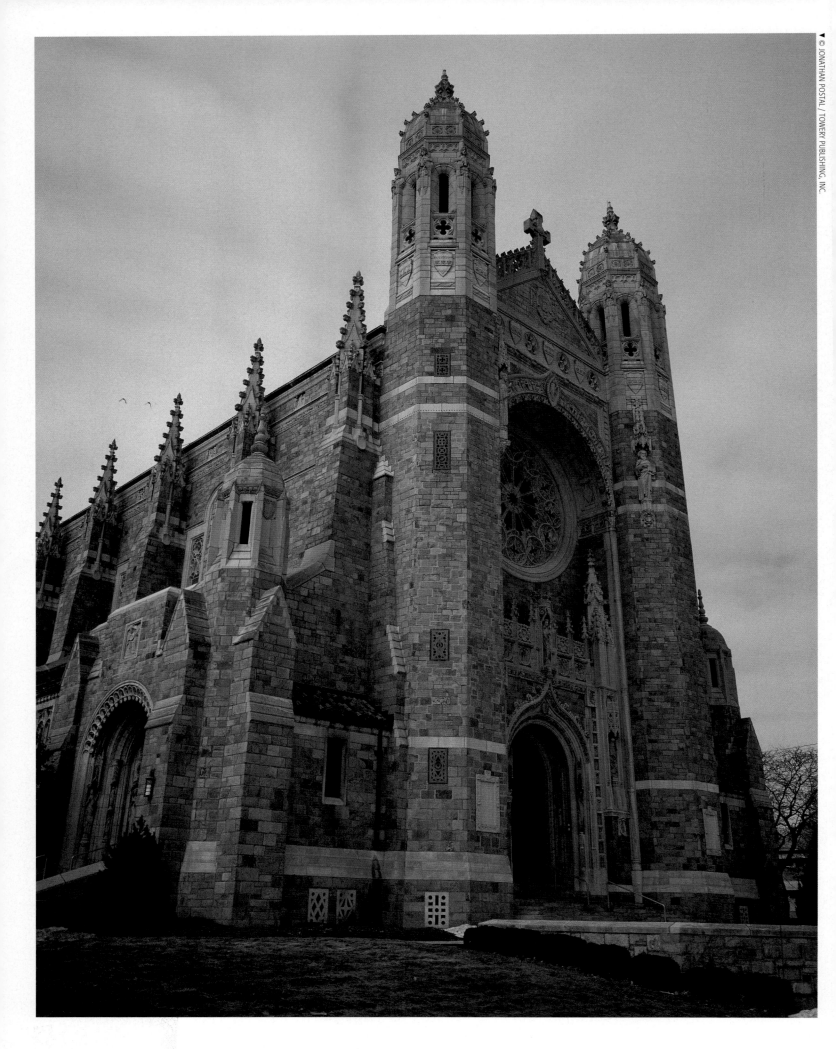

THE ONLY CATHEDRAL IN THE world built in the Plateresque style, the Queen of the Most Holy Rosary Cathedral is one of the city's most breathtaking architectural gems. Under the guidance of priests like Father Ron Warnimont (LEFT), it is also a spiritual home to a strong congregation of area Catholics and, as the seat of the Catholic Diocese of Toledo, serves as the mother church for more than 160 parishes throughout Northwest Ohio.

TOLEDO

SINCE THE EARLY 19TH CENTURY, emigrants from across the globe have settled in Toledo, and their diversity of cultures and religions has contributed to the city's unique personality. Designed by architect Talat Itil and opened in 1983, the Islamic Center of Greater Toledo (OPPOSITE) has become one of the largest facilities of its kind in the country, serving Northwest Ohio's Muslim population.

194

THE ISLAMIC CENTER OF GREATER Toledo's continuous growth and increased activity can be credited to dedicated leaders like Imam Farooq Abo-Elzahab (LEFT) and Cherrefe Kadri (OPPOSITE). A Lebanese second-generation Muslim and a local attorney, Kadri was the first woman in the United States to be appointed a leadership role in a mosque.

© JONATHAN POSTAL / TOWERY PUBLISHING, INC.

© JONATHAN POSTAL / TOWERY PUBLISHING, INC.

SUNDAYS AT THE INDIANA AVE-nue Baptist Church are spirited affairs, as the Rever-end Dr. J.E. Roberts (OPPOSITE LEFT) preaches to one of Toledo's largest African-American congregations.

TOLEDOANS COMMEMORATE their heroes with sculptures and memorials throughout the city. Designed by Wil Clay and Constancia Gafeney-Brown, *Radiance* (RIGHT) honors the sacrifices of civil rights leader Martin Luther King Jr. and stands near the bridge that bears his name. Commissioned by the Toledo Policeman's Association, *The Guardian* (OPPOSITE), designed by Jack Greaves, depicts a local officer leading children safely across the street.

TOLEDO'S MEN IN BLUE— including Central District Sergeant Richard Murphy (LEFT)—face myriad challenges as they work to keep the city safe. But lawmen need not fear a series of celebrity murals downtown, some of which capture a celluloid time when Hollywood made crime a glamorous thing (OPPOSITE).

O THE RESCUE: MARKING THE bravery of the area's firefighters is the steel-and-brick sculpture *Fire Station No. 13*, which was designed by George Greenamyer and stands near the neighborhood of Birmingham. Battling blazes throughout the city since 1837, the Toledo Fire Division employs more than 530 uniformed and nearly 40 civilian employees.

BLAZE OF GLORY: ESTABLISHED in 1976, the Toledo Firefighters Museum preserves the history of the Toledo Fire Division and educates visitors and students about fire prevention and safety. Under the direction of Curator John F. Repp (RIGHT), the museum displays thousands of artifacts—including an 1899 alarm office (OPPOSITE TOP)—at the Old Number 18 Fire House, which was built in 1920.

© ROGER BICKEL

RETRACING 1.5 MILES OF THE original Miami & Erie Canal, the Canal Experience at Providence Metropark in Grand Rapids, Ohio—located just a short drive from Toledo—re-creates 1800s-era Ohio lock, stock, and barrel. *The Volunteer*, a mule-drawn canal boat, ferries visitors through historic Lock #44 to the restored Isaac Ludwig Mill, one of the last remaining buildings from the original canal town.

1936

I N ADDITION TO ACRES OF FOREST and tallgrass prairie, the Wildwood Preserve Metropark features several buildings comprising the former estate of local businessman Robert A. Stranahan. Built in 1938 in the Georgian Colonial style, the Manor House (ABOVE) contains antique furniture from the early 1900s and is surrounded by well-manicured gardens and picturesque gazebos, while the former stables now house the Metz Visitor Center (OPPOSITE).

210

SHOWCASING THE AREA'S NATUral beauty while providing a nice place for a walk, the Metroparks of the Toledo Area includes nine nature areas—such as Wildwood Preserve (LEFT AND OPPOSITE TOP) and Swan Creek Preserve (OPPOSITE BOTTOM)—as well as a number of historical sites, all located within a short drive of the city.

THE MERCURIAL COLORS OF autumn, along with Ohio's varied fauna, provide the inspiration for local artist H. Pete Beckmann (OPPOSITE), whose im- pressionistic paintings appear in private and public collections throughout North America and Europe.

214

A S EACH DISTINCT SEASON cycles through, families converge on the city's parks for a quick game of catch or a bike ride down a scenic trail, discovering that Toledo is the perfect place to enjoy the great outdoors.

T O L E D O

WHILE SOME BIRDS FLY south to escape Ohio's icy winters, others cry fowl and pull the wool over their eyes. Embracing snow days with open arms, many Toledoans take to the hills for some sledding or sight-seeing.

ALL ABOARD: TRAIN TRACKS RUN throughout Toledo, from the murals gracing the Charter One Bank (OPPOSITE) to the trolleys that loop through down- town. During the summer, the Toledo Area Regional Transit Au- thority conducts tours of down- town and Maumee aboard its 1880 streetcar replicas (ABOVE).

WHOLLY TOLEDO: ALL around this All-America city, residents display a friendly, welcoming hospitality that reveals the region's unique treasures and traditions.

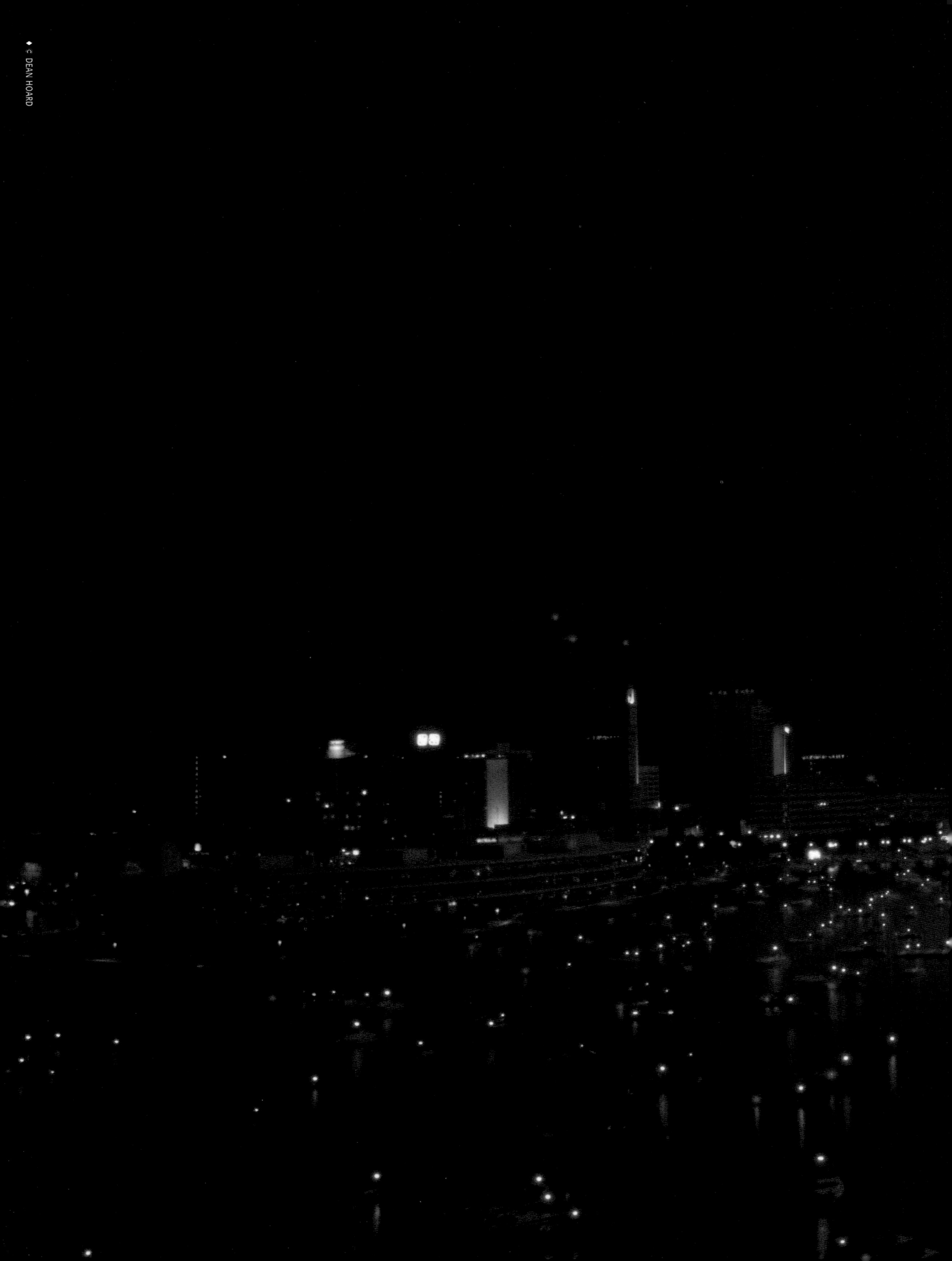
© DEAN HOARD

NO
STOPPING
ANY
TIME

ALASKA
Ireland
Quebec
HAWAII
MEXICO

PROFILES IN EXCELLENCE

A look at the corporations, businesses, professional groups, and community service organizations that have made this book possible. Their stories—offering an informal chronicle of the local business community—are arranged according to the date they were established in the Toledo area.

❖ AAA Northwest Ohio ❖ ALLTEL ❖ The Andersons, Inc. ❖ Anderzack-Pitzen Construction, Inc. ❖ Bax Global Inc.

❖ The Blade ❖ The Bostwick-Braun Company ❖ BP Toledo Refinery ❖ Brush Wellman Inc. ❖ Buckeye CableSystem

❖ Buckeye TeleSystem ❖ Calphalon Corporation ❖ Cavista Corporation ❖ Children's Discovery Center / Discovery

Express ❖ The Clarion Hotel Westgate ❖ Columbia Gas of Ohio ❖ Dana Corporation ❖ EISC, Inc. ❖ Faurecia Exhaust

Systems ❖ Fifth Third Bank ❖ General Motors Corporation, Powertrain Division, Toledo Transmission ❖ Great Lakes

Window, Inc. ❖ Harold Jaffe Jewelers ❖ HCR Manor Care ❖ Hickory Farms ❖ Hilton Hotel & Dana Conference Center

❖ The Hylant Group ❖ International Brotherhood of Electrical Workers Local #8 ❖ Kiemle-Hankins Company ❖

The Kroger Company ❖ Laborers' International Union Local #500 ❖ Libbey Inc. ❖ Lucas County Board of

Commissioners ❖ Master Chemical Corporation ❖ Maumee Valley Country Day School ❖ MedCorp, Inc. ❖ Medical

College of Ohio ❖ Metal Forming & Coining Corporation ❖ Midwest Environmental Control, Inc. ❖ Mosser

Construction, Inc. ❖ National City Bank ❖ Northwest Ohio Building and Construction Trades Council ❖ OmniSource

Corporation ❖ Owens Corning ❖ Owens-Illinois ❖ PepsiAmericas ❖ Pilkington North America, Inc. ❖ Poggemeyer

Design Group ❖ ProMedica Health System ❖ The Radisson Hotel-Toledo ❖ Regional Growth Partnership ❖

Riker Products, Inc. ❖ Romanoff Electric Corp. ❖ Sky Bank ❖ The Spieker Company ❖ SSOE, Inc., Architects •

Engineers ❖ Sunoco MidAmerica Marketing & Refining ❖ TARTA ❖ Teledyne Continental Motors-Turbine Engines

❖ Toledo Area Chamber of Commerce ❖ Toledo Edison Company ❖ Toledo-Lucas County Port Authority ❖

Toledo Lucas County Public Library ❖ United Association Local #50 Plumbers & Steamfitters ❖ The University of

Toledo ❖ White Family Dealerships ❖ Willis Day Properties, Inc. ❖

PROFILES IN EXCELLENCE

1835-1900

The Blade

WHEN THE *BLADE* WAS BORN IN 1835, LUCAS COUNTY WAS BRAND NEW. THE MAUMEE RIVER WAS CROSSED BY WAY OF BOAT OR BARGE, AND A DEBATE WAS RAGING IN CONGRESS AS TO WHETHER TOLEDO AND LUCAS COUNTY BELONGED IN OHIO OR MICHIGAN. TOLEDO ITSELF

was just two small villages—Port Lawrence and Vistula. Citizens realized there was a need to merge together, and there was a feeling among businesses that a newspaper with no ties to either village was needed. The city of Toledo incorporated just two years later.

Just as the city took its name from a city in Spain, the *Blade* took its name from the most famous of the Spanish city's products. By way of explanation, George Way, the first editor of the young newspaper, asserted: "We may be accused of challenging the rest of the world. No. We should prefer to keep our blade always in its scabbard, and hope not to be compelled to use it often in the offensive. We should not like, however, to have it rust in its sheath so that it will not easily leap forth when necessity or honor demand that we should use it. Our blade has

no elasticity—it will break before it will bend. . . . We hope it will always leap from its scabbard whenever the rights of individuals, or of the community, shall be infringed."

THE EARLY YEARS

The *Blade* changed owners and editors quite frequently in those early years. In 1844, Jesup Scott became editor. He was convinced that Toledo would one day become America's "great city," and in his case, this went far beyond civic boosterism. He recognized the importance of Toledo's port and railroad development. Scott also bequeathed 160 acres of land at what are now Bancroft and Westwood streets to create the Toledo University of Arts and Trades—better known today as the University of Toledo. He later became the first *Blade* editor to have a school in Toledo named

for him: Jesup W. Scott High School.

During the Civil War, the *Blade* was a steady supporter of the Union and an early backer of Abraham Lincoln. The newspaper had been founded as a voice for the Whig Party, which later became the Republican Party. The *Blade* followed the party line through the Civil War and into Reconstruction.

After the war, the owner of the *Blade*, Alonzo Pelton, was searching for a new voice. He settled upon David Ross Locke, whose witty editorial writings as Petroleum V. Nasby were popular with both the Union soldiers in the Civil War and the president himself. Two years later, Locke was a partner in the *Blade*, and by 1874, was owner and president of the company.

The *Weekly Blade* had a circulation of some 117,000 by 1883, and, in 1884, reached some 200,000. The

THOUGH THE *BLADE* CHANGED OWNERS AND EDITORS IN ITS EARLY YEARS, THE BUILDING IN WHICH IT BEGAN ON MAY 1, 1927, STILL SERVES AS ITS HEADQUARTERS IN TOLEDO.

Circulation of the *Weekly Blade* had climbed to some 230,000 by 1913, but, by 1924, it had dipped to some 114,000 subscribers. This was common of weekly papers of the 1920s—Sunday editions had taken the place of many of these. In October 1924, the *Blade* ceased publication of its weekly edition.

NEW LEADERSHIP

In 1926, the *Blade* was sold to Paul Block and Associates, one of the nation's largest publishers' representative firms. The paper continues to be owned by the Block family today.

Paul Block was an emigrant from East Prussia who came to the United States in 1885. To help provide for his family, Block, as a young teenager, went to work selling advertising for the *Elmira Telegram* in New York. In 1895, he moved on to New York City to work as an advertising representative for newspapers. Block established his own advertising representative firm in 1900.

National advertising was growing rapidly in the early 1900s, and Paul Block and Associates did well. With the profits he gained, Block bought newspapers around the country, including the *Pittsburgh Post-Gazette*. Block's friendships in those days read like a who's who of the late 1920s: newspaper mag-

newspaper was headquartered in a building at Superior and Jefferson streets that had been built for $125,000, a fortune at that time.

In 1888, Locke died at the age of 54, and his son, Robinson Locke, took over as editor. While his father's interests had first been the abolition of slavery and later the politics of reconstruction, Robinson Locke was intensely interested in music, art, and theater. He was influential in the founding of the Toledo Museum of Art and was active in arts organizations within Toledo.

Robinson Locke remained as editor until 1908, having seen Toledo grow from a just-established small town to a lively municipality. During his editorship, he saw the rise of Toledo under Mayors Samuel "Golden Rule" Jones and Brand Whitlock, two municipal reformers. At Robinson Locke's retirement, the Locke family leased the newspaper to N.C. Wright and Harry Thalheimer of Cleveland. They, in turn, hired as editor Grove Patterson, who would remain with the *Blade* for nearly 50 years.

Under these new editors, the *Blade* continued to support the Republican Party and its candidates.

nate William Randolph Hearst, Flo Ziegfeld, and New York Mayor Jimmy Walker.

Block paid $4.5 million for the *Blade* in 1926, and kept Patterson as his right-hand man. Patterson, for whom Grove Patterson Academy in west Toledo is named, in turn hired Fred Mollenkopf as city editor. Mollenkopf had recently been fired from the competing *News-Bee*, and was eager to scoop the paper that had ousted him. He remained as the *Blade*'s city editor from 1926 to 1949.

The *Blade*'s building at Superior and Jefferson was, by this time, inadequate for the newspaper's needs. The Toledo Blade Company purchased several lots at the intersec-

tions of Superior and Huron streets with Beech street, and hired the Henry J. Spieker Company to build a new headquarters location at a cost of nearly $650,000.

The building, where the *Blade* still stands today, opened on May 1, 1927. Legendary baseball player Babe Ruth attended the ceremonies, and President Calvin Coolidge, a friend of Block's, touched a golden key in the White House to start the presses in Toledo.

GROWTH AND PROSPERITY

The Great Depression hit Toledo hard, yet the *Blade* continued. The newspaper covered the Electric Auto-Lite strike, the exploits of the Licavoli gangsters,

and the adoption of the city manager form of government. Under Block's leadership, the *Blade* was a leader in the community not only as a business, but also as a bully pulpit to improve the city.

In 1941, Block died. He had been owner of the *Blade* for 15 years, and had bequeathed his company in equal shares to his sons, Paul Block Jr. and William Block. Both sons had been brought up in the newspaper business, but neither was available to take over the *Blade* at that time. Paul Jr. was studying for his doctorate in chemistry at Columbia University, and William was in the U.S. Army. The two brothers were named as copublishers of the *Blade* and the *Pittsburgh Post-Gazette*.

Paul Block Jr. returned to Toledo in 1944 as active publisher. Because the rival *News-Bee* had gone out of business, Toledo no longer had a newspaper that favored the Democratic Party. Block insisted that the *Blade* discontinue espousing the views of the Republican Party, and begin treating the two parties equally.

The *Blade* grew and prospered through the years, surviving when other newspapers were going under. Due to Block's interest in chemistry, the *Blade* became a leader in reporting on science. *Blade* bureaus were established in Washington, D.C.; Europe; and Columbus, Ohio. Block worked hard to establish the Medical

THE VALUES THE *BLADE* ESPOUSES TODAY— INCLUDING A FREE PRESS, INTEGRITY, CUSTOMER FIRST, CORPORATE CITIZENSHIP, TEAMWORK, AND CONSTANT IMPROVEMENT— REFLECT THE WORDS OF THE PUBLICATION'S FIRST EDITOR.

230

College of Ohio in Toledo and the Toledo-Lucas County Port Authority.

In 1987, Paul Block Jr. died. Today, the *Blade* is headed by co-publishers William Block Jr., son of William Block, and John Robinson Block, son of Paul Block Jr. William Block Sr. serves as chairman. As the Block family's holdings in other media grew, the Toledo Blade Company became a part of Block Communications, Inc. The Block family recently celebrated its 100th year in the communications business.

COMMUNITY PRIDE

The *Blade*'s position as a bully pulpit for the community has not changed much over the years. The paper lobbied vociferously and successfully for a return to the strong mayor form of government, as well as for greater freedom of the press through open records laws. The newspaper continues to push community leaders for greater local improvement, and has become outspoken in its fight for recognition by the state legislature of the Other Ohio—communities other than Cleveland, Cincinnati, and Columbus.

In the mid-1990s, the *Blade* formulated a mission statement, one that is certain to take it through the

new century: "We are dedicated to being the leaders in providing news, information, and advertising to Northwest Ohio and Southern Michigan."

The values the *Blade* espouses today—including a free press, integrity, customer first, corporate citizenship, teamwork, and constant improvement—reflect the words of the publication's first editor, and will continue to do so in the future.

WHEN THE BLADE WAS BORN IN 1835, LUCAS COUNTY WAS BRAND NEW. TODAY, THE NEWSPAPER AND THE GREATER TOLEDO AREA ARE THRIVING.

Lucas County Board of Commissioners

HE LUCAS COUNTY BOARD OF COMMISSIONERS PROVIDES THE COMMUNITY'S SOME 450,000 RESIDENTS WITH MANY BENEFITS THAT ENHANCE THEIR OVERALL QUALITY OF LIFE. THE LUCAS COUNTY BOARD OF COMMISSIONERS, AS LUCAS COUNTY'S MAIN GOVERNING BODY, IS RESPONSIBLE FOR MANY OF THE MOST IMPORTANT SERVICES

the county's 11 municipalities and 11 townships have come to depend upon.

Those vital services range from public safety and criminal justice to transportation and infrastructure, from workforce development and human services to recreation and recycling, from solid waste to sanitary water and sewer service. Whatever the need, the elected commissioners are committed to providing quality service to the community in a prompt and efficient manner.

THE EARLY DAYS

Lucas County was organized in 1835—two years before Toledo officially became a city—and was named after then-Ohio Governor Robert Lucas. But the birth of the county did not occur without a fight.

Prior to the county's organization, both Michigan and Ohio laid claim to the region. The area, along with a large portion of Michigan, most of northwestern Ohio, and part of eastern Indiana, was originally part of Wayne County, with Detroit named as its county seat. With the Michigan Militia prepared to strike, the Toledo War, as it had been called, ended

MOST PEOPLE THINK OF LUCAS COUNTY GOVERNMENT AS THE COUNTY COURTHOUSE (RIGHT) AND ONE GOVERNMENT CENTER (IN BACKGROUND), BUT LUCAS COUNTY IS BUILDING A FRAMEWORK FOR THE FUTURE WITH A NEW 2 MILLION GALLON WATER TOWER AND A CONSOLIDATED EMERGENCY COMMUNICATIONS CENTER.

peacefully when a secret court meeting established Lucas County on the orders of the Ohio General Assembly.

In Lucas County's early days, the first courthouse consisted of a small log schoolhouse located in downtown Toledo. The courthouse was later moved two more times to other downtown sites, moves that only proved temporary. In 1840, the county seat was moved to nearby Maumee, where a new courthouse was built using private donations. A great rivalry between the citizens of Maumee and Toledo was finally squelched when the Ohio General Assembly called for a referendum, and citizens voted to move the county seat back to Toledo in 1852.

The present-day courthouse was built in 1897, and covers two city blocks in downtown Toledo. Designed in a neoclassic architectural style, the main entrance of the court-

house welcomes visitors with a unique, hand-laid frog mosaic in the floor, paying homage to Lucas County's heritage as the Great Black Swamp, where frogs once lived and thrived. After an extensive face-lift in 2000, the exterior of the Lucas County Courthouse remains much as it did when it was first built. The beautiful landscaping and monuments surrounding the courthouse add a majestic touch to Toledo's Civic Center.

PROVIDING VITAL SERVICES

Contrasting with the old courthouse, several new building projects are being added to the downtown Toledo landscape. The new Lucas County Juvenile Justice and Detention Center brings court, detention, probation, and program services into one central location to provide a safer community, as it addresses the needs of the county's troubled youth and their families.

Lucas County Commissioners were also instrumental in centralizing the county's emergency services with the new Consolidated Emergency Communications Center. This facility, located near downtown, houses 911 call-takers and dispatchers, emergency planning and response personnel, and state-of-the-art communications technology, all which add up to faster response times to emergencies large and small.

SUPPORTING COMMUNITY ACTIVITIES

One of the community's most exciting projects is the construction of the new Lucas County Ballpark. Located in downtown Toledo's Warehouse District, the new ballpark is intended not only to be the home field of the world-famous Toledo Mud Hens baseball club, but also to spur economic development and serve as the centerpiece of a revitalized entertainment district.

As a public-private partnership, the Lucas County Board of Commissioners has ensured that local tax dollars serve as the catalyst for state and federal funding, as well as private investment. Local companies bought up all the existing luxury suites at the new ballpark within days of their sale, showing their community support of this exciting new entertainment venue.

The Lucas County Board of Commissioners has also enthusiastically backed hiking and biking trails that crisscross the region. The Wabash

Cannonball Trail, for example, links communities together in western Lucas County, allowing hikers and bikers to experience the wondrous beauty of the Oak Openings region, an area of native plant life unique to northwest Ohio.

FOCUSED ON ECONOMIC DEVELOPMENT

Through projects like the Lucas County Ballpark, Lucas County Commissioners have taken a leadership position in providing services and incentives that create and retain jobs, and spur development throughout the area. Lucas County government is one of the area's top-ten employers with more than 4,300 workers.

The Lucas County Board of Commissioners has committed to providing economic opportunities through

affordable housing. For example, Lucas County has partnered with Habitat for Humanity by providing land that the outreach organization has used to build homes for those who traditionally could not afford a mortgage on their own. Lucas County also offers down payment assistance and home repair grant programs.

The Westwinds Business Center began in the 1960s when the Lucas County Board of Commissioners purchased 400 acres of land with the hope of bringing companies to the area. Today, the complex offers small to midsize industries an ideal location. With the utility infrastructure already in place, businesses have been able to buy portions of the complex that are strategically located near the Toledo Express Airport and the Ohio Turnpike interchange.

From the early days to the 21st century, from providing vital services to supporting the community's quality of life, from focusing on economic development to promoting a productive local workforce, the Lucas County Board of Commissioners continues to build a framework for the future in an effort to ensure the county's success.

THE ORNATE ARCHES OF THE LUCAS COUNTY COURTHOUSE WERE PRESERVED AS AN EXAMPLE OF THE REBIRTH OCCURRING IN DOWNTOWN TOLEDO.

THE NEW LUCAS COUNTY BALLPARK (LEFT) WILL ENHANCE THE REVITALIZATION OF DOWNTOWN TOLEDO, WHILE PROVIDING FAMILIES AN AFFORDABLE ENTERTAINMENT VENUE.

Toledo-Lucas County Public Library

Lucas County residents have benefited from organized library service that has been provided for more than a century. Several library organizations joined together to form the organization known today as the Toledo-Lucas County Public Library and, as the community grew and evolved, each library

organization in the area went through its own set of changes.

From the beginning, libraries have fulfilled a quest for knowledge and a need for an entertainment venue by citizens of all ages. Throughout history, libraries have served a variety of readers—from the browser just looking for a good book to the scholar interested in research. Each reader has certain expectations, and those expectations set the compass for the future direction of library service in the area. Today, the library structure has taken on new and exciting dimensions, reaching a larger population of the community by offering more services, larger collections, and the latest technology.

The home of the old Toledo Public Library was located at Madison Avenue and Ontario Street (1890-1940).

EARLY YEARS

As settlers came to Ohio, they brought with them the concept of libraries, which they had experienced farther east. So it was no surprise that when Toledo officially became a city in 1835, the same year Lucas County was formed, a library organization was soon to follow.

In 1838, even before there were

sidewalks along major city streets, telegraph connections, and streetcars, library service in Lucas County was established. The Young Men's Association of Toledo began with just 66 charter members, each paying an annual fee of $2 to utilize the subscription service. This annual fee helped to provide a small array of resources to its members, including a collection of fewer than 500 volumes, a lecture series, and a

reading room equipped with newspapers and magazines.

As a new city, Toledo enjoyed this early library and saw it as an asset to the area. Townspeople encouraged potential investors and residents to support the area by supporting the library. As the community grew, so did the library association's membership pool. This cooperative relationship became a model for the future of library service,

Shelving at the old main library, circa 1937, was primitive (left).

Computer terminals replaced card catalogs in the historic main library, relics from a bygone era, with instant access to the library's entire collection (right).

and Toledo residents understood that service to the community and support by the community must take place simultaneously.

In 1864, a number of members from the Young Men's Association resigned to form their own organization called the Toledo Library Association (TLA). Three years later, the two organizations merged, keeping the TLA name.

Association members began to feel that, since many local citizens could not afford the annual membership fee, TLA's services were not reaching the majority of the city. There was a general belief by the townspeople that local governments should support libraries and enable use by everyone in the community. In 1853, the General Assembly of Ohio passed a law requiring cities and towns to levy taxes to support local libraries. The Toledo City Council passed a resolution in 1873 to create the Toledo Public Library (TPL), and agreed to levy a .5 mill property tax to support it.

TOLEDO PUBLIC LIBRARY

As soon as local legislation passed and funding sources were developed, TPL trustees set out to learn more about library operations. Concurrently, the Toledo Library Association's

collection of nearly 5,000 books, maps, and engravings was merged with some 1,320 books from the Toledo Board of Education. Located on the upper floor of the King Block building—now the site of the Toledo Edison building—TPL was open for business.

Open from 9 a.m. to 9 p.m. Mondays through Saturdays and from 1:30 to 9 p.m. on Sundays, the library soon began loaning materials to the public. TPL's policy allowed patrons to borrow only one item at a time and to keep that item for no more than two weeks before renewal. Within its first year of operation, the library's collection grew by 25 percent. And by 1890, when the library moved into its own building, nearly 29,000 volumes were included in the collection.

Toledo was also growing at a rapid pace. The streetcar network expanded, a municipal water system was installed, and the city was changing daily. Industry was booming and many local citizens were reaping the financial rewards. As the city grew, the library's funding base and number of patrons grew as well.

To accommodate additional usage, TPL decided to construct a new building. Designed by local architect Edward O. Fallis, the new library building was funded by bonds that paid investors 4 percent interest. Among the new building's attributes was its entire second floor, which was often referred to as the Children's Department. This feature was a new concept for libraries at the time.

Other new features were added to the TPL collection over the

THE VITROLITE MURALS IN CENTRAL COURT REMAIN A HALLMARK OF HISTORIC MAIN LIBRARY'S ARCHITECTURAL FEATURES. THE 19,000 SQUARE FEET OF VITROLITE PANELS ARE COMPOSED OF MORE THAN 80 DIFFERENT COLORS. LIBBEY-OWENS-FORD COMPANY ORIGINALLY PRODUCED VITROLITE, BUT IT IS NO LONGER AVAILABLE. THE MURALS WERE DELICATELY PRESERVED DURING CONSTRUCTION AND RENOVATION OF MAIN LIBRARY AND ARE THE ONLY REPRESENTATIONS OF VITROLITE ON SUCH A GRAND SCALE IN AMERICA.

years, including music rolls for player pianos in 1911 and expanded services. By 1903, patrons were permitted to borrow two books at a time. In 1907, the limit was raised to four books.

As TPL's collection and services continued to expand, the need for additional space became evident. In 1914, construction began on the library annex, which was opened to the public in October 1915. Additionally, the library's branch system was initiated in 1915, which further expanded TPL's community reach.

GROWTH OF THE LIBRARY BRANCH SYSTEM

In 1916, communities outside of Toledo benefited from the creation of the Lucas County Library (LCL). Headquartered in Maumee, LCL was funded by a $10,000 grant from library philanthropist Andrew Carnegie.

With two area library systems in place, the number of citizens served increased dramatically. For TPL, the first full-service branch was located in Glenwood School and opened in 1915. Then, when Toledo received a $125,000 grant from the Carnegie Foundation, five branches were built across the Toledo area.

TPL's first branch, opened in east Toledo in December 1917, was named in honor of David Ross Locke, a famous editor of the *Blade*. The Glenwood School branch was closed when the second Carnegie-funded branch opened in west Toledo. The Kent Branch, named after Eliza M. Kent, who was the first manager of TPL's Children's Department, officially opened on December 11, 1917.

In January 1918, three other TPL branches opened: the Mott branch, named after Anna C. Mott and located in the southwest part of the city; the north end's Jermain Branch, named after longtime TPL director Frances. D. Jermain; and the South Toledo Branch.

Additional in-school branches were added to the LCL system as new neighborhood schools were erected. Other branches were opened in the area. The Birmingham Branch, for example, opened in 1920 in the East Side Community House, and by 1925, the branch had its own building. The West Toledo Branch also opened in a leased building, but moved to its own home by the late 1920s.

LCL branches differed from each other in appearance, but served the same purpose of extending library services to new areas of the community. Small collections of approximately 100 books each were set up in drugstores in Waterville and Sylvania; the F.J. Holliker store in Whitehouse; and the post office in Monclova. By 1924, every school in the LCL district had service from the county library.

EXPANSION OF SERVICES

All three area libraries—TLA, TPL, and LCL—offered their patrons a variety of services that surpassed traditional book circulation. Through the years, these services have been adjusted and increased to meet the needs of the community.

As early as 1899, when the Children's Department opened its shelves for browsing, TPL was meeting the needs of the area's youngsters. In 1905, the library tradition of children's story time was initiated. And in 1919, librarians began visiting Toledo schools, reading stories,

THE STATE-OF-THE-ART MCMASTER FAMILY CENTER FOR LIFELONG LEARNING, MADE POSSIBLE THROUGH AN $850,000 GIFT FROM HAROLD AND HELEN MCMASTER, OFFERS GLOBAL VIDEOCONFERENCING FOR UP TO 275, AND IS USED IN NUMEROUS DISTANCE LEARNING PROGRAMS.

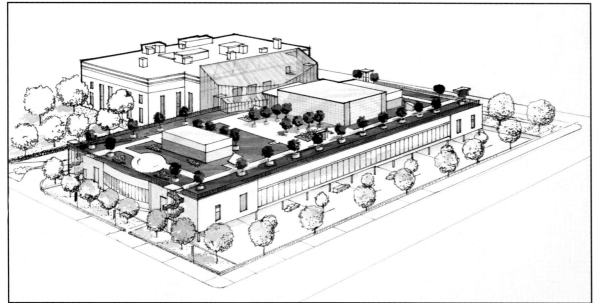

reviewing books, and encouraging students to sign up for a library card.

In 1926, when local industry was expanding, TPL's main library offered a new Technology Department, which focused on the natural and practical sciences, manufacturing, and business.

LCL began offering a bookmobile service in 1937. Through a federal grant and an increase in the county commissioners' appropriation, LCL purchased a vehicle, stocked it with nearly 3,000 volumes, and sent a librarian along for the ride. Patrons not only could come on board to make their selections, but also could request items for delivery on the next bookmobile visit.

NEW HOME FOR THE MAIN LIBRARY

While the depression wreaked havoc on the financial state of many local citizens, these citizens began to utilize TPL more. Financial problems also hit the library, causing a reduction of service hours, the closure of in-school branch libraries, and the reduction of salaries. But these reductions did not hamper the growth of the library system. With the help of the Public Works Administration (PWA), the Toledo Heights and Locke Branch libraries were also built in the 1930s. The Kent Branch expanded, and the Point Place Branch was opened later that decade.

The main TPL library was bursting at the seams. Because of insufficient shelving, librarians were forced to stack some books on the floor and the window ledges. With these new shelving concerns in mind, librarians and patrons began planning to build a new main library building.

The PWA came on board with the planning, and the board of education offered to sell an entire block of land framed by Michigan Street, Madison Avenue, 10th Street, and Adams Street to the library. This land not only allowed for a larger building site, but also provided enough space for future expansion.

Ground was broken for TPL's new

building in 1938, 100 years after the formation of the Young Men's Library Association. The Enoch Pratt Free Library in Baltimore was used as a model for the floor layout and organization of departments, and the exterior of the building bore a striking resemblance to the facade of the Folger Shakespeare Library in Washington, D.C.

The new TPL building was designed to allow not only for future expansion, but also for visitors to browse the collection, as well as to store additional items in nonpublic stacks. The library's departments grew from one children's and three adult departments to two children's and nine adult departments, including the new local history and genealogy departments. The new

library was open to the public on September 4, 1940.

THE LIBRARIES' MERGER

The continued growth of the area's library systems and the demands of their patrons began to take its toll on all three library organizations. In 1962, more than $1.7 million was requested from the county commissioners by the three libraries combined. But since the districts of the systems overlapped and many of the services were the same, it made sense to consider a merger. A consolidated system would provide more resources to more citizens.

For the next eight years, proposals were discussed by librarians and patrons, steering committees were

formed, and studies were performed. But the three systems remained separate. In 1970, however, the three systems merged to form the Toledo-Lucas County Public Library (T-LCPL). As a combined system, it served some 500,000 people in 343 square miles of Lucas County.

Combining the three systems, thus consolidating financial and material resources, resulted in the introduction of many new services to the community in the 1970s. For example, the Homebound Service, initiated in 1973, provided for a librarian to deliver materials to county residents who were unable to visit the library. Additional outreach to the Child Study Institute, Lucas County Jail, and Toledo House of Corrections began in 1977.

INTRODUCTION OF NEW TECHNOLOGIES

Even before the merger of the three library systems, the trend toward increasing technology within the libraries had begun. In October 1948, for example, TPL added 16mm education films to its collection for loan by churches, civic and social organizations, and individuals. Nonmusical recordings, including poetry, drama, speeches, and language instruction, were added in 1950. In 1971, the Records Lending Service began operations, offering cassettes by 1976. Other technological additions to the collection included videocassettes in 1980 and compact discs in 1985.

New items and ideas followed the technology expansion in the area of library operations. In 1973, T-LCPL became the first public library in Ohio to go on-line with the Ohio College Library Center (OCLC). In 1975, the public had access to a computer terminal at the main library, where individuals could check for titles throughout the catalog of OCLC member libraries.

In 1982, T-LCPL began to input data into a system that would eventually eliminate the card catalog drawer system. It took four years to input the card catalog information for each item in the collection, attach a bar code to each item, and build a database of library patrons. But by 1986, the system was up and running.

In 1991, patrons with computer and modem capabilities could dial into the Toledo Electronic Library, reserve items, check library hours and locations, and learn about library activities. In 1995, dial-up patrons could also access Toledo's Information Gateway to Electronic Resources (TIGER). This service provides bibliographic information from some 13,000 journals and access to Internet resources. Additional information has been available through the Internet since 1996.

THE LIBRARY TODAY

Technological advances, growth of T-LCPL's branch system, and other improvements were made possible by a number of levies passed in the 1970s and 1980s. In 1995, a $38.6 million bond issue was approved by county voters that would prepare the library for the new century.

This bond issue would allow for much needed upgrades and improvements at many of T-LCPL's branches. But undoubtedly the most impressive projects included in the capital improvements plan involved the addition to and refurbishing of the main library.

In August 2001, T-LCPL rededicated the main library, which constituted the culmination of five years of planning and hard work. While the large addition to the library opened in 2000, the renovation of the historic main library building was still not complete. With everything in place, the library held a gala rededication, complete with tours of the new facilities. Highlights included the 13,470-square-foot Children's Library, a dramatic increase in space compared to the former 3,312 square feet. In total, the main library formerly operated within 186,000 square feet of space; the addition and renovation project expanded the library to 271,000 square feet. This additional space opens new doors for new services and an ever expanding collection.

When the main library first opened its doors in 1940 at its present location, circulation stood at approximately 1.6 million. In the 2000-2001 year, circulation topped 6.1 million. At one point, state-of-the-art technology included the library's air-conditioning system. Today, T-LCPL boasts its satellite for videoconferencing. These changes and more are reflective of the entire history of libraries in the Toledo area. As the community requested more information, it provided the library with the funding and support to meet its needs. The community realized early on the benefits of a local library system and have supported that system—now ably represented by the Toledo-Lucas County Public Library—for more than 125 years.

The Bostwick-Braun Company

ESTABLISHED IN 1855 BY TWO BROTHERS FROM RACINE, WISCONSIN—WILLIAM AND CHARLES B. ROFF—THE BOSTWICK-BRAUN COMPANY IS TODAY ONE OF THE COUNTRY'S OLDEST AND LARGEST FULL-SERVICE, GENERAL-LINE HARDWARE DISTRIBUTORS. THE COMPANY'S VISION STATEMENT—"QUALITY IS OUR CORNERSTONE, SERVICE IS

our mission, people are our pride"—is indicative of its success in professionally and efficiently serving a 10-state region as a wholesale hardware distributor for commercial, industrial, and retail customers.

The Bostwick-Braun Company has a long history of continued growth in Toledo. As the population increased in Ohio in the mid-19th century, so did the itch of prospective entrepreneurs. The Roffs were two such businessmen who saw the potential for success in Toledo. In 1855, after traveling by horseback to begin a new life in the city, they established W. & C.B. Roff & Company, a retail and wholesale hardware business located at 130 Summit Street.

After only two exceptional years, the Roff brothers' business grew out of its first building. With only 13,000 people living in Toledo, the 1858 city directory listed the annual sales for W. & C.B. Roff & Company as $75,000.

The growth of the firm attracted a number of quality employees. Among the new faces was Oscar Alonzo Bostwick, hired in 1862 as the company's first traveling salesman. Bostwick became a principal in 1865 and remained active with the company until 1893. German-born Carl F. Braun came on board in 1866, followed by his cousin George A. Braun in 1868. The Braun cousins purchased an interest in the company in 1868, after the retirement of William Roff. Ultimately, after Charles B. Roff retired in 1873, the company became known as The Bostwick-Braun Company.

A COMPANY ON THE MOVE

Exceptional sales, as well as growing out of its building, became the norm for W. & C.B. Roff & Company. In 1865, the business again moved to a larger building on Monroe Street, giving it access to the Maumee River. As business and industry continued to grow in the United States, so did the demand for hardware.

With Bostwick and the Brauns at the helm, the renamed Bostwick-Braun Company remained at the corner of Monroe and St. Clair streets until after the turn of the century, when the firm built its own building. The Bostwick-Braun Company building was completed in 1908. The 300,000-square-foot, eight-story structure could hold more than 200 million pounds of merchandise.

With the majority of its business coming from the West, the company expanded out of state in 1985, when its 280,000-square-foot distribution center opened in Ashley, Indiana. After several more moves, The Bostwick-Braun Company settled into its current headquarters on 13th Street in late 1990.

QUALITY IS THE CORNERSTONE

Every year, The Bostwick-Braun Company hosts its Fall Market. Held in Toledo, this event welcomes more than 300 manufacturers who show more than 1,000 dealers and retailers the latest innovations in the hardware business.

Yet another testimony to the company's vision are the employ-

THE BOSTWICK-BRAUN COMPANY'S HEADQUARTERS IS LOCATED IN DOWNTOWN TOLEDO AT THE CORNER OF WOODRUFF AND 13TH STREETS.

THE COMPANY'S SOME 250 EMPLOYEE-OWNERS RECEIVED THE NORTHWEST OHIO ENTREPRENEUR OF THE YEAR AWARD IN 2000, GIVEN BY THE ACCOUNTING FIRM OF ERNST & YOUNG.

ees themselves. Since 1980, The Bostwick-Braun Company has been employee-owned. Because of this corporate structure, each Bostwick-Braun employee sees his or her role in the overall company as a step to individual prosperity. Each employee-owner is committed to excellence, innovation, and professionalism. Everyone understands that the success the company enjoys will directly affect, and benefit, the employee-owners. This attitude results in qual-

ity products, exceptional service, and an outstanding reputation with the company's customers.

The Bostwick-Braun Company believes in the value of having a knowledgeable staff. All employees are required to obtain a minimum of 32 hours of corporate-sponsored training annually. This knowledge, tied with the employee-owners' commitment to their company, was recognized by local accounting firm Ernst & Young in naming

Bostwick-Braun the Northwest Ohio Entrepreneur of the Year in 2000—an award that is based on a company's innovation, financial performance, and commitment to its businesses and its community. Upon receiving the award on behalf of the firm's some 250 employee-owners, Bill Bollin, president, said, "This award is truly a tribute to all the employee-owners of the company. An entrepreneur by definition is one who owns and operates a business, and we have more than 250 of them working towards common goals. They made the difference."

As evidenced by the company's accomplishments and accolades, the future promises continued success. The Bostwick-Braun Company is a great success in Toledo and beyond.

CLOCKWISE FROM TOP:
FOR ITS EXCEPTIONAL BUSINESS PRACTICES AND SERVICE, BOSTWICK-BRAUN RECEIVES SEVERAL AWARDS EACH YEAR FROM VARIOUS VENDORS AND AFFILIATIONS.

ELAINE CANNING, EXECUTIVE VICE PRESIDENT OF BOSTWICK-BRAUN, CONGRATULATES 1999 EMPLOYEE OF THE YEAR, SCOTT WOLFRUM, SHIPPING SUPERVISOR. THE COMPANY'S ANNUAL OWNER'S CELEBRATION RECOGNIZES OUTSTANDING EMPLOYEE-OWNERS, AND PAYS TRIBUTE TO THOSE WHO MADE BOSTWICK-BRAUN'S ESOP POSSIBLE IN 1980.

ALL EMPLOYEE-OWNERS ARE REQUIRED TO OBTAIN 32 HOURS OF CORPORATE-SPONSORED TRAINING ANNUALLY, WHICH ENABLES THEM TO PROVIDE THE BEST SERVICE POSSIBLE TO VALUED CUSTOMERS.

BOSTWICK-BRAUN HOLDS ITS ANNUAL DEALER MARKET AT THE SEAGATE CONVENTION CENTRE IN DOWNTOWN TOLEDO. ON AVERAGE, IT DRAWS SOME 1,000 CUSTOMERS AND 400 VENDOR BOOTHS.

Fifth Third Bank

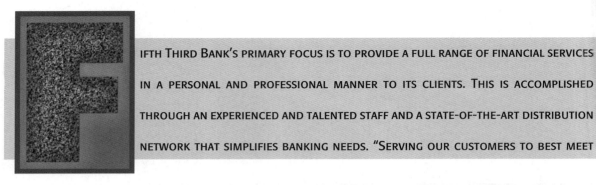

IFTH THIRD BANK'S PRIMARY FOCUS IS TO PROVIDE A FULL RANGE OF FINANCIAL SERVICES IN A PERSONAL AND PROFESSIONAL MANNER TO ITS CLIENTS. THIS IS ACCOMPLISHED THROUGH AN EXPERIENCED AND TALENTED STAFF AND A STATE-OF-THE-ART DISTRIBUTION NETWORK THAT SIMPLIFIES BANKING NEEDS. "SERVING OUR CUSTOMERS TO BEST MEET

their needs is why we're in business and what we do best," says Robert A. Sullivan, president and CEO, Fifth Third Bank (Northwestern Ohio). "We strive to make banking convenient by providing consumers and businesses with numerous locations, longer hours, and products and services to meet individualized needs."

Fifth Third Bank (Northwestern Ohio) has $4.1 billion in assets and operates 45 full-service banking centers in the Greater Toledo area, Bowling Green, Findlay, Tiffin, Fostoria, Fremont, Gibsonburg, and Sandusky, plus Lambertville and Monroe in Michigan. Nine of those centers are Bank Mart® locations, which are open seven days a week inside select Kroger stores. For added convenience, the bank offers more than 80 Jeanie® 24-hour ATMs in northwestern Ohio and southeastern Michigan.

Fifth Third also offers Jeanie Telephone Banking and Online Banking at www.53.com. With Fifth Third

Online Banking, personal and business customers have access to their accounts 24 hours a day, and can check account balances, transfer funds, pay bills, open a checking or savings account, and apply for a loan or credit card.

HARDWORKING PRODUCTS AND SERVICES

A diversified financial services company, Fifth Third provides a broad array of products and services to every type of customer through four primary businesses: retail banking, commercial banking, investment advisory services, and Midwest Payment Systems (MPS), the bank's data processing subsidiary.

Retail banking encompasses the full range of products and services provided at Fifth Third banking centers, including totally free checking and other lifestyle checking options, savings accounts, certificates of deposit, mortgage and installment loans, home equity loans and lines of credit, credit cards, small-business banking, and investment services.

Fifth Third's commercial customers appreciate the breadth of financial products available. The bank offers traditional funding for expansion, real estate, and venture capital projects, as well as financing for leasing and international opportunities, initial public offerings, and closely held services.

Investment Advisors, Fifth Third's money management arm, is in the business of managing money for individuals, companies, and not-for-profit organizations. One of the largest money managers in the Midwest, Fifth Third has more than $190 billion in assets, $36 million of which is actively managed by the bank. Fifth Third offers investment, brokerage, trust, and private banking services, including underwriting and public financing services to its clients.

Fifth Third's fourth primary business, MPS, provides data processing solutions to more than 85,000 retail locations and financial institutions around the world. MPS processes some 5 billion transactions in 18 different currencies annually. For individual consumers, that means

FIFTH THIRD BANK (NORTHWESTERN OHIO) PRESIDENT AND CEO ROBERT A. SULLIVAN (LEFT) AND CHAIRMAN JOHN SZUCH

FIFTH THIRD CENTER IN DOWNTOWN TOLEDO SERVES AS THE HEADQUARTERS FOR FIFTH THIRD BANK'S NORTHWESTERN OHIO AFFILIATE.

Fifth Third is there when they use their credit or debit cards to purchase a suit at Saks Fifth Avenue or a book at Barnes & Noble.

WORKING HARD IN THE COMMUNITY

Fifth Third Bank is dedicated to enhancing the quality of life in the communities it serves, including involvement by employees, as well as corporate support. Through private trusts and foundations managed by Fifth Third and its own Fifth Third Foundation, the bank supports programming in education, the arts, community development, and human services.

Fifth Third is proud to perform its fiduciary responsibility with the highest degree of professionalism and to work in partnership with the philanthropic community to ensure a better quality of life for all.

ONE OF THE HARDEST-WORKING BANKS IN THE BUSINESS

Fifth Third Bank, one of the nation's premier financial institutions, has a rich banking heritage of more than 100 years. Founded in Cincinnati as the Bank of Ohio Valley in 1858, it acquired its unusual name as a result of its 1871 acquisition by the Third Na-

tional Bank, which combined with the Fifth National Bank in 1908. Today, it is comprised of 16 banking affiliates located in Ohio, Kentucky, Indiana, Michigan, Illinois, and Florida. The Northwestern Ohio affiliate headquartered in Toledo was established in 1989.

Fifth Third has enjoyed phenomenal success for the last quarter century. Despite the ups and downs of the economy and the banking industry, Fifth Third has reported record earnings and dividend growth every year since 1973. Today, the bank has more than $69 billion in assets and more than 15,000 employees. It operates more than 950 full-service locations and nearly 2,000 Jeanie ATMs. During the past quarter century, the bank has increased earnings at an average rate of 16 percent, outperformed the Standard & Poor's 500 by 16-fold, and reported revenue growth that is twice the industry average.

That success, combined with the bank's high capital ratios and consistently strong credit quality, has led industry analysts to name it the number one bank in the country for nine consecutive years. Fifth Third Bank management attributes the bank's performance to hard work, sales effort, teamwork, cost control, and employees' willingness to give more than 100 percent to their jobs, a principle referred to as hustle. Hence, Fifth Third's tag line, Working Hard To Be The Only Bank You'll Ever Need.®

DRIVE-UP JEANIE® ATMS PROVIDE 24-HOUR CONVENIENCE TO CUSTOMERS.

CUSTOMERS CAN BANK SEVEN DAYS A WEEK AT BANK MART® LOCATIONS INSIDE SELECT KROGER STORES.

FIFTH THIRD IS A FINANCING LEADER FOR COMMERCIAL REAL ESTATE THROUGH THREE FINANCING VEHICLES—CONSTRUCTION LOANS, CONVENTIONAL FINANCING, AND PLACEMENT WITH CAPITAL ENTITIES.

The University of Toledo

STABLISHED IN 1872, THE UNIVERSITY OF TOLEDO (UT) HAS GROWN TO BE THE ONE OF THE LARGEST PUBLIC UNIVERSITIES IN OHIO. WITH APPROXIMATELY 19,000 STUDENTS, THE UNIVERSITY REMAINS COMMITTED TO THE FOUNDING PRINCIPLES THAT WERE SET MORE THAN A CENTURY AGO: THE PURSUIT OF ACADEMIC EXCELLENCE AND THE DESIRE

for all students to reach their highest potential.

Located in the heart of a thriving residential community, UT's campus includes residence facilities; a 150,000-square-foot Student Recreation Center; and the impressive Glass Bowl Stadium. Throughout the campus, several world-class teaching facilities have been built and are staffed with world-renowned faculty members who focus on personal attention.

With approximately 80 percent of UT's instructors holding doctorates, students not only benefit from their vast knowledge, but also from small class sizes with an average student-to-faculty ratio of 17-to-1. The university also offers a full range of financial aid options, including scholarships that recognize and reward academic achievements and leadership skills.

WEB TECHNOLOGY HAS ALLOWED THE UNIVERSITY OF TOLEDO TO OFFER QUALITY EDUCATION THROUGH DISTANCE LEARNING TO MEET THE DIVERSE NEEDS OF TODAY'S STUDENTS.

NATIONAL RECOGNITION

Living up to the university's founding principles has not only resulted in a history of more than 125 years, but also garnered several national accolades for UT. The university's programs, faculty, and facilities have been highlighted in a number of media venues, including the *Wall Street Journal*,

THE UNIVERSITY OF TOLEDO (UT) WAS RECENTLY NAMED ONE OF THE 22 MOST BEAUTIFULLY LANDSCAPED CAMPUSES IN THE NATION BY THE AMERICAN SOCIETY OF LANDSCAPE ARCHITECTS.

USA Today, Consumer Reports, CNN, C-SPAN, and *The Today Show*. UT was also recently listed in *The 100 Best Colleges for African-American Students,* and was recognized by the American Society of Landscape Architects as one of the 22 most beautifully landscaped campuses in the country.

In recognition of its technology advancements, *Yahoo! Internet Life* magazine has dubbed UT one of America's 100 most wired colleges.

EMPHASIS ON DIVERSITY

As a nationally recognized institution, UT offers certificates and associate's, bachelor's, master's, and doctoral degrees within eight colleges: Arts and Sciences, Business Administration, Education, Engineering, Health and Human Services, Pharmacy, Law, and University College. Each college offers programs of study to attract students with diverse career goals.

UT offers its students and the community a unique opportunity through its University College. The college's mission is to provide lifelong access to education for the success of students and the community by offering quality academic programs and learning services. University College serves both traditional students and adult learners seeking baccalaureate and associate's de-

grees, as well as credit certificate programs. In addition, the college responds to the needs of the community through outreach programs, distance learning, and continuing education.

UT's diverse academic offerings are balanced with a wide range of activities for students. With more than 200 campus organizations, students are free to pursue many interests. And, as a member of the Mid-American Conference (MAC), UT supports 19 varsity sports. Cheered on by the local community, UT's football, baseball, and basketball games have become popular events in the area.

UT's students hail from all areas of Ohio, the United States, and nearly 90 countries around the world. The International House, one of UT's residential facilities, provides an opportunity for students from around the nation and the world to live and learn together. Additional global experiences can occur through partnerships with businesses and organizations, which provide students with co-op, internship, and international study opportunities.

With an extensive list of accolades and ever expanding educational opportunities, the University of Toledo stands to make a lasting impact on the Greater Toledo area for years to come.

BUILDING ON ITS RICH HISTORY, MAUMEE VALLEY COUNTRY DAY SCHOOL HAS MAINTAINED ITS REPUTATION AS A PREMIER COLLEGE PREPARATORY EDUCATIONAL INSTITUTION, SERVING STUDENTS AGED THREE THROUGH 18 YEARS WHO COME FROM COMMUNITIES IN NORTHWEST OHIO AND SOUTHEAST MICHIGAN.

Sisters Marian and Mary Smead moved their private day school from western New York State to Toledo in 1884. The Smead School for Girls, predecessor to today's Maumee Valley Country Day School, officially opened that year with 35 day students, eight boarders, and eight faculty members. In 1930, the 72 wooded acres of the school's current home on Reynolds Road were offered by one of the school's board members. When the doors opened in September 1934, the school was renamed the Maumee Valley Country Day School, and male students were permitted to enroll. Presently, the enrollment is approximately 500 students.

It works to develop the whole child—including intellectual, physical, aesthetic, emotional, social, and ethical development—through a challenging liberal arts core curriculum.

Students from preschool through high school are offered a multitude of hands-on learning opportunities in a nurturing, supportive environment, which includes a 10-to-1 student to teacher ratio, emphasiz-ing personal attention from a dedicated and creative faculty. Each student has a faculty advisor who is attentive to his or her academic, social, and emotional well-being. Part advocate, cheerleader, disciplinarian and friend, the advisor works with other faculty members to help guide students through the challenges of school and becoming young adults.

With a no-cut participatory athletics program and an outstanding fine arts program showcased in the Wolfe Gallery and the new Millennium Theatre, Maumee Valley Country Day School students are encouraged to develop all of their talents. The curriculum is multi-disciplinary and project-oriented with an emphasis on critical thinking and discussion. Technology is appropriately integrated throughout the curriculum. Students in third through eighth grade take a week-long trip each year that helps their learning come to life.

The upper school Winterim program is the capstone of Maumee Valley's experiential education pro-gram. Each January, upper school students enroll in a three-and-one-half week intensive study—either a campus-based course, educational travel, independent study or exchange at one of 27 network schools across the country. Through courses ranging from building computers to filmmaking, or from cycling the Mayan route in Mexico to interning in a medical laboratory, students experience new ways to learn outside the classroom. They develop a willingness to take risks, learn to think and act for themselves, and become more familiar with the world and their role in it.

Today, a diverse student body—30 percent students of color—comes from miles around to attend this independent, liberal arts school. The combined SAT scores of its students are among the highest in the area and the percent of seniors recognized by the National Merit program is second to none. Generally, 100 percent of graduates go on to higher education, many being accepted into the most selective colleges and universities in the nation.

MAUMEE VALLEY COUNTRY DAY SCHOOL IS COMMITTED TO ITS MISSION "TO ENABLE STUDENTS TO BECOME ENLIGHTENED, COMPASSIONATE, AND CONTRIBUTING CITIZENS OF OUR GLOBAL COMMUNITY, WHILE PREPARING GRADUATES FOR THEIR BEST POSSIBLE OPPORTUNITIES IN HIGHER EDUCATION."

Libbey Inc.

has its roots in East Cambridge, Massachusetts, and was once known as the New England Glass Company.

The Libbey name first became associated with the New England Glass Company in 1870, when William L. Libbey was hired as a sales manager. His son Edward Drummond Libbey joined him in 1874, working as a clerk. In 1878, when competition forced the company to close, William Libbey saw an opportunity, took over the New England Glass Company, and renamed it the New England Glass Works, Wm. L. Libbey & Sons Props. Libbey moved the company to Toledo in 1888 and, in 1892, renamed the company the Libbey Glass Company.

STRIVING TO DELIVER QUALITY PRODUCTS THROUGH INNOVATIVE TECHNOLOGY AND RESPONSIVE CUSTOMER SERVICE, LIBBEY INC. IS A LEADER IN THE DESIGN, MANUFACTURE, AND MARKETING OF HIGH-QUALITY GLASSWARE AND TABLEWARE.

In 1893, when the World's Columbian Exposition opened in Chicago, Edward Libbey built a fully operational glass factory at the fair. The exposure Libbey received at the exposition resulted in worldwide name recognition for the company. That recognition has grown as the company has spanned three centuries of operation.

DIVERSIFICATION

In the early years, hand-cut glass was the company's main product. Because of the time and skill necessary to create glass pieces, the cost was high, with glass considered a luxury item by many. The development of today's functional household uses for glass was spurred by Michael Owens' invention of the first automatic glassmaking machine, which produced stemware faster and cheaper than ever before.

Today, Libbey serves the retail, foodservice, and specialty markets with a variety of tableware products. To better position itself as an industry leader, Libbey has made some strategic investments over the years, including the acquisition of Syracuse China Company and World Tableware Inc., and the firm's partnership with Vitrocrisa.

Since acquiring Syracuse China in 1995, Libbey has become known as a leader not only in glassware, but also in ceramic dinnerware as well. The World Tableware Inc.

acquisition in 1997 added to Libbey's ceramic dinnerware line, as well as providing metal flatware and hollowware to the company's foodservice customers.

Since 1997, Libbey has partnered with Vitrocrisa, the largest glass tableware manufacturer in Mexico. The joint venture expanded Libbey's production and distribution capabilities in Latin America, and also enabled Libbey to become the exclusive distributor of Crisa products in the United States and Canada.

CUSTOMER FOCUSED

Libbey is driven by its vision to be "World-Class, second to none." This vision is supported by the company's mission to be a customer-focused organization delivering world-class performance through the ideas and achievements of motivated people, winning together through teamwork. Libbey values include teamwork, change, performance, respect, and development. To that end, the company strives to deliver quality products through innovative technology and responsive customer service.

As new products and ideas are developed, Libbey Inc.'s customers benefit from the company's new designs, exciting colors, and dramatic shapes. The name and leadership of Libbey will continue to hold a preeminent position in the industry for years to come.

S A WHOLLY OWNED OPERATING UTILITY OF THE FIRSTENERGY CORP., TOLEDO EDISON COMPANY HAS BEEN SERVING CUSTOMERS IN THE TOLEDO AREA FOR MORE THAN 100 YEARS. "WHEN FOLKS IN TOLEDO THINK OF ELECTRIC SERVICE, THEY THINK OF TOLEDO EDISON, OR, AS MANY CALL IT, 'THE

Edison,'" says James Murray, president of FirstEnergy's Western Region, which includes Toledo Edison's service area.

Its predecessor, Toledo Traction Company, was a horse-drawn trolley operation owned by Albion Lang in the 1890s. With Thomas Edison's invention of the three-wire system for electric distribution, Lang could power his trolleys by electricity. In 1895, Lang received the exclusive Toledo license for Thomas Edison's three-wire system, along with the right to use Edison's name in the corporate title. Thus, Toledo Edison Company was born.

The company's first power plant, Water Street Station, was named for its Toledo location and built in 1898. The 4,000-kilowatt plant was expanded several times to meet Toledo's electricity demand in the early 1900s.

Water Street Station's generating units were supplemented and later replaced by other coal-fired plants, such as Acme Station on Front Street and Bay Shore Station in Oregon, Ohio. By 1977, the company that once had used horse-drawn line trolleys began making electricity with atomic power at its Davis-Besse Nuclear Power Station, near Oak Harbor, Ohio.

"Like the technology used to make electricity, the company itself has changed with the times," Murray says.

CREATING FIRSTENERGY

The electric utility industry, having undergone regulation in the 1930s, began deregulating in the 1990s. To prepare for competition, Toledo Edison joined with Cleveland Electric Illuminating to form Centerior Energy in 1986, and in 1997, merged with Ohio Edison, creating FirstEnergy.

Headquartered in Akron, FirstEnergy is the nation's 10th-

largest investor-owned electric utility. Its other operating companies include Cleveland Electric Illuminating Company and Ohio Edison in Ohio, and Penn Power in Pennsylvania. FirstEnergy's 16 power plants have a capacity of more than 12,000 megawatts and serve some 2.2 million customers within 13,200 square miles of northern and central Ohio, and western Pennsylvania. FirstEnergy's proposed merger with Morristown, New Jersey-based GPU, Inc. will make it the nation's fourth largest, nearly doubling its number of customers and tripling its service area.

Being part of a larger operation also provides Toledo Edison the resources to continue its time-honored tradition as a socially responsible corporate citizen.

"We've always been an integral part of the communities we serve," Murray says. Noting that Toledo Edison has contributed millions of dollars since 1990 to the local United Way campaign, he adds that, "We've consistently been a leader in those kinds of programs, but we also have a long history in the area's economic development arena."

When building restoration, such as the Valentine Theater, and con-

struction projects, such as the new Mud Hens stadium, are occurring, Toledo Edison is one of the first to come forward with significant contributions. The company is also playing a significant role in the development of the city's east side riverfront.

Water Street Station, decommissioned in the mid-1980s, was donated to the city for redevelopment as a restaurant-retail facility. Likewise, Toledo Edison Company's now-closed Acme power plant site will be redeveloped.

"We're deeply committed to these kinds of projects and, as part of FirstEnergy, we're steadily diversifying our services," Murray says. "But delivering reliable electricity is still our core business. And, here in Toledo, we're still 'the Edison.'"

CLOCKWISE FROM TOP:
TUCKED WITHIN THE CITY'S SKYLINE, THE TOLEDO EDISON COMPANY BUILDING REFLECTS THE MAUMEE RIVER.

WHITE LIGHTS WHOSE POWER IS SUPPLIED BY TOLEDO EDISON PLANTS DOT THE OUTLINE OF THE ARCH-STYLE CHERRY STREET BRIDGE AT DUSK.

TOLEDO EDISON'S BAY SHORE POWER PLANT GENERATES ELECTRICITY BY BURNING PETROLEUM COKE, A WASTE PRODUCT THAT COMES FROM THE NEARBY BP TOLEDO REFINERY.

TOLEDO EDISON LINE CREWS SAFELY MAINTAIN THE COMPANY'S ELECTRIC SYSTEM TO ENSURE RELIABLE SERVICE FOR THE COMPANY'S SOME 370,000 CUSTOMERS.

RICK ZAIDAN

United Association Local # 50 Plumbers & Steamfitters

HE UNITED ASSOCIATION LOCAL UNION 50 WAS CHARTERED IN 1890 WITH 12 ORIGINAL CHARTER MEMBERS. LOCAL 50 IS NOW ONE OF 400 CHARTERED LOCAL UNIONS OF THE UNITED ASSOCIATION THROUGHOUT THE UNITED STATES AND CANADA. TODAY, LOCAL 50 HAS GROWN TO MORE THAN 900 ACTIVE MEMBERS AND APPRENTICES, AND BOASTS

TODAY, UNITED ASSOCIATION LOCAL # 50 PLUMBERS & STEAMFITTERS HAS GROWN TO MORE THAN 900 ACTIVE MEMBERS AND APPRENTICES, AND BOASTS 350 RETIREES WHO HAVE SERVED THE ORGANIZATION WITH PRIDE, SKILL, AND DEDICATION.

350 retirees who have served the organization with pride, skill, and dedication. Local 50 offers a variety of well-trained workers: certified welders, licensed plumbers, and heating and air-conditioning service technicians who are fully capable of servicing every need in the plumbing, heating, and mechanical construction industry.

Local 50, along with more than 110 contractors, services an area of northwest Ohio from the Indiana line east to Sandusky Bay, and from the Michigan line to south of Findlay. Local 50, along with the Mechani-

cal Contractors Association and the Plumbing Contractors Association, is ready and able to serve any need of business and industry for new construction, renovation, and remodeling.

For more than a century, the United Association (UA) Local Union 50 Plumbers & Steamfitters has been providing its membership with a multitude of benefits, including pension plans and a self-insured health and welfare plan, as well as a credit union for the membership and their families.

HIGHLY TRAINED, SKILLED CRAFTSMEN

Members of Local 50 have a vested interest in the training of future workers. In support of its goals to have highly trained and skilled craftsmen, Local 50 maintains quality and

safety standards on the job. The organization provides an extensive apprenticeship program for individuals who apply and are interested in training in this specialized industry.

Because recertification for certain skills is required, journeymen in Local 50 have the opportunity to participate in continuing training and education. Such programs foster the spirit of building a career with the union, rather than of just meeting job requirements.

When Local 50 Plumbers & Steamfitters began, it focused on plumbers and gasfitters, but over time expanded to pipefitters, steamfitters, welders, and heating and air-conditioning service mechanics. Now, approximately 200 students are enrolled in Local 50's apprenticeship program each year, which consists of a five-year program requiring 264 training hours each year.

After working all day in the industry, the students attend classes from one to three nights a week, three hours each night. The school offers courses that provide students with expertise in various aspects of the industry. Upon graduation, each apprentice not only has earned journeyman status, but also has

earned 26 credits with Owens Community College toward an associates degree.

With the need for skilled workers growing steadily each year, Local 50 is preparing to open a new, larger training center. This 32,000-square-foot facility will accommodate approximately 300 students.

The extensive training that journeymen receive throughout the apprenticeship program qualifies them to be able to work anywhere in the United States and Canada. Through a partnership with the UA, Local 50 Plumbers & Steamfitters members are provided with the best training, which assures contractors and customers of quality workmanship.

Local 50 workers and their fellow union members from all over the country are able to handle a wide range of projects, from residential to large industrial assignments, utilizing both small and large work teams. The workers have contributed to the success of a number of projects at local facilities including the new Jeep Plant; North Star Steel

in Delta, Ohio; Defiance Central Foundry; Sun Oil; BP Refinery; and Davis Besse Nuclear Power Station.

BEST VALUE CONTRACTING PROGRAM

Local 50 Plumbers & Steamfitters also participates in the Best Value Contracting Program, a national program that promises to deliver quality performance the first time, every time. With this program, workers are more conscientious and efficient—a benefit to the contractor, the customer, and the community.

The Best Value Contracting Program stresses the use of qualified contractors, making customers and general contractors aware that the lowest bid is not always the best. While unqualified contractors can end up as the lowest bidder on a job, they can often end up costing owners more through hidden expenses such as poor workmanship, schedule delays, and substandard materials.

The Best Value Contracting Program relies on an intensive examination of competing, qualified

contractors in all critical performance areas, including staffing, training, financial stability, and technical qualifications. This program further assures contractors and customers that when using Local 50 craft workers, they are dealing with quality, trained people who deliver quality service every time.

SUPPORTING LOCAL INITIATIVES

In addition to its commitment of quality work, Local 50 Plumbers & Steamfitters has an ongoing commitment to the support of local charities and organizations. Throughout the years, countless volunteer hours have been donated to assist many worthwhile charities, including the Sunshine Children's Home, Habitat for Humanity, and Camp Miakonda, a Boy Scouts facility.

Members of the union also participate in job fairs and presentations to middle and high school students in an effort to publicize the industry. Through these efforts, Local 50 members hope to spark the interest of young men and women to enter the trade, get the proper schooling, and train to become future craft workers.

Local 50 Plumbers & Steamfitters has been committed to quality of life, a fair wage, and stability throughout the area for more than 110 years. Local 50 has the ability to handle any job, whether it requires one person or 1,000 people, and provides builders and developers peace of mind in the knowledge that they have access to a skilled workforce who are fully trained and have an outstanding work ethic. United Association Local Union # 50 continues to provide unparalleled service to fill the needs of the industry.

LOCAL 50, ALONG WITH MORE THAN 110 CONTRACTORS, SERVICES AN AREA OF NORTHWEST OHIO FROM THE INDIANA LINE EAST TO SANDUSKY BAY, AND FROM THE MICHIGAN LINE TO SOUTH OF FINDLAY.

LOCAL 50 OFFERS A VARIETY OF WELL-TRAINED WORKERS: CERTIFIED WELDERS, LICENSED PLUMBERS, AND HEATING AND AIR-CONDITIONING SERVICE TECHNICIANS WHO ARE FULLY CAPABLE OF SERVICING EVERY NEED IN THE PLUMBING, HEATING, AND MECHANICAL CONSTRUCTION INDUSTRY.

International Brotherhood of Electrical Workers Local 8

INTERNATIONAL BROTHERHOOD OF ELECTRICAL WORKERS LOCAL 8 (IBEW 8) HAS BEEN PROVIDING NORTHWEST OHIO WITH QUALITY RESIDENTIAL, INDUSTRIAL, COMMERCIAL, AND TELEDATA/ TELECOM ELECTRICAL WORKERS SINCE 1891. ■ WITH ITS OFFICES LOCATED ON A 30-ACRE COMPLEX IN ROSSFORD, IBEW 8 CONSISTS OF SOME 2,000 MEMBERS IN 12 COUNTIES OF NORTHWEST

Ohio and three counties in southeast Michigan. Performing nearly 70 percent of the residential, industrial, commercial, and teledata/ telecom electrical work in the entire 15-county area, some 80 percent of the work in Lucas County, and almost 90 percent of the work in Toledo, Local 8 workers are an integral part of industry in Toledo.

INNOVATION SUPPORT

While the names most associated with the history of electricity include Benjamin Franklin, Thomas Edison, and George Westinghouse, the dedicated, often forgotten linemen and wiremen who risked their lives to erect poles and string wires have contributed greatly to the success and accessibility of electric power, but with fewer accolades.

INTERNATIONAL BROTHERHOOD OF ELECTRICAL WORKERS (IBEW) LOCAL 8'S RETIRED WORKERS PARTICIPATE IN THE ANNUAL LABOR DAY PARADE.

As the industry began to grow and prosper, the experienced linemen and wiremen were not reaping adequate benefits. Employers often hired inexperienced men who were hungry to learn the trade and willing to work for low wages. Lack of experience made these men more dangerous to their skilled co-workers and ruined the trade's reputation.

Desperate for an effective apprenticeship program to train new workers properly and ensure fair wages, a group of experienced workers in St. Louis began to meet in 1890 to discuss common concerns and share industry notes. This group sought to bring together all members of the trade into one unified voice.

Representative F.J. Heizleman from Toledo was there in 1891 when the National Brotherhood of Electrical Workers (NBEW) convened in St. Louis. He was among representatives from seven other midwestern cities representing some 300 electrical workers. By its second con-

vention in 1892, the organization was comprised of 43 local unions and some 2,000 members. In 1893, those numbers jumped to 61 and 10,000, respectively. As the organization continued to grow in numbers and more local unions were forming throughout the country, NBEW went international in 1899, when it welcomed its first Canadian local union.

Today, IBEW is an industrial union comprised of workers in the building trades, utilities, railroad, broadcasting, telephone, manufacturing, and other industries. The union offers contract negotiation information, and administers pension funds and health and welfare funds. Training programs and apprenticeships to help members improve their skills are also available. Since its inception, IBEW has grown to more than 750,000 members throughout the United States and Canada.

A HOST OF MEMBER BENEFITS

Although membership in IBEW is not required for all electrical workers, it is strongly recommended because of the significant benefits for dues-paying members. In addition to standardized pay rates, health care, and pension plans, the union offers an outstanding apprenticeship program and ongoing training opportunities to help workers become the most qualified, innovative, and skilled in their field.

Through the Toledo Electrical Joint Apprenticeship and Training Committee (JATC), IBEW Local 8 supports the men and women who desire to become skilled electrical workers. By providing pre-apprenticeship and apprenticeship programs, JATC offers quality training to equip workers with the skills and knowledge necessary to succeed in the field.

IBEW LOCAL 8 MEMBERS AND THEIR FAMILIES GATHER FOR THE ANNUAL LABOR DAY PARADE.

These apprenticeship programs are challenging, but the rewards are great. After receiving 8,000 hours of on-the-job training and 900 hours of classroom training during the five-year program, journeymen electricians are qualified and certified to lay out, install, repair, and test electrical systems, and can earn a substantial living at the same time. A complete understanding of the National Electrical Code and OSHA regulations is taught during the five-year program, as safety is the primary goal of the union.

IBEW also acts as an advocate for its members through bargaining groups and regular meetings with local contractors. Local 8 has bargaining relationships with more than 100 employers in the area, and union representatives meet regularly with these contractors to handle on-site problems. IBEW also recruits unorganized contractors and employees, and educates unorganized people on the union benefits for both employees and employers.

A CONTINUING COMMITMENT TO THE COMMUNITY

Offices for Local 8's insurance and pension programs, administrative offices for contractors, a credit union, a rental hall, and a training facility overflow area are located at IBEW 8's 30-acre headquarters complex in Rossford. But the facility is used for more than day-to-day business; it is used as a community outreach tool. Local organizations are invited to use the facility and surrounding land to host meetings and other outings.

"It's our way of being good corporate citizens," says Dennis Duffey, Local 8 business manager. And Local 8 workers can be seen throughout the community volunteering and providing support to numerous local organizations. "Not a week goes by that someone isn't doing something," says Duffey.

Through their commitment to quality work and community support, Local 8 workers have achieved the kind of progress that would make the pioneers who met in St. Louis more than 100 years ago proud of the foundation they laid for a successful electrical construction trade. Today, the apprenticeship program they dreamed of has become a reality. IBEW is turning out highly qualified journeymen each year, and improved working conditions, fair wages, and pension programs have become industry standards.

INSTRUCTORS AT THE IBEW LOCAL 8 TRAINING CENTER TEACH APPRENTICES THE SKILLS NEEDED TO SUCCEED IN THE WORKPLACE.

Toledo Area Chamber of Commerce

SINCE ITS ESTABLISHMENT IN 1893, THE TOLEDO AREA CHAMBER OF COMMERCE HAS PLAYED A CRITICAL ROLE IN THE ECONOMIC PROSPERITY OF NORTHWEST OHIO. IT WAS IN THAT YEAR THAT THE MANUFACTURER'S ASSOCIATION AND THE CHAMBER OF COMMERCE CLUB MERGED TO CREATE AN ORGANIZATION TO ADVOCATE FOR

CLOCKWISE FROM TOP:
AMBASSADORS FOR THE TOLEDO AREA CHAM-
BER OF COMMERCE, DONNED IN THEIR SIGNA-
TURE RED JACKETS, ARE OFTEN ON HAND AT
AREA RIBBON-CUTTING AND GROUND-BREAKING
CEREMONIES, AS WELL AS OTHER CELEBRATIONS.

THE CHAMBER PROVIDES MANY OPPORTUNITIES
FOR MEMBERS TO HEAR FROM LOCAL, STATE,
AND FEDERAL OFFICIALS ABOUT LEGISLATION
THAT COULD IMPACT THE BUSINESS COMMUNITY.

A BENEFIT OF CHAMBER MEMBERSHIP IS THE
EXCHANGE OF IDEAS BETWEEN BUSINESSPEOPLE
THROUGH A VARIETY OF MENTORING EVENTS,
EDUCATIONAL PROGRAMMING, AND VOLUNTEER
ACTIVITIES.

COMPANIES DEPEND ON THE CHAMBER FOR
ALL SORTS OF NEWCOMER AND RELOCATION
MATERIAL, MAPS, BUSINESS PUBLICATIONS,
AND OTHER ECONOMIC AND COMMUNITY
INFORMATION.

business, promote the economic growth of the region, and stimulate the community's progressive public spirit. This mission has remained constant ever since.

The Toledo Area Chamber of Commerce's many accomplishments have been made possible by the thousands of volunteers from member companies who have served in key leadership roles and as chairmen and members of committees assisting the professional staff in guiding the organization's direction. Today, the chamber has built a solid membership of more than 4,200 businesses in its multicounty service area, spanning from Fortune 500 corporations to small businesses with only one employee. Members gain a return on their dues investment from the chamber's focus on economic and business development; leadership and business advocacy; and member benefits and services.

A significant part of the chamber's economic and business development efforts is the Northwest Ohio

Small Business Development Center (SBDC), which provides personal business counseling and offers educational programs to help start-up companies, as well as existing businesses. Thanks to funding from the U.S. Small Business Administration, the Ohio Department of Development, and the chamber, the SBDC is able to provide its services at no cost to clients.

The chamber focuses on economic development in two ways. First the chamber's SBDC, with several full-time counselors, assists entrepreneurs with the business-

planning and problem-solving process, including financial, human resources, and marketing issues. Second, by forming strategic relationships with other area organizations, the chamber strives to ensure continued funding, leadership, and representation to provide successful economic development for the entire region.

The Toledo Area Small Business Association (TASBA) is the small-business division of the chamber—sharing the overall mission of the chamber, but narrowing its focus to the specific needs of businesses

with 150 or fewer employees. TASBA's activities and policies are set by a 25-member board of directors, who represent a cross section of the chamber's small-business members. One of association's goals is to act as the advocate of small-business interests on public policy issues.

The chamber's economic development initiative also includes supporting minority business development. The chamber's Minority Business Services (MBS) department encourages minority entrepreneurs to become more involved with the chamber as a way to increase access to valuable benefits and services. In collaboration with the Northern Ohio Minority Business Council (NOMBC), the chamber assists in the national certification of minority business enterprises (MBE). Certification provides minority business owners access to procurement opportunities with corporate and government entities.

Creating a nurturing climate for doing business is a goal of the chamber's advocacy initiative. By working to reduce or eliminate onerous business regulation, the chamber can help members reduce the cost of doing business. The chamber is the only entity in northwest Ohio that lobbies for the entire business community on legislative issues such as tax reform, workforce development, and workplace regulations. The chamber's political action committee, the Leadership Fund, was launched in 2001 with the goal of promoting good government and probusiness candidates.

The chamber's very active volunteer structure works to monitor legislation and regulations, and takes positions on important key issues affecting business. This is a vital chamber service, since the majority of members are small to medium-sized companies that do not have the resources to perform this function individually.

Part of establishing a business-friendly climate is providing opportunities for member companies to prosper and grow. Saving money on basic business expenses has become routine for members participating in the chamber's selection of cost-cutting benefit programs. These programs deliver substantial group

discounts on health insurance, workers' compensation group ratings, cellular phone service, overnight delivery plans, life and disability insurance, dental insurance, natural gas plans, on-hold messaging packages, and an Internet employee recruitment program. These benefit programs have helped fuel a 25 percent increase in chamber membership since 1998, and more than 81 percent of the membership participate in one or more of the programs.

Many of the chamber's member services programs are designed to help companies come together, stay informed, and ultimately make better business decisions. Initiatives such as Business After Hours, the Entrepreneurial Roundtable, the TASBA Breakfast and Luncheon Speaker Series, the Candidates' Forum, the annual clambake, and the annual golf outing help keep members and local businesses abreast of important issues, provide a setting for productive networking, and offer companies a chance to promote their products and services.

The chamber's current initiatives and long history of service have been recognized by various organizations. The U.S. Chamber of Commerce has bestowed its certificate of accreditation on the Toledo Area Chamber of Commerce, a status earned by only 12 percent of chambers nationwide. In 2000, the chamber received the National Association for Membership Development's (NAMD) Award for Excellence, the highest achievement in the membership development profession, which recognizes excellence in financial performance, internal operations, and organizational mission. The chamber also won the award in 1995 and placed as a finalist in 1997.

For more than a century, the Toledo Area Chamber of Commerce has acted as a regional, private sector catalyst, bringing together resources and organizations that are necessary for the continued progress of the local business community. Today, as northwest Ohio speeds into the 21st century, the chamber is well positioned to continue its leading role in creating economic prosperity and a higher quality of life for the entire region.

Sunoco MidAmerica Marketing & Refining

OR AREA RESIDENTS, THE MOST VISIBLE ASPECT OF SUNOCO'S TOLEDO OPERATION IS ITS WOODVILLE ROAD REFINERY, WHICH HAS PLAYED A VITAL ROLE IN SUNOCO'S PETROLEUM PRODUCT BUSINESS FOR MORE THAN 100 YEARS. WHAT MAY NOT BE OBVIOUS, HOWEVER, IS THAT ADJACENT TO THE REFINERY SITE IS THE HEADQUARTERS OF

Sunoco MidAmerica Marketing & Refining, the young and dynamic organization that oversees both the marketing and refining segments of Sunoco's business throughout the Midwest region.

The formation of the regional business unit in the mid 1990s represented a unique change in approach for Sunoco. It underscored the fact that it is an American company, serving the country's heartland—the Midwest. The new name also signified an increased emphasis on marketing, integrating it with the function of refining. Sunoco MidAmerica is one of seven business units of Sunoco, which is one of the larger petroleum companies in the Unites States in terms of refining capacity.

SUNOCO TANKER TRUCKS HELP DISTRIBUTE THE VARIETY OF PRODUCTS PRODUCED AT THE REFINERY, INCLUDING GASOLINE, DIESEL, JET FUEL, KEROSENE, AND PETROCHEMICALS.

A HISTORY OF INNOVATION

The Sunoco name was first introduced to Toledoans in 1895 when the Sun Oil Company assumed ownership of the refinery. In just three years, the regional nature of the business was already becoming apparent as the company began to sell its variety of oils, paraffin, and greases throughout Indiana, Michigan, Ohio, and Wisconsin.

In the early 1900s, the refinery played an important role in the development of innovative petroleum-based products. Sunoco research efforts resulted in several important discoveries, which allowed higher quality gasoline to be produced in greater quantity. During World War I, the refinery provided the Allies with military supplies. Later, refinery engineers were also responsible for developing a process to recover a key ingredient in synthetic rubber. The discovery proved to be timely as rubber shipments from the Far East had been halted because of World War II.

Over the years, Sunoco continued to expand refinery operations. In 2000, the facility underwent a major maintenance and renovation project. Today, the latest in petroleum technology helps optimize production at the rate of 140,000 barrels-per-day or 53 million barrels-per-year. More than 60 percent of the refinery's production is gasoline. Other significant products include diesel and jet fuel, kerosene, and petrochemicals.

Sunoco opened its first retail gas station in Toledo in 1919. It pioneered the use of an innovative pump that allowed customers to select the grade of gasoline they would receive. Now, approximately 900 retail gasoline outlets sell more than 800 million gallons of Sunoco gasoline per year. A majority of the retail outlets have undergone major upgrades, renovation, and image enhancement since the formation of Sunoco MidAmerica. These sites are located in Indiana, Kentucky, Michigan, Ohio, and West Virginia.

A GOOD NEIGHBOR

Sunoco MidAmerica continues to demonstrate a long-term public commitment to environmentally responsible business activities. It was the first Fortune 500

MORE THAN 800 MILLION GALLONS OF GASOLINE ARE SOLD AT SUNOCO STATIONS EVERY YEAR (LEFT).

SUNOCO MIDAMERICA MARKETING & REFINING HAS MORE THAN 900 RETAIL GASOLINE LOCATIONS IN FIVE STATES (RIGHT).

company to adopt principles promoted by the Coalition for Environmentally Responsible Economies (CERES). Endorsing CERES principles represents the company's commitment to continuous environmental improvement and a desire to be publicly accountable for the environmental impact of its activities. Among the areas covered by CERES principles are health, environment, and safety practices; public accountability; relationships with external stakeholders; business processes and culture; and public policy.

In keeping with the CERES business approach, Sunoco MidAmerica has taken steps to ensure it is a good neighbor in the communities it serves. The company has formed a Community Advisory Panel (CAP) in an effort to enhance regular communication with the community. The panel is made up of neighborhood residents along with representatives from businesses, educational institutions, and governments from the cities of Oregon, Northwood, and East Toledo. The CAP provides a forum for discussion on topics of concern to the community and gives Sunoco the ability to share information about safety, health, environmental education, and civic concerns. Similar efforts are underway in other areas served by Sunoco.

Part of being a good neighbor means taking on the responsibility of supporting the events and activities that make up the fabric of the community. Sunoco MidAmerica actively promotes the annual United Way campaign. Many employees support the campaign with financial donations and by giving their time as volunteers to help respond to community needs.

The safety of its employees is a top priority of Sunoco MidAmerica. The company is committed to the health and well-being of its employees. The employees attend regular company-sponsored safety training meetings. Routine safety audits and inspections provide important data that can be used to recognize unsafe conditions before they develop into problems.

NEW CHALLENGES AND OPPORTUNITIES

Sunoco MidAmerica recognizes that changes are constantly occurring in today's marketplace. In an effort to respond to these challenges and opportunities, the company recently adopted a new vision statement and set of core values. These principles will guide the company as it begins its journey through the new millennium.

Sunoco MidAmerica Marketing & Refining is proud to call Toledo home. The company has renewed its commitment to building on its strong foundation of good, responsible, and honest business, with unwavering support to the community.

▲ STEVE GRAND

THE MOST VISIBLE ASPECT OF SUNOCO'S TOLEDO OPERATION IS THE WOODVILLE ROAD REFINERY, WHICH PROCESSES SOME 53 MILLION BARRELS PER YEAR.

PROFILES IN EXCELLENCE

1901-1940

FOR SOME 100 YEARS, AAA NORTHWEST OHIO HAS BEEN ONE OF THE AREA'S MOST WIDELY RECOGNIZED NAMES. WHETHER A TRAVELER IS STRANDED ON THE SIDE OF THE ROAD, WANTS TO PLAN A TRIP TO ARUBA, OR IS SHOPPING FOR COMPETITIVE INSURANCE RATES, AAA PRIDES ITSELF ON OFFERING EXCEPTIONAL CUSTOMER SERVICE,

comprehensive member benefits, and unwavering commitment to public safety.

Before the American Automobile Association (AAA) was formed, smaller, separate groups sprouted up in the late 1800s in cities such as Chicago, New York, and Philadelphia. These tight-knit groups supported automobile owners when most people still relied on the traditional horse and buggy for transportation.

In 1902, Frank C. Webb of the Long Island Automobile Club suggested forming a federation of clubs that would be represented. In March of that same year, the American Automobile Association was organized. Later that year, 15 Toledo citizens met at the old Boody House and formed a social organization called the Toledo Automobile Club. At their first official meeting on September 14, 1902, the group elected Dr. Lewis A. Liffrin as its first president and George Palmer as secretary.

From that time on, the goal of the Toledo Automobile Club, now AAA Northwest Ohio, has always been to support its members. As transportation by car became more popular, so did the need for touring information. In the 1920s, AAA began offering maps and travel books to its members. In 1934, the Triptik® was introduced, and in 1945, AAA began to handle international reservations.

AAA NORTHWEST OHIO: 100 YEARS OF SERVICE

Just as the national organization's services expanded year after year, so too did those of the local organization. As more services were offered, the value of membership increased. Today, AAA Northwest Ohio remains affiliated with AAA National, but operates as a separate entity, offering additional services specifically for residents of northwest Ohio. Currently, the organization's main office is located on Central Avenue in Toledo, and it operates 11 branches—six in the Toledo area, with additional offices in the nearby cities of Perrysburg, Bowling Green, Bryan, Defiance, and Port Clinton.

As a not-for-profit organization, AAA Northwest Ohio feeds its member fees back into the club, offering newer and better services to its members. Since its inception, AAA Northwest Ohio has kept emergency road service as its primary focus, but the organization now offers its members two additional services: a travel agency and an insurance agency.

Helping the stranded driver is AAA's number one concern. The organization pledges to respond to emergency road service requests within 30 minutes. Whether towing a vehicle to safety, changing a flat tire, boosting a battery, or delivering emergency gas, AAA will assist members wherever they are. AAA has also partnered with a number of auto manufacturers as the provider of choice for the manufacturers' roadside assistance programs for vehicle owners.

As a full-service travel agency,

A. KARL HALBEDL IS PRESIDENT AND CEO OF AAA NORTHWEST OHIO (LEFT).

AAA NORTHWEST OHIO'S MAIN OFFICE IS LOCATED ON CENTRAL AVENUE IN TOLEDO. IT ALSO OPERATES 11 BRANCHES THROUGHOUT THE AREA (RIGHT).

AAA provides its members with free maps, Tourbook®, and the popular Triptik routings, which map out the best route to the vacationer's desired destination, alerting him or her to any potential road construction or other delays. The travel service also includes vacation planning, complete with bookings for air and train travel, car rentals, hotels, and cruise lines. Through the club's Show Your Card & Save program, members can also benefit by receiving discounts at participating local and national hotels, restaurants, retail stores, and theme parks.

In addition, AAA offers competitive insurance rates for automobiles, boats, motorcycles, and RVs, as well as home owner's and life insurance. A team of professionals is on hand to provide members with personalized insurance counseling and free quotes.

COMMUNITY SAFETY

AAA maintains a strong commitment to public safety. This commitment is evident in the organization's many safety programs designed for pedestrians, motorists, and bicyclists alike. By working hand in hand with local police departments, schools, and various organizations, AAA encourages safety within the community, both on and off the road.

Child safety is a priority for AAA as well. Each year, AAA Northwest Ohio provides materials and supplies for more than 3,000 local grade schools. In addition to these supplies, AAA hosts safety patrol reward events for those fourth through sixth graders who participate as safety patrollers throughout the year.

Another kid-friendly program provided by AAA is on bike safety. Each year, a Bike Rodeo is held that features an obstacle course, a helmet fitting, and a free bike check. At the event, parents and children view a safe-bike-riding video to learn the basics of bike safety.

AAA Northwest Ohio hosts Car Care Clinics periodically, where representatives from the Toledo Police Department present safety tips, a personal defense trainer demonstrates basic self-defense techniques, and auto technicians offer suggestions to avoid major car problems and unexpected breakdowns.

Numerous national campaigns are endorsed by AAA, including Buckle Up America! and the Don't Drink & Drive! campaign. To support these efforts, AAA sponsors billboards and arranges for public service announcements to air on local radio stations. During the holiday season, AAA works with area restaurants that agree to distribute Designated Driver stickers and offer free soft drinks to designated drivers.

The wide variety of services and programs offered by AAA Northwest Ohio is a testament to the

organization's dedication not only to the automobile owner and traveler, but to local citizens of all ages. "Everything we do is for our members," says Kathryn Pencheff, managing director of marketing/public affairs. With this specific goal guiding the organization, AAA is poised to continue offering newer and better services to its members, while maintaining its traditions of support and customer service well into the future.

AAA NORTHWEST OHIO'S CONCERN FOR PUBLIC SAFETY IS EVIDENT IN THE ORGANIZATION'S MANY SAFETY PROGRAMS DESIGNED FOR PEDESTRIANS, MOTORISTS, AND BICYCLISTS ALIKE.

SINCE ITS INCEPTION, AAA NORTHWEST OHIO HAS KEPT EMERGENCY ROAD SERVICE AS ITS PRIMARY FOCUS, BUT THE ORGANIZATION NOW OFFERS ITS MEMBERS TWO ADDITIONAL SERVICES: A TRAVEL AGENCY AND AN INSURANCE AGENCY.

Owens-Illinois

HILE THE SPECIFIC ORIGIN OF GLASSMAKING IS UNKNOWN—THERE IS EVIDENCE OF BLOWN GLASS DATING BACK MORE THAN 2,000 YEARS— MUCH OF WHAT THE WORLD KNOWS TODAY ABOUT GLASS CONTAINER MANUFACTURING CAN BE TRACED TO ONE MAN: MICHAEL J. OWENS.

Owens, who began his career in the glass industry at the age of 10—shoveling coal into a furnace in a Wheeling, West Virginia, glass factory—developed the industry's first fully automatic bottle-making machine. Operational by 1903, the Owens machine yielded bottles faster, cheaper, and better than the semiautomatic machines of the 19th century. With this successful invention, the Owens Bottle Machine Company was born. By 1919, the company was not only building glassmaking machines, but had begun producing bottles, and it changed its name to Owens Bottle Company. In 1929, Owens Bottle Company merged with the Illinois Glass Company to form Owens-Illinois (O-I), known today as a leader in glass and plastics packaging.

TECHNOLOGY AND INNOVATION

Described by colleagues as a brilliant man and a mechanical genius, Owens was a hard worker who saw a need for a better way to make glass bottles. His pioneering spirit created a legacy of innovation that continues to drive O-I today. As a leader in glass and plastics technology, the company has always been willing to accept new challenges, resulting in numerous patents to its credit.

Innovative plastics packaging is one of O-I's fortes, as it has introduced multilayer containers using recycled plastics, bottles with enhanced barrier protection to increase shelf life, and closure systems with tamper-evident, child-resistant, and dispensing features. Innovations like these, coupled with high productivity and low-cost production capabilities, have made O-I the leading supplier in nearly all of the markets it serves.

With operations on five continents, O-I is one of the world's leading manufacturers of glass and plastics packaging. It is estimated that approximately one of every two glass containers used worldwide is manufactured by O-I, its affiliates, or its licensees.

CONSERVATION AND RECYCLING

Continuous improvement to manufacturing processes has always been a focus for O-I. The company has developed ways to make products better and at a lower cost, while remaining kind to the environment by incorporating more recycled materials into glass and plastics production. O-I engineers have also refined and made improvements to the company's glassmaking furnaces to make them more energy efficient, and have found ways to reduce the weight of products to conserve raw materials.

O-I is considered the largest user of recycled glass containers in the country, utilizing nearly 1 million tons annually. Further, the company is the largest purchaser of bottle-grade post-consumer recycled polyethylene terephthalate (PET), as well as being one of the largest purchasers of bottle-grade post-consumer recycled high-density polyethylene (HDPE) plastic resins in the country. These efforts have conserved

WITH OPERATIONS ON FIVE CONTINENTS, OWENS-ILLINOIS (O-I) IS ONE OF THE WORLD'S LEADING MANUFACTURERS OF GLASS AND PLASTICS PACKAGING PRODUCTS.

raw materials and helped to prolong the life of landfill sites.

FOCUS ON MINORITY EDUCATION

In addition to the products and processes O-I has developed, the company prides itself on its commitment to improve the quality of life in communities where it does business. Since 1992, O-I's primary focus for corporate contributions has been minority education.

O-I provides educational opportunities for minority and disadvantaged youth, as well as new experiences that help young people achieve their full potential. Scores of students from junior high through university-level schools have benefited from O-I's scholarships and other company-sponsored minority education programs.

Included among O-I's company-sponsored education programs is the University of Toledo's Prep/Tech Program, a math and science program for junior high students in Toledo Public Schools; Toledo EX-CEL, a scholarship incentive program established by the University of Toledo for minority high school students in Toledo Public Schools; and the 50 Men & Women of Toledo, an organization of community leaders who promote educational opportunities for minority students. O-I also supports the Toledo Technology Academy (TTA). Through financial and equipment donations, and by offering part-time and summer employment opportunities for students in TTA's plastics technology program, O-I assists students in

Toledo Public Schools who are interested in manufacturing and technology careers.

Monetary gifts benefit local schools through O-I's matching gifts program. The company also offers financial support to various organizations to encourage the development of new minority education programs, such as a summer art/employment program for inner-city youth with the Arts Commission of Greater Toledo; education support programs with Boys and Girls Clubs of America; instructional television programming with the Public Broadcasting Foundation of Northwest Ohio; and summer day camp for inner-city children at the Toledo Botanical Gardens. O-I has also

partnered with the Toledo Museum of Art and its Community Learning Resource Center designed for underserved populations, the Toledo Opera Association's Young Audience Program, and the Owens-Illinois Music Education Program and the Community Music Lessons Program with the Toledo Symphony Orchestra.

Initiated at the direction of Joseph H. Lemieux, who became chairman of Owens-Illinois in 1991, the company's minority education program has targeted some $6 million toward current and future minority education efforts. By addressing root problems, O-I's program is an investment in the future—both for the young people involved and for the Toledo area.

TODAY'S TECHNIQUES FOR HIGH-PRODUCTIVITY GLASSMAKING (LEFT) ARE THE LEGACY OF MICHAEL J. OWENS, WHO DEVELOPED IN TOLEDO THE FIRST FULLY AUTOMATIC BOTTLE-MAKING MACHINE.

O-I STRIVES TO PROVIDE ENVIRONMENTALLY FRIENDLY PACKAGING, SUCH AS FULLY RECYCLABLE PLASTIC BEER BOTTLES (RIGHT). BY USING RECYCLED MATERIALS IN ITS GLASS AND PLASTIC CONTAINERS, O-I HELPS CONSERVE RAW MATERIALS AND PROLONG THE LIFE OF LANDFILL SITES.

LESSONS FOR YOUNG MUSICIANS, PROVIDED BY MEMBERS OF THE TOLEDO SYMPHONY ORCHESTRA, ARE AMONG THE MANY MINORITY EDUCATION PROGRAMS SPONSORED BY O-I IN THE TOLEDO AREA (BELOW).

Dana Corporation

OR NEARLY A CENTURY, TOLEDO-BASED DANA CORPORATION HAS BEEN ONE OF THE GLOBAL AUTOMOTIVE SUPPLY INDUSTRY'S LEADING INNOVATORS. FOUNDED IN 1904, THE COMPANY HAS GROWN FROM ITS INITIAL LOCATION IN A GARAGE TO MORE THAN 300 FACILITIES IN SOME 35 NATIONS, BECOMING ONE OF THE WORLD'S LARGEST SUPPLIERS

to vehicle manufacturers and the aftermarket.

Dana is a leader in the development of modular systems technology, and a worldwide resource for engineering, research, and development. It is also a global leader in the manufacture of diverse vehicular components and systems. As a quality leader, Dana operations have twice won the nation's highest quality honor, the Malcolm Baldrige National Quality Award, which recognizes performance excellence and focuses on an organization's overall performance management system. These awards came in 1996 and 2000.

But perhaps most importantly, Dana is more than 75,000 people focused on finding innovative solutions for the diverse needs of its customers, whether they are located around the corner or around the world.

UNCHAINING THE AUTOMOTIVE INDUSTRY

Dana was initially established as the Spicer Manufacturing Company in Plainfield, New Jersey. The company's founder, Automotive Hall of Fame inductee Clarence Spicer, unchained the automotive industry by patenting and providing the first practical automotive driveshaft, which replaced the chain-and-sprocket drive system previously in use. To this day, Spicer's name is associated with several of the company's primary brands, including Spicer® axles and driveshafts.

In 1914, Charles A. Dana—a lawyer, politician, and businessman—joined Spicer to provide financial backing and management guidance. In recognition of these contributions, the company was renamed Dana Corporation in 1946.

INNOVATION: A CLARENCE SPICER LEGACY

True to the nature of Clarence Spicer, innovation and technology growth have been hallmarks of the Dana Corporation over the past century. Each year, Dana engineers earn hundreds of patents related to innovative products and processes. Dana operates more than 70 product research and development centers worldwide to support this effort.

Today's Dana is a thriving multinational company. Its primary businesses, which it terms foundation businesses, include axles, driveshafts,

CLOCKWISE FROM TOP:
COMPANY NAMESAKE CHARLES A. DANA (RIGHT) ONCE SAID, "STONE AND MORTAR, BRICKS AND MACHINERY CAN BE DUPLICATED, BUT THE WORKERS CANNOT."

THE DANA TRUCK FLEET BENEFITS FROM A LOGISTICS SYSTEM THAT CAN TRACK VEHICLES DOWN TO A CITY BLOCK AND COMMUNICATE WITH DRIVERS TO ENSURE TIMELY AND EFFICIENT CUSTOMER SERVICE.

DANA CORPORATION'S WORLD HEADQUARTERS IS LOCATED IN TOLEDO.

AT A DANA FACILITY IN TAIWAN, TRAINING CLASSES SHOW THAT THE DANA STYLE IS IN ACTION.

structures, brake and chassis products, fluid systems, filtration products, and bearings and sealing products. Dana provides these products to original equipment manufacturers and the service sectors of three basic markets: automotive, commercial vehicle, and off-highway. To better serve these global markets, Dana provides customers with a series of services ranging from systems integration and logistics management to replacement parts and services.

PEOPLE FINDING A BETTER WAY™

Despite the myriad of leading products that Dana engineers and manufactures, and the many markets it serves, its people still credit the Dana Style for the corporation's continued growth and success. Charles A. Dana himself once said, "There is only one thing really worthwhile about an organization and that is its men and women. Stone and mortar, bricks and machinery can be duplicated, but the workers cannot."

It was Dana's commitment to a decentralized, people-oriented organization that ultimately led the company to adopt a new corporate slogan—People Finding a Better Way—in the early 1990s. The slogan reflects the central principle of the Dana Style: The company's people are its greatest asset. Fueled by this unique mix of style and substance, Dana is one automotive supplier that has benefited by letting its people take the wheel on the road to global success.

Dana is a Fortune 500 company that may be as renowned for its style as for its continued global growth. And that's no small accomplishment, considering that its increasingly global sales have grown by an average of nearly $1 billion annually since 1993.

While the Dana Style is clearly focused on the company's people, its positive effects spill over into many other areas such as planning, communication, and quality—all of which ultimately benefit Dana's customers.

From encouraging employees to provide two ideas monthly—with a goal of implementing 80 percent of those ideas—to advocating that all Dana people complete at least 40 hours of education annually, the company has taken an aggressive approach to empowering and helping its people grow. Dana even has its own university system, Dana University, where accredited instructors teach business, industrial, and technical classes. The tangible results have included increased innovation, productivity, responsiveness, and pride.

Another element of the Dana Style is contributing to the communities in which Dana people live and work. Along with the many charitable efforts of Dana people, the Dana Foundation contributes annually to a wide variety of organizations in Toledo and other communities, including United Way, various school programs, museums, and many other groups.

As Dana Corporation comes upon its centennial anniversary, its people remain committed to supporting customers, shareholders, and communities alike for another century and beyond.

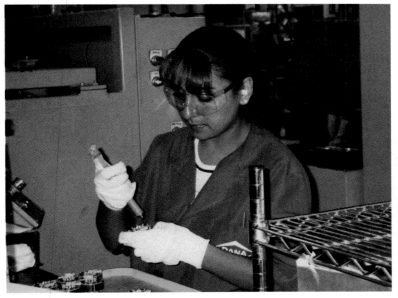

AT THE COMPANY'S FACILITY IN CHIHUAHUA, MEXICO, A DANA WORKER ASSEMBLES A CONNECTOR (LEFT).

WORKERS TEST AUTOMOTIVE AXLE GEARS FOR QUALITY AT THE DANA FACILITY IN VÖLKEMARKT, AUSTRIA (RIGHT).

General Motors Corporation, Powertrain Division, Toledo Transmission

ENERAL MOTORS CORPORATION BEGAN OPERATIONS IN TOLEDO IN 1916, UNDER THE DIRECTION OF CHEVROLET MOTOR DIVISION. ORIGINALLY LOCATED ON CENTRAL AVENUE, THE PLANT PRODUCED MANUAL TRANSMISSIONS IN THE 1920S AND 1930S FOR PASSENGER CARS AND TRUCKS. THROUGHOUT

World War II, the plant continued operations, manufacturing truck transfer cases and transmissions for four- and six-wheel military trucks. General Motors (GM) purchased the Alexis Road property in 1956 from the Martin-Parry Corporation and the Brown Trailer Company. Operations were halted at the Central Avenue site in 1957, and employees were transferred to the Alexis Road location to begin production of automatic transmissions.

The Toledo plant currently utilizes more than 1.8 million square feet of manufacturing space on Alexis Road. Additions to the property include a powerhouse, a quality assurance center, an employee park, a wellness center, and an employee skill development center. As General Motors attempted to align operations, the Hydra-matic Division acquired management responsibility of the Toledo plant in 1983. In 1990, the Hydra-matic Transmission and General Motors Engine Divisions

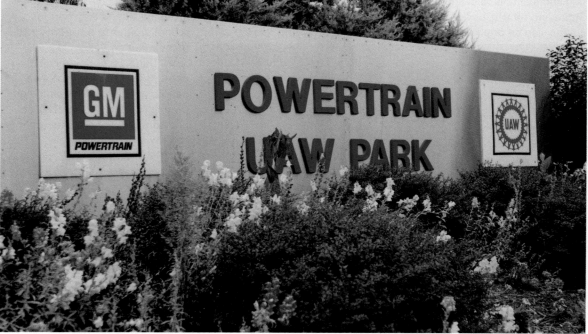

were integrated to form the GM Powertrain Division.

Over the years, Toledo's GM products have included the Turboglide automatic, rear-mounted Corvair automatic, rear-mounted Pontiac Tempest models, two-speed Power- glide automatic, THM 350 three-speed automatic, Hydra-matic 4L60 hydraulic four-speed automatic transmission, and Hydra-matic 4L60-E electronic four-speed automatic transmission (one-piece case). The Toledo Transmission Plant cur-

GENERAL MOTORS CORPORATION'S POWERTRAIN DIVISION, TOLEDO TRANSMISSION EMPLOYEES NOT ONLY HAVE COMBINED TEAMWORK, DEDICATION, AND SAFETY PERFORMANCE TO PRODUCE A HIGH-QUALITY TRANSMISSION, BUT ALSO ARE DEDICATED TO SERVING THEIR COMMUNITY.

WITH A PLANT POPULATION OF APPROXIMATELY 4,000 HOURLY AND SALARIED EMPLOYEES, GM POWERTRAIN TOLEDO RANKS AS ONE OF THE LARGEST EMPLOYERS IN NORTHWEST OHIO.

rently manufactures and assembles the two-piece-case Hydra-matic 4L60-E transmission, and maintains a three-shift manufacturing and assembly operation.

THE PLANT AND ITS PEOPLE

With a plant population of approximately 4,000 hourly and salaried employees, GM Powertrain Toledo ranks as one of the largest employers in northwest Ohio. GM Powertrain's hourly employees are represented by the United Automobile, Aerospace, and Agricultural Implement Workers of America (UAW), Local 14. UAW Local 14 is rich in history and is distinguished as one of the earliest local unions established in the international union.

The people of GM Powertrain Toledo work together, applying skills that require the highest degree of precision and workmanship. Manufacturing methods, machinery, and materials used at the Toledo plant have often been described as the industry's finest. This recognition contributes to GM Powertrain's reputation for performance in safety, quality, reliability, and efficiency.

DEDICATED TO THE COMMUNITY

GM Powertrain is not only committed to the production of high-performance transmissions; the plant is equally dedicated to its community. Every year since 1992, the plant and UAW Local 14 have received the Pillar Award from United Way in recognition of combined corporate and employee contributions totaling more than $100,000. In 2000, the plant received the Community Builder award from United Way in appreciation for its continued employee commitment to the organization's campaign.

Powertrain employees also support local Red Cross Blood Drives, Junior Achievement, and Christmas Charity campaigns. In 2000, the Toledo plant was recognized with the Gold Award from the local NAACP in acknowledgement of the plant's commitment to promoting diversity in the workplace. The plant also boasts a strong co-op student pro-

gram with various universities, including the University of Toledo Engineering Student Co-op Program.

ACCOMPLISHMENTS

GM Powertrain has been honored with numerous statewide and national awards, including recognition by Ohio Governor George Voinovich, who designated the plant as one of the top six businesses in the state that have made outstanding efforts in the prevention of pollution. In 1995 and 1999, Powertrain Toledo was ranked as the most productive transmission plant in North America by manufacturing consultants Harbour and Associates. The Toledo Transmission plant was also recognized in 2000 by the Powertrain Division for outstanding performance in both quality and safety.

General Motors Corporation's Powertrain Division, Toledo Transmission employees not only have combined teamwork, dedication, and safety performance to produce a high-quality transmission, but also are dedicated to serving their community. Through these commitments, GM Powertrain Toledo has achieved its great success and has earned respect within the Toledo area.

OPERATIONS WERE HALTED AT THE CENTRAL AVENUE SITE IN 1957, AND EMPLOYEES WERE TRANSFERRED TO THE ALEXIS ROAD LOCATION TO BEGIN PRODUCTION OF AUTOMATIC TRANSMISSIONS.

BP Toledo Refinery

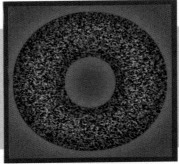

HIO MAY BE ONE OF THE LAST PLACES TO COME TO MIND WHEN THINKING OF OIL FIELDS, BUT IN THE LATE 19TH CENTURY, NORTHWEST OHIO WAS A THRIVING OIL PRODUCING CENTER. IN FACT, TOLEDO WAS ONCE HOME TO FOUR REFINERIES. THE BP COMPANY'S TOLEDO REFINERY HAS ROOTS THAT REACH BACK TO

that oil boom. Built by John D. Rockefeller in 1919, the Toledo Refinery joined the growing family of Standard Oil of Ohio and has supplied quality petroleum products ever since. In 1988, the red, white, and blue Sohio brand was replaced with the now familiar green and gold as Toledo Refinery became part of the global oil giant BP.

Though referred to as the Toledo Refinery, the plant is actually located on nearly 585 acres in the Toledo suburb of Oregon; its myriad towers and vessels form the city's northern skyline. The Toledo Refinery is among Oregon's largest employers, with approximately 500 permanent employees and several hundred contract employees.

The Toledo Repositioning Project— a $235 million upgrade commissioned by Toledo Refinery in 1999— includes a new coking unit, additional sulfur recovery units, and other improvements that allow the processing of heavy sour crude oil. Part of this project involves supplying petroleum coke to FirstEnergy's Bay Shore Power Plant, a partnership

that improves both facilities' long-term viability. Such synergy is typical of Toledo Refinery's progressive thinking in adapting to the challenging global petroleum business.

With a capacity to process 160,000 barrels of oil per day, BP Toledo Refinery is a major producer of gasoline, diesel, and jet fuel for the Ohio market. It produces clean fuels—currently gasoline and soon diesel—that are extremely low in sulfur content and help improve the air quality of many major metropolitan areas by reducing tail pipe emissions. It is no coincidence that the BP Green stands for environmental excellence.

A FOCUS ON SAFETY

No other issue receives more attention and concern than does safety at the Toledo Refinery. BP employees receive many hours of job-related training each year. Through Process Safety Management and other initiatives, identification and abatement or elimination of risks takes place. The refinery's Joint Union/Management

Safety Committee reviews safety data, procedures, and develops and implements programs to make the workplace a safe and healthy environment. Millions of hours worked without a lost-time accident are a testament to these efforts.

Emergency preparedness is another top priority. The Toledo Refinery maintains three Emergency Response Teams skilled in fire fighting, first aid and rescue, and hazardous materials handling and industrial hygiene. These team members re-

WITH A CAPACITY TO PROCESS 160,000 BARRELS OF OIL PER DAY, BP TOLEDO REFINERY IS A MAJOR PRODUCER OF GASOLINE, DIESEL, AND JET FUEL FOR THE OHIO MARKET.

ceive many hours of specialized training and participate in drills with outside agencies each year. Through preventative measures and emergency preparedness, the Toledo Refinery provides not only a safe facility for its employees, but a safe neighbor to the community residents.

ENVIRONMENTAL PERFORMANCE

Perhaps one of the most critical issues by which a facility is judged by the community is its environmental performance. Operating an environmentally sound facility is of the utmost importance to the Toledo Refinery. The refinery maintains a staff of full-time professionals who monitor processes, the soil, air, and water in and around the refinery. They are also responsible for studying and reporting environmental data to the EPA and developing and implementing plans to ensure compliance with regulations and waste reduction. The

Toledo Refinery's efforts were recognized at the state level when it was the recipient of the prestigious Governor's Award for Outstanding Pollution Prevention for its flare meter system. This innovative system allows the refinery to closely monitor its flare system and identify and correct flaring sources.

Since 1990, Toledo Refinery has invested nearly a quarter-billion dollars in environmental controls. The Toledo Refinery has reduced its EPA-regulated Toxic Release Information (TRI) emissions by 75 percent. Further, BP's Volatile Organic Compound (VOC) emissions—such as the fumes seen rising from gasoline nozzles—have been reduced by 90 percent. BP embraces the reduction of greenhouse gasses and is committed to being an industry leader in environmental responsibility and operation.

In 1999, BP's Toledo Refinery was certified as being in compliance with the ISO 14001 standard. This

certification came after an in-depth audit of environmental policies, programs, and procedures. Each year, an independent auditor examines refinery operations for re-certification. Toledo Refinery is one of only two refineries in the country to be so designated.

A PART OF THE COMMUNITY FOR MORE THAN 80 YEARS

BP's Toledo Refinery strives to be the neighbor of choice in the Oregon community. It values its community's thoughts and maintains two groups to foster an effective dialogue. The Community Advisory Board consists of elected and appointed officials, representatives of regulatory agencies, and prominent members of the community. This group, formed in 1990, meets quarterly. The Citizen Advisory Panel is comprised of private citizens and small business owners and meets monthly. Both groups provide an excellent forum to discuss issues of importance to the community and refinery alike.

The Toledo Refinery is also a generous benefactor to the area. Each year, more than $100,000 is spent in the community for educational, civic, and humanitarian causes. But it's not just financial support. BP encourages its employees to participate in community projects and other volunteer activities. BP employees have helped build playgrounds, participated in mentoring programs in local schools, and have adopted needy families during the holidays. As any good neighbor, the BP Toledo Refinery recognizes the need to reinvest in the community which helped make it strong.

IN 1999, BP's TOLEDO REFINERY WAS CERTIFIED AS BEING IN COMPLIANCE WITH THE ISO 14001 STANDARD; IT IS ONE OF ONLY TWO REFINERIES IN THE COUNTRY TO BE SO DESIGNATED.

Laborers' International Union Local 500

From building bridges and laying highways to erecting large industrial buildings and other institutions, members of the Laborers' International Union of North America (LIUNA) have been an integral part of the building trades and heavy and highway construction industry since its founding on April 13, 1903.

Founded in 1919, Laborers' International Union Local 500, the local union of which the Toledo area is a part, today retains a membership roster of more than 1,200 men and women. These workers represent a variety of building trades and hail from the six-county area that includes Defiance, Fulton, Henry, Lucas, Williams, and Wood counties.

A HISTORY OF LEADERSHIP

Headquartered in Washington, D.C., LIUNA is known as one of the most innovative unions in the building trades industry, with a reputation of leadership in the areas of labor management cooperation, worker training, and health and safety. With 650 local chapters scattered throughout the United States and Canada, LIUNA is also one of the largest unions affiliated with the American Federation of Labor and Congress of Industrial Organizations (AFL-CIO). LIUNA's local chapters are supported by the union's international headquarters, as well as by 10 regional offices in the United States and Canada, and more than 60 district councils responsible for bargaining on behalf of their affiliated local unions.

The international union represents a diverse array of industries, including Alaskan pipeline workers, airplane machinists and mechanics, poultry processing employees, mail handlers, national park rangers, maintenance and display workers, nurses, and construction workers. Local 500, however, represents more general laborers.

MEMBER BENEFITS

Just as with many other labor unions, LIUNA offers its members a number of important benefits, including a political voice, health and welfare coverage, a prevailing wage, collective bargaining representation, and training, including an apprenticeship program.

LIUNA works hard to defeat antiworker/antidignity legislation in Congress, and strives to promote legislation that ensures the safety and health of all workers. Local 500 members have initiated a political action committee made up of members who work to assist politicians in favor of passing legislation on the national, state, and local levels that benefit workers.

The international union uses

Members of Laborers' International Union Local 500, which is part of Laborers' International Union of North America (LIUNA), pour and grade concrete on Monroe Street in Toledo.

Local 500 members prepare a deck for concrete on the overpass of Interstate 75 South (left).

The Toledo Museum of Art gets a facelift as Local 500 members take part in a massive renovation project (right).

LOCAL 500 MEMBERS REPRESENT A VARIETY OF BUILDING TRADES AND HAIL FROM THE SIX-COUNTY AREA THAT INCLUDES DEFIANCE, FULTON, HENRY, LUCAS, WILLIAMS, AND WOOD COUNTIES.

the combined purchasing power of its members to negotiate benefits and services. The leverage its members provide also assists in wage and collective bargaining issues.

Through the international union's labor-management cooperatives, management and labor representatives work together to solve the issues union members and employers may have. LIUNA operates three such cooperatives: Laborers-Employers Cooperation and Education Trust (LECET); Laborers-Associated General Contractors (L-AGC) Education and Training Fund; and Laborers' Health and Safety Fund of North America (LHSFNA). Each of these cooperatives operates under specific missions and provides unique services. The mission of LECET is to expand the market for unionized construction. L-AGC works to provide education and training programs to individuals and organizations. LHSFNA is divided into five divisions: occupational safety

and health, health promotion, research, computer services, and administration.

Members of LIUNA also benefit from a variety of training opportunities. The international union has endorsed some 69 training centers across the country. Local 500 members utilize the Millwood, Ohio, site, and conduct training locally on topics ranging from OSHA compliance and safety training to hazardous waste removal.

The U.S. Department of Labor has recently named construction craft laborer as an apprenticeable trade. LIUNA's three-year apprenticeship program requires participants to complete 4,000 hours of classroom and on-the-job training. Subscribing to the earn-while-you-learn philosophy, the union considers apprenticeship training a worthwhile investment. Further, through a partnership with Owens Community College, local apprentices are able to receive college credits toward an associate degree for some of their training.

PERFORMING A VALUABLE SERVICE

While LIUNA's general labor focus is broad, Local 500's membership base is found in the commercial and residential construction area. These local members perform general labor and cleanup—including operating small power tools, demolition, and mixing mortar—which are valuable, timesaving efforts that assist other tradesmen, including carpenters and bricklayers. Local laborers have assisted their fellow tradesmen on many major projects in the area, including the new Jeep plant, the I-280 bridge, and the downtown stadium.

The United Labor Program, a unique program supported by Local 500, is operated through United Automobile Workers Local 12 and provides training for volunteer members. The six-week training course prepares the volunteers to act as counselors for their fellow workers. This counseling may include talking with a member about depression, or walking a fellow member through the steps needed to obtain public assistance.

Both on the job and off, Laborers' International Union Local 500 members have made and continue to make significant contributions to the community, including active participation in Big Brothers/Big Sisters of Northwest Ohio, the Red Cross, and the YMCA. In the Toledo area and beyond, Local 500 is making an impact in the community.

The Kroger Company

T WAS 1883 WHEN A YOUNG MAN NAMED BARNEY KROGER FIRST OPENED HIS GROCERY STORE IN CINCINNATI. THROUGHOUT THE EARLY 1900S, THE GROCERY STORE CHAIN WAS BEGINNING TO MAKE A PRESENCE IN OTHER MAJOR OHIO CITIES, AS WELL AS IN NORTHERN KENTUCKY. BY 1924, THE TOLEDO MARKET HAD WELCOMED ITS FIRST KROGER STORE. ■ TODAY, THE KROGER COMPANY

is the largest retail food company in the nation in terms of sales. In northwest Ohio, the company employs more than 3,100 workers in its 20 stores.

PRODUCTS AND SERVICES

Part of Kroger's mission statement indicates that the company "will satisfy consumer needs better than the best of [their] competitors." To assure this satisfaction, each Kroger store offers its customers a full line of national brands, the Kroger brand, and the company's high-quality Private Selection line, as well as delicatessen, bakery, and produce departments. Most stores even offer a pharmacy and a banking center.

In addition to a large selection of quality grocery items, Kroger has recently begun offering its customers a free benefit program called the Kroger Plus Card. This program gives cardholders special in-store discounts on a number of selected items each week. Through partnerships with other establishments in the area, Kroger Plus Cards also provide customers with additional discounts on products and services.

Customer satisfaction is also realized through Kroger's second-to-none customer service philosophy and training system. All Kroger employees, from baggers and cashiers to department managers, are required to go through specialized, computer-based training before ever setting foot on the sales floor. This training not only outlines the company's vision of customer service, but also gives detailed descriptions of the how-tos of individual jobs.

Food safety is another high priority at Kroger. The company is leading the way in the industry in terms of maintaining and surpassing industry standards for food safety. In

fact, all of Kroger's store managers are required to attend a three-day seminar, complete a home study program, and pass a state test to be certified in food safety by the National Registry of Food Safety Professionals.

LINKED TO THE COMMUNITY

Locally, Kroger supports many community organizations through sponsorships, donations, and volunteer hours. The company even encourages managers to be involved. In the Toledo area, many board positions of local non-

profit organizations are filled by Kroger store management staff.

While Kroger actively supports the local food bank, Salvation Army, United Way, and Scouting for Food, the company is best known for its involvement in the annual Jamie Farr Kroger Classic. This annual LPGA tournament has helped to raise more than $3.2 million for local children's charities. Providing excellent customer service and caring for its community through local involvement are two of the pillars on which The Kroger Company has maintained its stand for more than a century.

CLOCKWISE FROM TOP:
THE KROGER COMPANY RECENTLY RESTORED THIS 1934 TRACTOR TRAILER RIG FOR USE IN PARADES.

KROGER ASSOCIATES TAKE GREAT PRIDE IN SUPPORTING LOCAL CHARITIES.

KROGER'S MASCOT IS PEPE THE PENGUIN, KNOWN FAR AND WIDE TO AREA CHILDREN.

Kiemle-Hankins Company

IEMLE-HANKINS COMPANY PROVIDES INDUSTRIAL ELECTRICAL SOLUTIONS TO MANUFACTURING COMPANIES, MACHINERY BUILDERS, ELECTRICAL CONTRACTORS, UTILITIES, AND COMMERCIAL CUSTOMERS IN TOLEDO AND THE OHIO-MICHIGAN-INDIANA TRISTATE AREA. THIS FAMILY-OWNED BUSINESS IS ROOTED IN TOLEDO, BUT IT ALSO

operates nine locations in Michigan and Ohio, and serves customers in Indiana as well. Company associates provide electric motor and apparatus repair, new automation controls, new electrical supplies, and power systems equipment and repair.

TWO DIVISIONS, ONE THRIVING COMPANY

When Fred Kiemle started the company in 1928, and Bill Hankins expanded it in 1954, they could only imagine the successes the firm would generate. Now, with two distinct and vibrant divisions that are leaders in their fields, Kiemle-Hankins can tell its customers with conviction that it is a total electrical solutions provider.

As the company's older division, Services includes associates who have been servicing the electric motor repair needs of many Toledo-area customers for more than 70 years. Industrial clients include Chrysler, Ford, General Motors, and almost every large or small manufacturer in the area.

Supply Division associates provide products made by world leader Rockwell Automation (Allen-Bradley) and most other leading electrical manufacturers. Through these sales,

Kiemle-Hankins helps its customers automate their new or replacement manufacturing machines or systems, or provides full maintenance and repair to their broken equipment.

CUSTOMER SERVICE

The trend in industry for more companies to outsource various electrical repair and maintenance functions has also led to strong growth for Kiemle-Hankins. As a total electrical solutions provider, the company's qualified staff can provide broad services to customers while saving them overhead.

"Our associates set us apart," says Steve Martindale, chairman and CEO. "We have the best-trained, most talented workers, and they care about customers. Our repairmen or on-call associates will get up at 2 a.m. in a snowstorm to provide service if necessary. They take real pride in solving problems for clients."

This partnership with customers has become one of the keys to the company's success. With this approach, Kiemle-Hankins works with customers to fix the immediate problem, and then conduct product training or education seminars to

provide suggestions for avoiding the problem in the future.

Customers appreciate this service. In 1997, Chrysler awarded Kiemle-Hankins its service excellence Pentastar Award, an unusual honor for an electrical MRO supplier. Kiemle-Hankins' collaboration with Chrysler results in substantial savings for the company, and Kiemle-Hankins' associates continue to apply the same award-winning problem-solving approach to every customer.

COMMUNITY SERVICE

The successes and continued growth Kiemle-Hankins has seen through the years have made the company keenly aware of its commitment to the Toledo community. The company's leaders have been active on and supported local boards and charities. Kiemle-Hankins and its associates have also participated in supporting United Way and other local charities. The company's philosophy advocates service and the Golden Rule as a means of community enrichment.

With a firm commitment to quality, service, and growth, Kiemle-Hankins Company will continue to prosper in its industry and in Toledo for years to come.

WITH A FIRM COMMITMENT TO QUALITY, SERVICE, AND GROWTH, KIEMLE-HANKINS COMPANY IS A TOTAL ELECTRICAL SOLUTIONS PROVIDER. ITS CLIENT LIST INCLUDES MANUFACTURING COMPANIES, MACHINERY BUILDERS, ELECTRICAL CONTRACTORS, UTILITIES, AND COMMERCIAL CUSTOMERS IN TOLEDO AND THE TRISTATE AREA.

Faurecia Exhaust Systems

OW A GLOBAL MEGASUPPLIER OF AUTOMOBILE EQUIPMENT, FAURECIA—A $7.4 BILLION, INTERNATIONAL, TIER 1 AUTO SUPPLIER—DESIGNS AND MANUFACTURES ESSENTIAL AUTOMOTIVE COMPONENTS THROUGH THREE MAIN OPERATING DIVISIONS: SEATING, INTERIOR SYSTEMS AND FRONT-END MODULES, AND EXHAUST

systems. The seating division designs and supplies seats for all types of vehicles, including cars, minivans, and sport utility vehicles.

The interior systems and front-end modules division includes dashboards and cockpits, door panels, soft trim, and acoustic parts. Faurecia's North American Exhaust Division, headquartered in Toledo, is a design, development, and manufacturing source of exhaust systems. Faurecia Exhaust Systems is a global original equipment manufacturer (OEM) supplier.

In addition to Faurecia's North American Exhaust headquarters operations, Toledo is also home to a technical center, a customer program center, and one of five North American manufacturing plants for the company.

COMPANY EVOLUTION

Northwest Ohioans may not realize that the company known as Faurecia Exhaust Systems is rooted in a company familiarly known in Toledo as the former AP Automotive Systems. Faurecia, as it is today, is a company whose history began on both sides of the Atlantic.

In 1882, a French company called Cycle Peugeot was formed and began manufacturing the *grand bi* (big bicycle). By 1910, Cycles et Automobiles Peugeot was created in the French region of Montbeliard, and produced cars, bicycles, and components for cars. In 1926, Cycles et Automobiles Peugeot split into two companies: Société Automobiles Peugeot for cars and Cycles Peugeot for bicycles and motorcycles,

as well as tube components for exhaust systems, steering columns, and related products.

Concurrently, back in the United States, John Goerlich of Toledo was distributing automotive parts from his car. In 1927, Goerlich founded Associated Parts, known later as AP Parts, promoting a muffler called the Taylor Loud Speaker as his main product.

The following decades resulted in a series of product and company name changes, mergers, and acquisitions for these companies in both countries. In Europe, Cycle Peugeot began producing exhausts in 1956. Then, in 1987, Cycle Peugeot and the tooling and plastic components manufacturer Société Aciers et Outillage Peugeot (AOP) merged to create Equipements et Composants

pour L'Industrie Automobile (ECIA). From 1987 to 1997, strong development and growth occurred in Europe, and expansion into China, India, Brazil, and the United States began. During that time period, additional acquisitions of European companies were added to the group. When ECIA and Bertrand Faure, a French company specializing in seating, merged in 1998, the new company became known as Faurecia. The goal for this new company was to create a world-class automotive components group.

Meanwhile, in the United States, AP was also going through significant changes. It became known in the exhaust industry for product innovations. The company also experienced ownership changes, both as a public company and as a private company. In 1996, a Dayton-based company, Tube Products, which was owned by Questor, bought AP Parts and renamed the combined entity AP Automotive Systems. In 1998, AP Automotive Systems divested its aftermarket operations to focus exclusively on original equipment.

By 1999, these changes, which had occurred thousands of miles apart and spanned more than a half century, resulted in Faurecia's 1999 acquisition of AP Automotive Systems. The merger allowed Faurecia to become one of the three world leaders in exhaust systems.

PRODUCTION EXHAUST SYSTEM

PRODUCTS AND SERVICES

Faurecia's Exhaust Division provides full-service engineering solutions, including design, development, and validation. Through the company's Tier 1 Global Program Management, products can be engineered and manufactured in multiple geographies. In addition, the firm has a comprehensive manufacturing infrastructure, as well as supply base management capability. Faurecia has the ability to develop and manufacture all of the major components of exhaust systems.

The company is committed to customer satisfaction, continuous improvement, technical innovation, safety, quality, and profitable growth. These commitments are supported by management principles outlined in Excellence by Faurecia, a comprehensive quality system that assists employees in assessing performance and continuous improvement to achieve individual and corporate excellence.

Faurecia has been built on the excellence of several companies that have come together to make one of the world's largest suppliers of automotive products.

DURABILITY TEST LAB

Romanoff Electric Corp.

OUNDED IN TOLEDO IN 1927, ROMANOFF ELECTRIC CORPORATION IS ONE OF THE NATION'S LARGEST ELECTRICAL CONTRACTORS. OFFERING A HIGHLY TRAINED, EXPERIENCED WORKFORCE, ROMANOFF IS A FULL-SERVICE ELECTRICAL CONTRACTOR WITH FOUR GROUPS TO MEET CUSTOMER NEEDS. ITS POWER, SERVICE, HIGH VOLTAGE, AND

telecommunication groups serve industrial, commercial, and institutional customers. Essential to the company's growth has been its unwavering commitment to the customer. Romanoff's dependability, dedication, quality workmanship, and high ethical standards have earned the trust of its customers.

BEGINNING WITH A FRIENDSHIP

Max Romanoff met Jack Romanoff in Cleveland in the spring of 1925 while working on the Cleveland Terminal Tower. Ironically, these two men who shared a common last name—but were not related—would end up becoming close friends. In 1927, the two moved to Toledo and opened Romanoff Electric. At that time, the company specialized in residential and commercial projects.

Surviving the Depression years required conservative spending and a constant concern for maintaining a good reputation, but the company managed to grow. In 1935, Romanoff expanded into the industrial area, which later became its key market.

Throughout the next five decades, Romanoff continued to grow and make a name for itself, both locally and nationally. By 1988, Romanoff

FROM TOP:
ROMANOFF ELECTRIC CORP.'S OFFICE BUILDING IS LOCATED IN TOLEDO.

HEALTH CARE IS ONE OF ROMANOFF'S LARGEST MARKETS.

LOCATED IN THE TOLEDO MUSEUM OF ART, THE GREAT GALLERY IS ANOTHER ROMANOFF PROJECT.

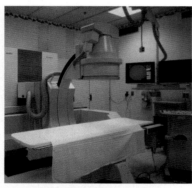
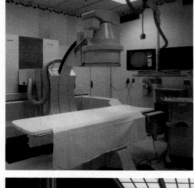

Electric ranked as the 20th-largest electrical contractor in the country. In the 1990s, the company expanded its services by starting its utility and telecommunications groups.

CUSTOMER FIRST PHILOSOPHY

As a full-service contractor, Romanoff strives to meet all of its customers' electrical contracting needs. By offering four diverse groups, Romanoff's customers benefit from a one-stop shop.

The power group offers various installations that include lighting, power, equipment hook-up, fire alarm, and temperature control. It works to save customers money by performing both design/build and plan/spec projects, and by utilizing its state-of-the-art, in-house equipment.

Romanoff's services group provides its customers with a fleet of service vehicles, which are on call 24 hours a day and ready to handle all maintenance and emergency situations. This group specializes in fast response and efficient resolutions.

A highly trained, well-equipped crew keeps Romanoff's high-voltage group running smoothly. Trained by the American Line Builders Association, these individuals manage outside electrical projects such

as power distribution via overhead lines, substations, underground lines, streetlights, and traffic lights.

Specializing in the design and installation of low-voltage communication cabling, the telecommunications group offers its customers the specialized skills and equipment to satisfy cabling needs including fiber-optic installation, computer networking, security, voice, and video.

All of Romanoff's projects, big and small, are executed with professionalism, expertise, and timeliness. Romanoff's employees strive to build strong customer relationships. Its reliable, hardworking, motivated staff is willing to go the extra mile to earn a customer's trust and loyalty.

The importance of strong relationships emphasizing trust also carries through the company among Romanoff's employees. Romanoff creates a family atmosphere where people work as a team and look out for one another. The company's structure is essentially flat, with few high-level managers, where all employees are treated equally. It's a symbiotic relationship that works for Romanoff.

As part of its commitment to its employees, Romanoff puts a great deal of emphasis on safety by striving for a zero-injury workplace. While

taking the proper safety precautions is of both monetary and human value, the company realizes that the human value is far more important to the employer and the community.

Romanoff electricians receive safety training in a variety of ways. Initially, they attend a 16-hour construction safety program provided to them by the Joint Apprenticeship Training Committee. Romanoff employees also obtain safety training through weekly safety talks, monthly foremen meetings, and a weekly newsletter highlighting safety issues. All of this allows Romanoff to meet and exceed industry standards, often going beyond stringent Occupational Safety & Health Administration (OSHA) requirements.

COMMITTED TO THE COMMUNITY

As important as its employees and customers are to the company, Romanoff remains aware of its responsibility to be a good corporate citizen. The company has been actively involved in United Way efforts and has been a Pacesetter in its annual campaign. Local Habitat for Humanity projects have benefited from donated materials and labor from Romanoff as well.

Further, Romanoff has been key to many of the electrical projects for several local businesses including the Toledo Museum of Art, the Toledo Zoo, and the new Jeep plant. The Jeep project alone involved providing and distributing power

and installing lighting in two structures totaling more than 700,000 square feet of space.

In 1998, Romanoff became part of a national company, Encompass Services Corporation. This merger has not changed Romanoff's commitment to northwest Ohio. Instead, Romanoff looks at the relationship as a way to build a national identity, pool resources and best practices, and serve nationally through its sister companies. Romanoff believes in supporting the community that supports it by buying materials locally and utilizing local workers.

Commitment to the community will remain a goal for Romanoff well into the future. As technology changes, Romanoff continues to adjust to new and innovative products and procedures. In the telecommunications area, for example, the company is striving to remain the regional leader. And Romanoff will continually train and update employees in this exciting new area. It is this philosophy of meeting and exceeding customers' needs and expectations that has resulted in continued growth for the company.

While Romanoff Electric will move forward as Encompass Electrical Technologies, it will remain committed to its employees, customers, and the local community.

DAIMLER/CHRYSLER CALLED ON ROMANOFF'S EXPERTISE FOR ITS NEW $600 MILLION PLANT TO PRODUCE JEEPS.

AMONG THE COMPANY'S OTHER PROJECTS ARE TOLEDO ZOO'S NEW PEDESTRIAN BRIDGE (LEFT) AND FIBER-OPTIC CABLING INSTALLATION BY TELECOMMUNICATIONS GROUP.

Willis Day Properties, Inc.

ILLIS DAY PROPERTIES, INC. IS A FAMILY-OWNED COMPANY THAT HAS BEEN PROVIDING TOLEDO-AREA BUSINESSES WITH VALUABLE SERVICES FOR MORE THAN EIGHT DECADES. THROUGH THE YEARS, SERVICES MAY HAVE CHANGED, BUT THE COMPANY'S REPUTATION FOR HONESTY,

integrity, trustworthiness, and fairness has remained constant.

Today, Willis Day is a full-service real estate development and leasing company. From office space to storage space, small office suites to large warehouses, Willis Day can provide its customers with the facilities they need at a fair price.

A LONG HISTORY IN TOLEDO

Willis Day can trace its roots back to 1929, when Willis Day Jr. founded Willis Day Storage Company. At that time, the business was operated out of a large office and warehousing building on Monroe Street in downtown Toledo. As the years passed and demand increased, additional buildings were added to the company's roster.

Willis Day withstood the financial tests that came with the Great Depression, and emerged as a viable enterprise, offering needed services to area businesses. Willis Day Jr.'s three sons—Willis III, Thomas, and Richard—became involved in the company business in the mid-1940s. These four men worked together to build the business. Their hard work and dedication resulted in the company's growth and evolution into its present form as Willis Day Properties, Inc.

EXPANSION OF SERVICES

The family's original storage company centered around residential, commercial, and office moves. As a company with a favorable reputation, Willis Day was contracted to handle some important moves for area businesses. The Toledo Public Library, for example, hired Willis Day to transfer all of the books from the Main Library's Ontario Street location to the new facility at its present location on Michigan

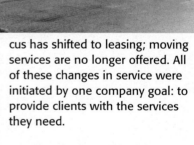

Street. The move required the organized coordination of nearly 350,000 volumes. The process was estimated to take more than 130 hours to complete, but Willis Day completed the entire move in only 72 hours. High-profile moves such as this illustrate the company's flexibility and values, as well as its integrity in getting the job done right and on time.

Willis Day eventually expanded into the machinery moving and rigging business. Another new business line, Willis Day Freight Systems, offered clients a time and cost savings by supplying a freight service for warehousing clients needing to ship products on a regular schedule.

In the 1980s, the company's main focus was on warehousing. Today, although warehousing is still a significant part of the business, the fo-

cus has shifted to leasing; moving services are no longer offered. All of these changes in service were initiated by one company goal: to provide clients with the services they need.

THE SCOPE OF BUSINESS TODAY

To remain successful and profitable in its industry, Willis Day has had to focus its services. Today, the company's main concentration is on storage and leasing facilities. With a large amount of its business devoted to leasing to third parties, Willis Day owns more than 2.5 million square feet of storage/industrial space.

One of the company's largest facilities is the Willis Day Business Center, located on Bennett Road.

FROM ITS FOUNDING IN 1929 TO ITS CURRENT SUCCESS, WILLIS DAY PROPERTIES, INC. HAS PROVIDED CUSTOMERS WITH THE FACILITIES THEY NEED AT A FAIR PRICE.

This facility alone accounts for more than 1 million square feet of leasing space. Willis Day purchased the 1.2 million-square-foot complex—formerly the home of the Dana Spicer Transmission Plant—in 1986 and transformed it into a business/industrial park. This facility now houses the company's headquarters.

Operating with fewer than 20 employees, the family's second and third generations occupy key positions within the company. Yet, it is Willis Day Jr.'s values of service, courteousness, and common sense that still guide the firm.

Willis Day is still a client-focused company that is willing to do whatever it takes. The company works to make storage and leasing easy for the client. Whether it's leasing an existing building or building to suit a client's specifications, Willis Day can provide custom spacing. Tenants and prospective tenants know that if they ask for something, it will get done because it is the company's goal to accommodate all customers—whether they need a high-profile facility or a small, economical space.

STRONG ATTACHMENT TO NORTHWEST OHIO

Just as the company's services have expanded through the years, Willis Day has had opportunities to expand its service area. However, the Day family has intentionally kept the company grounded in northwest Ohio. Willis Day IV, president, explains that "although there are plenty of locations to expand the business, the family remains committed to Toledo and the surrounding communities. In addition, given Toledo's proximity to business and industry, and its location at the crossroads of two major interstates, the area is perfect for the industries who can benefit from the services Willis Day Properties offers."

Rooted in family ties and dedicated to serving the needs of a variety of clients, Willis Day Properties, Inc. has grown with the Toledo area. The company's strong reputation and record of success will continue well into the future.

THROUGH THE YEARS, SERVICES MAY HAVE CHANGED, BUT THE COMPANY'S REPUTATION FOR HONESTY, INTEGRITY, TRUSTWORTHINESS, AND FAIRNESS HAS REMAINED CONSTANT.

IN AN EFFORT TO MAKE STORAGE AND LEASING EASY, THE COMPANY REMAINS A CLIENT-FOCUSED ORGANIZATION WILLING TO DO WHATEVER IT TAKES.

Pilkington North America, Inc.

ILKINGTON NORTH AMERICA, INC.'S ROOTS IN TOLEDO RUN DEEP, EVIDENCE OF A PROUD HISTORY THAT DATES BACK OVER A CENTURY AGO. IN THE LATE 1800S, GLASS TECHNOLOGY PIONEER EDWARD FORD FOUNDED THE EDWARD FORD PLATE GLASS COMPANY IN ROSSFORD, OHIO. IN 1916, EDWARD DRUMMOND LIBBEY

CLOCKWISE FROM BOTTOM RIGHT:
FOR DECADES, PILKINGTON NORTH AMERICA HAS WORKED WITH AUTOMAKERS TO IMPROVE GLASS PERFORMANCE AND CHARACTERISTICS, TAKING GLASS FROM ITS MOST BASIC STATE TO A SOPHISTICATED, FUNCTIONAL DESIGN TOOL.

PILKINGTON PLC IS ONE OF THE LARGEST MANUFACTURERS OF FLAT AND SAFETY GLASS FOR THE BUILDING AND AUTOMOTIVE MARKETS IN THE WORLD, AND HAS SUCH A STRONG INDUSTRY PRESENCE THAT ONE IN EVERY FOUR CARS WORLDWIDE CONTAINS PILKINGTON PRODUCTS.

PILKINGTON'S ROOTS IN TOLEDO RUN DEEP, EVIDENCE OF A PROUD HISTORY THAT DATES BACK OVER A CENTURY AGO.

and Michael J. Owens formed the Libbey-Owens Sheet Glass Company. These two businesses merged in 1930 to form the Libbey-Owens-Ford Glass Company.

Glass accounted for almost all of the company's business from 1930 to the 1960s, when the company began to enlarge its scope of operations to include other products and markets. To reflect this expansion, the word "glass" was dropped from the corporate name in 1968 and the firm became Libbey-Owens-Ford Company. The corporation underwent a major transformation in 1986 when the glass division of Libbey-Owens-Ford Company and the Libbey-Owens-Ford name were acquired by Pilkington plc of St. Helens, England. At the same time, the company's fluid power and plastics operations were reorganized as operating units of a separate corporation. In 2000, the firm changed its legal name from Libbey-Owens-Ford Co. to Pilkington North America, Inc., and is now known as Pilkington.

With two main product areas—building and automotive products—Pilkington has operations in 25 countries on four continents. It is one of the largest manufacturers of flat and safety glass for the building and automotive markets in the world, and has such a strong industry presence that one in every four cars worldwide contains Pilkington

products. Pilkington's worldwide headquarters is located in St. Helens. Toledo is home to Pilkington's North American support office. Pilkington shares are traded on the London Stock Exchange under the ticker symbol PILK.

PILKINGTON NORTH AMERICA

Pilkington operates three main businesses in North America. The building products business makes clear float glass and proprietary tinted and on-line coated float glass for architectural and specialty applications around the world. Proprietary tints and on-line coating give Pilkington's architectural glass a distinct appearance, as well as excellent energy performance characteristics. Markets served include commercial glazing, residential glazing, and mirror, furniture, and specialty applications.

The automotive original equipment business manufactures both laminated and tempered automotive glass parts for automakers. For decades, Pilkington has worked with automakers to improve glass performance and characteristics, taking glass from its most basic state to a sophisticated, functional design tool. Pilkington's automotive product line includes clear, tinted, solar control, safety, and privacy glass products, as well as several advanced, functional, glass-glazing

products and systems.

The automotive glass replacement business unit is a distributor of automotive replacement glass from manufacture through wholesale. Pilkington's distribution center in Columbus, Ohio, supplies products to the firm's more than 80 company-owned service centers and more than 200 truckload customers. In addition to meeting customer needs for replacement glass products, business education and trading solutions are offered through a 24-hour-a-day, seven-day-a-week Internet-enabled customer value package, ePremier. Additional customer value is offered through Pilkington Classics, a vintage and classic auto glass source.

In addition, North America hosts a division of Pilkington Aerospace, a supplier of high-performance glass and plastic composite glazing for aircraft, locomotives, and cars.

The future looks bright for Pilkington. As a competitive glassmaker that strives to develop new products and technologies to benefit the industry and its consumers—working to become "first in glass"—the company will continue to see growth. Toledo-based Warren Knowlton, regional director for Pilkington North America, supports this outlook: "By 2003, it is our goal to be the most competitive, the most profitable, and the fastest-growing global glass company in the world."

2001 GENERAL MOTORS CORP., GM MEDIA ARCHIVES

HEN HUGH WHITE OPENED HIS FIRST CHEVROLET DEALERSHIP IN ZANESVILLE IN 1921, HIS GOAL WAS TO PROVIDE CUSTOMERS WITH THE BEST PURCHASE AND OWNERSHIP EXPERIENCE POSSIBLE. TODAY, THAT GOAL STILL STANDS TRUE. ■ CURRENTLY, THE WHITE FAMILY operates four dealerships in the Toledo area, offering the Chevrolet, Acura, Toyota, and Lexus brands. Through other family-owned dealerships in Dayton and Columbus, Ohio, and Casper, Wyoming, the company offers a variety of domestic and foreign automobiles.

OFFERING QUALITY BRANDS AND PREMIER SERVICE

Jim White moved into the Toledo market in the 1940s, and passed the torch of leadership on to his son. Now, with the fourth generation of Whites at the helm, the company remains committed to growth by offering quality automobiles.

Although the four White Family Dealerships in the area focus on different brands, the family doesn't consider each other the competition. Instead, the dealerships work together with the common goal of growth for the company as a whole. The different brands available at the White Family Dealerships have been chosen based on the strength of the manufacturer. Only quality, good-selling brands are associated with the White name.

Chevrolet remains one of the dealerships' major brands. At one point in the company's history, it had more than a dozen Chevrolet/ General Motors franchises in three states, and was considered one of the largest General Motors dealer chains in the country. Migration into the foreign market was an inevitable change, and the White Family Dealerships were some of the first Honda authorized dealerships in the country. Now that car buying has taken on a more global approach, the White Family Dealerships have products to fit every customer's needs.

FOCUSED ON SERVICE

Offering quality brands is only one important part of the car-buying equation. For a dealership to be successful, an attentive, courteous, accurate service department must be in place to satisfy customers after the sale. The White Family Dealerships have won several manufacturers' service awards, including Acura's customer satisfaction Precision Team Award and Toyota's President's Cup. Toyota has awarded its Service Excellence Award to the White Dealerships an

impressive 11 years in a row.

But perhaps the greatest testament to the White Family Dealerships' service philosophy is the relationship with the customer that results in repeat sales. The successes the dealerships have experienced are grounded in the idea that if a customer has a good experience, he or she will be back for future business.

Loyalty to customers, loyalty to employees, and loyalty to their community have always been important to the White family. "Our employees live here," says Dave White, president, Dave White Chevrolet/Acura. "We have a strong belief in giving back to the community. The more we can help to strengthen the community, the more the community will strengthen us."

LEADING THE WHITE FAMILY DEALERSHIPS ARE (CLOCKWISE FROM FAR LEFT) DAVE WHITE SR., DAVE WHITE JR., JIM WHITE JR., AND TIM WHITE.

OPERATING FOUR DEALERSHIPS IN THE TOLEDO AREA, THE WHITE FAMILY FOCUSES ON LOYALTY TO THE CUSTOMER, EMPLOYEES, AND THE COMMUNITY.

National City Bank

STABLISHED IN TOLEDO IN 1932 AS THE OHIO CITIZENS TRUST COMPANY, NATIONAL CITY BANK IS COMMITTED TO ITS CONSTITUENT COMMUNITIES. THROUGHOUT ITS HISTORY, THE BANK'S DEDICATION TO HELPING ITS CUSTOMERS MEET THEIR FINANCIAL GOALS AND ITS COMMUNITIES GROW AND PROSPER HAS REMAINED STEADFAST. ■ WITH SOME 30

branches throughout a five-county area in northwest Ohio and more than 340 branches in the state, National City's financial professionals serve as a gateway to the services and advice clients seek. It is the Ohio banking subsidiary of National City Corporation, the 10th-largest banking organization in the country, with more than $90 billion in assets. National City operates banks and other financial services subsidiaries in Michigan, Pennsylvania, Indiana, Kentucky, and Illinois.

HISTORICAL ROOTS

When the Ohio Citizens Trust Company opened in downtown Toledo, it employed 25 people and had some $300,000 in capital funds. After two years, the bank joined the Federal Reserve System and the Federal Deposit Insurance Corporation (FDIC). At that time, the bank's customers' only option was the headquarters office, but as the customer base grew, so did the number of branch offices; the bank's first branch office opened in 1949.

National City Bank has provided customers with many Toledo-area banking firsts throughout its history.

In 1952, for example, the Colony branch opened, featuring the area's first drive-through window. Then, in 1975, it became the first area bank to introduce a teller terminal system, giving tellers a direct connection with the computer for savings passbook customers.

The Ohio Citizens Trust Company acquired several banking institutions between 1959 and 1982, before merging with National City Corporation of Cleveland. Among the benefits to customers were an expansion of services and financial assistance to northwest Ohio and southeast

WITH CUSTOMERS AS ITS PRIMARY FOCUS, NATIONAL CITY REMAINS COMMITTED TO BEING MORE THAN THE TRADITIONAL BANK.

WITH SOME 30 BRANCHES THROUGHOUT A FIVE-COUNTY AREA IN NORTHWEST OHIO AND MORE THAN 340 BRANCHES IN THE STATE, NATIONAL CITY'S FINANCIAL PROFESSIONALS SERVE AS A GATEWAY TO THE SERVICES AND ADVICE CLIENTS SEEK.

Michigan. The name change to National City followed in 1992.

PRODUCTS AND SERVICES

With customers as its primary focus, National City remains committed to being more than the traditional bank. Bringing together myriad financial services and working with customers, the bank's relationship managers identify and offer the best solutions to meet financial needs at every stage of a client's business and personal life.

With strength in personal and corporate lending, National City's competitive edge is the staff expertise and the breadth of services offered. A top priority of National City has been to keep familiar faces in front of the customers. Convenience and variety of services prove to be a great benefit as well. Various checking and savings account options, loans, and lines of credit are available, as well as E-banking for customers' convenience.

Many of the region's prominent individuals look to National City's Private Investment Advisors for insightful and objective financial advice. Three business units—Sterling, Private Client Group, and NatCity Investments—deliver a suite of financial services that support each other to provide customers access to the services appropriate to their needs.

This team-based approach is critical to the successful managing of personal and family finances.

The corporate lending team at National City is one of the area's most respected, stable, and innovative groups. Its veteran corporate bankers have the experience and resources to solve a business' financial challenges and facilitate corporate growth. Companies benefit from an array of services—from commercial and real estate financing to investment banking and cash management services. While the scope of the group's services is global, every decision that concerns the business customer is made locally, resulting in fast and flexible service.

National City is a recognized leader in small-business programs. The bank's success in meeting the needs of small businesses is reflected in its status as a Small Business Administration (SBA) Preferred Lender in all six states where it operates. With a national reputation for leadership in financial services, National City has the flexibility and resources to deliver fast approvals, quick decisions, and personal service.

Whether managing personal finances or managing a company's assets, National City acts as a partner. Offering diverse products and services, the bank helps clients put financial plans into action, connecting them with savings and invest-

ment tools to reach financial goals. National City is committed to providing northwest Ohioans with bankers who listen.

COMMUNITY PARTNERSHIPS

Through the years, National City Bank has prioritized support of, and partnerships with, the community. From the bank's initial community project in 1935, which featured a weekly radio broadcast to acquaint people with various local civic organizations and industries, to being a Hall of Fame sponsor with the Jamie Farr Kroger Classic, the bank believes in bolstering Toledo-area causes.

In partnership with Mt. Vernon Elementary School for more than 10 years, National City has made monetary and human resource contributions to support supplemental programs for academic enhancements. Since 1998, 20 bank employees have volunteered to tutor 40 Mt. Vernon students through the OhioReads program.

National City is proud of its community revitalization investment. Working with the City of Toledo, Organized Neighbors Yielding Excellence (ONYX, Inc.), and the Local Initiative Support Corporation (LISC), National City Community Development Corporation has provided an equity investment for construction of the Washington Village project in central Toledo. The bank also provides low-down-payment, low-interest loans to home owners purchasing houses in central Toledo. National City also supports civic investment programs, such as participation in capital campaigns for the Symphony and Art Museum, as well as expansion of the Toledo Zoo and the Toledo Lucas County Library.

Building on its dedication to excellence in customer service and financial performance, and its reputation for community involvement, National City Bank will continue to be a high-performance organization for generations to come.

Riker Products, Inc.

TOLEDO-BASED RIKER PRODUCTS, INC. IS A MAJOR SUPPLIER OF HEAVY-DUTY PRODUCTS TO ORIGINAL EQUIPMENT MANUFACTURERS (OEMS), AS WELL AS TO THE AFTERMARKET. THE RIKER FAMILY FOUNDED THE COMPANY IN 1932, AND IT HAS BECOME WELL KNOWN IN THE INDUSTRY AS A MANUFACTURER AND DISTRIBUTOR OF

heavy-duty exhaust components and accessories.

In recent years, Riker has gone through ownership changes that have resulted in the company's affiliation with other OEM suppliers in the heavy-duty market. In 1990, the Brenlin Group of Akron purchased the company. A reorganization in 1995 placed Riker under the umbrella of its current parent company, Cypress Companies. Cypress Companies, also of Akron, is a privately owned holding company whose other holdings include Tredit Tire & Wheel Co. in Elkhart; Ausco Products in Benton Harbor, Michigan; Performix Technologies Ltd. in Warren, Ohio; and Prior Gaskets, Inc. in Dallas.

Riker designs and manufactures mufflers, spark arresters, pipes and tubes, flexible metal hosing, semitrailer exhaust stacks, clamps, brackets, and related parts. These products are mainly used for on- and off-road trucks; specialized vehicles for the construction, agricultural, and mining industries; and buses. The company also serves the aftermarket and manufacturers' catalytic converters for urban buses.

A recent emphasis for the company has been servicing other manufacturing firms on custom jobs. Riker will take on custom bending and cutting projects, providing these specialized clients with a tremendous savings in time and cost.

A REPUTATION FOR QUALITY AND VALUE

Riker is known for its high quality standards. These standards have earned the company both ISO 9001 and QS 9000 certification. Committed to designing high-quality products with maximum efficiency in mind, Riker utilizes an in-house design team and advanced computer applications, including AutoCAD and electronic design data transfer.

Riker's engineering staff is able to build to print and build directly from samples using state-of-the-art equipment. Follow-up on product performance through laboratory and road testing, as well as durability studies, assures a quality product. By involving Riker in the design process, maximum usage of formed tubing is utilized, which results in a cost savings for the customer.

In addition to design and production capabilities, Riker Products offers tube bending and cutting operations. Led by the slogan "Bend it—don't build it," Riker has shown its clients a cost savings in the design and manufacture of formed tubing that replaces expensive welded fabricators.

Custom bending for steel, brass, aluminum, and stainless steel tubes with diameters up to eight inches, as well as high-speed cutting capabilities, has opened up new doors for Riker, which now offers these services on a project-by-project basis. "Even though many customers think

RIKER PRODUCTS, INC.—BASED IN TOLEDO AND FOUNDED IN 1932—HAS BECOME WELL KNOWN IN THE INDUSTRY AS A MANUFACTURER AND DISTRIBUTOR OF HEAVY-DUTY EXHAUST COMPONENTS AND ACCESSORIES.

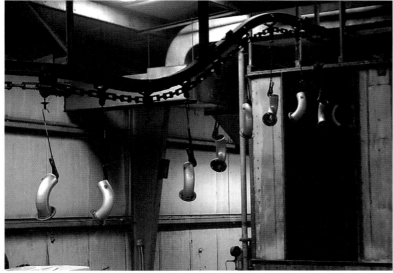

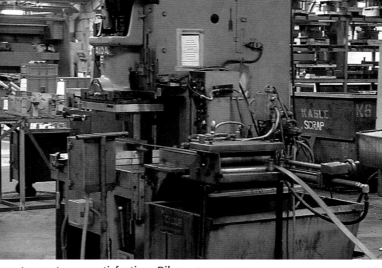

of us as a job shop, we also have the capabilities and resources to run high-production jobs," says Brian Douglas, CFO. Riker's 250,000-square-foot plant provides the capacity to take on these additional custom cutting and bending projects, while still serving the company's established customer base.

STATE-OF-THE-ART OPERATIONS

The manufacturing floor at Riker Products includes state-of-the-art metal forming, assembly, and welding equipment. With 18 bending machines—each with the capability to bend various diameters of tubing, which may range from 7/16-inch to eight-inch—as well as various gauges in tubing thickness, Riker's versatility is evident. Manufacturers of ski lifts and race car roll bars, for example, that require the bending of heavy-gauge tubing directly benefit from this versatility.

A high-speed Haven cutting machine, also available at Riker, can make multiple cuts per minute on tubing up to five inches in diameter. Advanced techniques are used in the washing, metal preparation, painting, and coating of every product that Riker produces.

CUSTOMER SATISFACTION

Riker offers these quality services and state-of-the-art equipment to ensure complete customer satisfaction. This philosophy is imperative for a company that works with many different industries and strives to help customers engineer products specific to their needs.

Through the years, Riker has developed partnerships with various suppliers to further demonstrate its commitment to customer satisfaction. The strong relationship Riker has with its suppliers assures high-quality materials, thus producing high-quality products, resulting in

greater customer satisfaction. Riker also supplies warehouses, to ensure optimum inventory levels for product availability on demand.

Partnerships with clients, such as the relationship Riker has with Johnson Matthey, Inc., for example, ensure quality production of catalytic exhaust mufflers for transit buses. Both companies work with the engine manufacturer to create a product that will meet EPA clean air standards.

Riker must continually strive to find new and innovative ways to build its client base. Taking on custom projects and offering each client the firm's focused attention, as well as such added services as design, testing, and warehousing, maintain the company's reputation for exemplary customer satisfaction. With such attention to detail and pursuit of success for each and every customer, it is clear that Riker Products, Inc. will continue to prosper for years to come.

RIKER DESIGNS AND MANUFACTURES MUFFLERS, SPARK ARRESTERS, PIPES AND TUBES, FLEXIBLE METAL HOSING, SEMITRAILER EXHAUST STACKS, CLAMPS, BRACKETS, AND RELATED PARTS.

COMMITTED TO DESIGNING HIGH-QUALITY PRODUCTS WITH MAXIMUM EFFICIENCY IN MIND, RIKER UTILIZES AN IN-HOUSE DESIGN TEAM AND ADVANCED COMPUTER APPLICATIONS, INCLUDING AutoCAD AND ELECTRONIC DESIGN DATA TRANSFER.

Hylant Group

T HE HYLANT GROUP PROVIDES INNOVATIVE RISK MANAGEMENT, INSURANCE, EMPLOY-EE BENEFITS, EXECUTIVE COMPENSATION, AND FINANCIAL SERVICES TO ITS LOCAL, NATIONAL, AND MULTINATIONAL CLIENTS. IN SUPPORT OF THIS EFFORT, HYLANT AGGRESSIVELY RECRUITS THE MOST TALENTED EMPLOYEES AT EVERY LEVEL, SETS HIGH

performance standards, and utilizes the latest knowledge and technology to live up to the company motto: The Best at What We Do. In short, the Hylant difference is in its people and their attitudes.

Hylant management prides itself on setting rigorous standards for quality, service, and ethical behavior. When working with clients, Hylant employees are encouraged to innovate in order to move beyond the typical interaction between a business client and their insurance agency. Hylant employees benefit from a company-wide climate that encourages and supports professional development and growth. The goal is simple—Hylant's retention of trained, knowledgeable, and valued people.

Today, the Hylant Group employs more than 350 people in nine locations. There are 170 employees in two Toledo offices—Jefferson Avenue and the Ohio Building—and an additional 180 in Cleveland, Columbus, and Cincinnati; Troy and Ann Arbor, Michigan; and Fort Wayne, Indiana.

A HISTORY OF GROWTH

F ounded in 1935 as Edward P. Hylant, Inc., the Hylant Group is a third-generation business with deep roots in Toledo. The company's first office was located in downtown Toledo in the old Toledo Trust Building on Summit Street. After two more moves to ever-larger quarters, the company still calls downtown home.

At Hylant, change means more than just moving into new offices. In 1942, following the death of founder Edward P. Hylant, John T. MacLean was hired to lead the business, and the company was renamed Hylant-MacLean. In 1946, Edward Hylant's son Robert joined the firm after service in World War II, even-

THE LEADERSHIP TEAM AT THE HYLANT GROUP, GATHERED BENEATH A PORTRAIT OF ROBERT HYLANT, INCLUDES (FROM LEFT) RICHARD HYLANT, PRESIDENT, HYLANT GROUP TOLEDO; SCOTT STEWART, SENIOR VICE PRESIDENT; BILL BUCKLEY, PRESIDENT AND CHIEF OPERATING OFFICER; AND PATRICK HYLANT, CHAIRMAN AND CHIEF EXECUTIVE OFFICER.

tually becoming CEO in 1957, when John MacLean retired. In 1982, the reins of the company were passed to a third generation: Patrick R. Hylant took over as chairman and CEO, and still occupies that position today. To reflect the changing nature of the business, the name MacLean was officially retired in 2000, and the company was renamed the Hylant Group.

Location, leadership, and name changes have not affected the company's history of growth. The Hylant Group enjoyed prosperity and moderate growth through the 1950s, 1960s, and 1970s, becoming an increasingly important part of the Toledo business insurance community.

Beginning in 1987 with expansion into Troy, Michigan, the company has grown significantly with subsequent expansions into markets throughout the Midwest.

PRODUCTS AND SERVICES

A s Hylant acquired firms, its goal was twofold: to offer its core products and services to new markets and to acquire companies with specific expertise that could benefit the entire client base. Through the Worldwide Broker Network (WBN), Hylant reaches into Europe, Africa, South America, and the Far East. In 1994, Hylant introduced a Managing General Agency operation in Toledo

compensation, general and product liability, professional liability, auto, crime, fiduciary, directors and officers, employee benefits and executive compensation, personal insurance, surety, 401(k), risk management consulting, title insurance, and personal financial planning. As business changes, Hylant will continue to innovate and meet the challenges faced by its client base.

STRATEGIC PROGRESS

The 1990s were a period of tremendous growth for the Hylant Group. Through various acquisitions and the opening of new offices, the company's workforce grew from 80 employees in 1990 to more than 350 in 2001. While this benchmark is a significant accomplishment by any standard, Hylant's position and importance within its industry also increased during this decade of growth. In 1990, the company was ranked 84th largest of 12,000 agencies nationwide by *Business Insurance*, a highly regarded industry publication. By the end of 1999, Hylant was ranked 43rd. The corporate goal is to be in the top 25 by 2004.

Through increasing market share in its current markets, moving into new markets, and through a program of strategic acquisitions, the Hylant Group is well positioned for sustained growth and profitability. As a new century begins, two members of the fourth generation of the Hylant family, great-grandchildren of the founder, have joined the agency. Along with the many dedicated employees at every level, they represent the future of a company poised for continued success for generations to come.

with the formation of Hylant Administrative Services (HAS). HAS currently operates as the Administrator for the Ohio Plan and the Ohio Fair Participating Plan, which insures more than 650 municipalities, townships, and fairs throughout Ohio.

In 1998, Hylant acquired Midland Title, expanding Hylant's business into title insurance. In 1999, Hylant Broker Services, headquartered in Columbus, was formed. In 2000, Hylant acquired O'Brien and Sanderson Insurance of Fort Wayne, Indiana, establishing a property/casualty and employee benefits presence in the Northeast Indiana market. Employee benefits and 401(k) operations were expanded with acquisitions in Ann Arbor, Michigan, and Cleveland, Ohio. The following year, Hylant Financial Services was formed to provide specialized financial planning and investment services.

Today, Hylant offers its clients a wide range of products and services including property, inland marine, ocean cargo, worker's

PepsiAmericas

PepsiAmericas, part of the multibillion-dollar beverage giant Pepsi-Cola, offers more than 1.4 million thirsty customers in 18 northwest Ohio counties and across the United States a wide variety of beverage options. Among those options are regular, diet, and caffeine-

free carbonated beverages, along with noncarbonated beverages such as sports drinks, tea, fruit juice, water, and even Starbucks' Frappuccino and SoBe healthy beverages.

PepsiAmericas has been a part of the Toledo-area community since 1935, when it first entered the region as Electro Pure Water, a franchise bottler with production and distribution capabilities. In 1952, the company became known as Variety Beverage Company, with a name change to RKO Bottling in 1967. Pepsi-Cola General Bottlers acquired the company in 1987.

As an active community supporter, the Pepsi name is associated with many of the area's best-known entertainment venues, such as Rally by the River and the annual Thanksgiving Day Parade. Pepsi has been—and plans to continue to be—the official beverage of the Jamie Farr LPGA Tournament, and has also

agreed to support the U.S. Senior Open in Toledo in 2003. Pepsi is also a big supporter of the Toledo Mud Hens baseball team, and is a member of the Founders' Club for the new downtown stadium. Additionally, Pepsi provides support to the Cherry Street Mission, Center of Science and Industry (COSI), Toledo Symphony, Mobile Meals, and Northwest Ohio Food Bank, just to name a few.

STATE-OF-THE-ART PRODUCTION CAPABILITIES

Pepsi's Hill Avenue production plant is state of the art. It features a highly automated system with the industry's fastest and most efficient equipment. The system is operated by three line operators and two forklift operators, while the automated machine itself performs the filling, sealing, and packaging parts of the process. With

the ability to output tens of thousands of cases per day and hundreds of thousands of cans per hour, the Hill Avenue plant still holds plenty of room for growth. In fact, the plant is currently working at only 70 percent of its maximum capability.

The company also operates a distribution center in Lima, Ohio. With both facilities combined, Pepsi employs more than 400 northwest Ohioans. The company considers these operations as another important part of its contribution to the area's prosperity.

THE HISTORY OF PEPSI

Pepsi has been part of Americana for more than a century. Just hearing the beverage's name brings to mind the clink of ice in a glass and the fizz that tickles the nose. It causes the mind to conjure up the image of a family sitting together at the kitchen

table, having dinner, playing games, or just talking, while sipping on cold, bubbly glasses of Pepsi-Cola.

The first Pepsi-Cola was produced in 1890 by Caleb Bradham, in his New Bern, North Carolina, drugstore. The product was first bottled in Chicago in 1935, in green or brown reused beer bottles with paper labels reading Refreshing and Healthful—Famous for over 30 Years. At that time, the fizzy cola was distributed by a network of enterprising distribu-tors with no set territories. Sales were booming until 1942, when wartime rations on sugar cut pro-duction. But as the rations were lifted and the years rolled on, con-sumption was on the rise.

Throughout the years, Pepsi's marketing involved using slogans like Reduced in Calories and Re-freshing Without Filling. The com-pany also hired spokespeople such as Michael Jackson and Britney Spears to help boost sales. Today, Pepsi products are the preferred soft drink throughout the country among many.

Recently, the company has begun to take a more global approach with its new slogan, Growing Across the Globe. With several operations in the United States, as well as in Puerto Rico, Jamaica, the Bahamas, Trinidad, Poland, Hungary, the Czech Repub-lic, and the Republic of Slovakia, PepsiAmericas is working to expand its presence around the globe.

PEPSIAMERICAS HAS BEEN A PART OF THE TOLEDO-AREA COMMUNITY SINCE 1935. BELOW, HILL AVENUE PLANT EMPLOYEES GATHER AT THE NEWLY BUILT FACILITY IN 1968. TODAY, THE COMPANY EMPLOYS MORE THAN 400 NORTHWEST OHIOANS.

Owens Corning

ESTABLISHED IN TOLEDO IN 1938, OWENS CORNING IS A $5 BILLION, GLOBAL INDUSTRY LEADER IN BUILDING MATERIALS AND COMPOSITE PRODUCTS. THE COMPANY HAS A LEADERSHIP POSITION IN EVERY MARKET IN WHICH IT PARTICIPATES. OWENS CORNING'S HISTORY BEGINS WITH THREE MEN: DR. GAMES SLAYTER, DALE KLEIST, AND "JACK"

THOUGH IT IS BASED IN TOLEDO, OWENS CORNING HAS MORE THAN 20,000 EMPLOYEES WORLDWIDE, WITH MANUFACTURING, SALES, AND RESEARCH FACILITIES IN MORE THAN 30 COUNTRIES ON SIX CONTINENTS.

Thomas. Slayter was known for his vision of expanding technology and innovation of glass fiber. He hired Thomas as his research assistant, and later hired Kleist to help Thomas. In 1932, Kleist, a young researcher, was attempting to weld together architectural glass blocks to form a vacuum-tight seal when a jet of compressed air accidentally struck a stream of molten glass. This resulted in fine glass fibers, which turned out to be thin enough to be utilized as a commercial fiberglass insulation.

Then, in 1933, Thomas began to conduct experiments using glass wool instead of natural fibers on textile machinery. This indicated the possibility of using glass fibers instead of natural or other synthetic fibers in textile applications. The discovery of fine glass fibers for use in the textile industry and Thomas' work involving glass wool spawned the still-thriving fiberglass insulation and glass fiber textile industries.

In 1935, Corning Glass approached Owens-Illinois to join forces in the production of glass fiber. For years, the companies worked together. But, in 1938, experimental costs prompted the companies to form a separate company to sink or swim on its own. Thus, borrowing from each of its parent companies' names, Owens Corning Fiberglas Corporation was announced.

In 1944, Owens Corning Fiberglas created a prototype boat hull made of fiberglass-reinforced plastic (FRP), a material that proved to require very little maintenance—a distinct advan-

and research facilities in more than 30 countries on six continents.

As the company grew larger and more successful, so too did its international arena. The company expanded in 1958 to Australia, and in the 1960s, began operations in New Zealand, South Africa, Sweden, and Colombia. On March 15, 1965, Owens Corning Fiberglas Europe, a wholly owned subsidiary, was formed, and stationed its headquarters in Brussels. The company also has a Science and Technology Center in Battice, Belgium, which is a source of technological innovation with its research and experimentation of new and improved products.

Owens Corning's newest approach and offering to the consumer is what it calls System Thinking. Introduced in 1996, this new approach presents complete project solutions, rather than offering expertise on just one individual product. Owens Corning is confident that this approach will benefit the consumer, as projects run smoother and quicker and become more cost-effective overall.

One example of this initiative is System Thinking Roofing Systems. A member of the roofing business since 1977, Owens Corning remains a top producer of residential asphalt roofing in the United States. The System Thinking Roofing System is made up of products that include shingles, underlays, ridge vents, and soffits, which, together, are superior to any one product alone.

The Owens Corning brand is recognized seven to one over the next leading competitor, and continues to lead the industry with constant research and technology to make better products for the consumer.

tage over wooden boat hulls. In 1953, use of FRP was expanded when the company, along with General Motors, announced the first production automobile with a body made entirely out of FRP—the Chevrolet Corvette. As a result of the company's growth and development, Owens Corning Fiberglas began moving its personnel into the Fiberglas Tower, the first high-rise building to use the open office concept, in 1969. Fiberglas Tower was home until 1996, when the company moved into its new world headquarters, located in downtown Toledo. The company also changed its name in 1996 to Owens Corning, a reflection of its growing interest in technology in other areas beyond fiberglass.

THE COLOR OF SUCCESS

Owens Corning is most widely known for its fiberglass products. Shortly after the discovery of the glass fiber, the first commercial fiberglass insulation was installed in October 1933. The product proved to have outstanding thermal performance, and has shown that it neither deteriorates over time nor absorbs moisture.

In response to requests for a way to distinguish Owens Corning fiberglass insulation from its competitors, red dye was added to the process, which resulted in the insulation turning pink. In 1980, the Pink Panther™ became the new "spokesman" of PINK Fiberglas Insulation, and is still recognized and associated with the company worldwide. In 1987, Owens Corning made legal history by becoming the first company to trademark a color—in this case, pink.

In 1993, the company unveiled PinkPLUS®, a new fiberglass insulation targeted to the do-it-yourself residential market, and marketed it as easy to install and handle. Its latest product, Miraflex® fiber, is used in the PinkPLUS insulation, and is virtually itch-free. This new product has proved to be very popular with the consumer, as it expands and conforms to fit in small spaces.

A WORLDWIDE LEADER

Though it is based in Toledo, Owens Corning has more than 20,000 employees worldwide, with manufacturing, sales,

©2001 UNITED ARTISTS

OWENS CORNING IS A $5 BILLION, GLOBAL INDUSTRY LEADER IN BUILDING MATERIALS AND COMPOSITE PRODUCTS.

PROFILES IN EXCELLENCE

1941-1970

OmniSource Corporation

COMPANIES SUCH AS FORT WAYNE-BASED OMNISOURCE CORPORATION PLAY AN INTEGRAL ROLE IN THE LIFE CYCLE OF FERROUS AND NONFERROUS METALS. THE COMPANY PROVIDES AN ESSENTIAL LINK BETWEEN THE SOURCES OF SCRAP METAL AND THOSE INDUSTRIES THAT CONSUME IT—MAINLY STEEL MILLS AND FOUNDRIES. AS A

ALUMINUM BAILING IS ONE OF SEVERAL NON-FERROUS PROCESSES PERFORMED AT THE OMNISOURCE HILL AVENUE FACILITY (TOP).

THE OMNISOURCE SCRAP MANAGEMENT BAILING FACILITY, LOCATED AT THE DAIMLER-CHRYSLER STAMPING PLANT IN STERLING HEIGHTS, MICHIGAN, PROVIDES DAIMLERCHRYSLER WITH A WORLD-CLASS SOLUTION FOR THEIR SCRAP HANDLING NEEDS (BOTTOM LEFT).

OMNISOURCE PROCESSES SCRAP COILS AT THE DETROIT AVENUE FACILITY (BOTTOM RIGHT).

processor and broker, the firm provides a steady market for those with scrap to sell. At the same time, OmniSource assures major consumers of scrap a reliable supply in the quantities and quality they need.

OmniSource has pioneered the concept of Scrap Management, and is the North American leader in providing Scrap Management services. Through the development of Scrap Management, OmniSource has expanded the traditional scrap process to encompass all factors that impact the net revenue companies receive for the scrap they generate. By developing facilities on-site at many scrap generators and providing a variety of business services, OmniSource has differentiated itself from competitors and offers customers a total solution to their scrap needs.

GROWTH AND CHANGE

In 1979, the Rifkin family's Superior Iron & Metal company acquired Kripke-Tuschman Industries Inc. In the early 1980s, the growing company was renamed OmniSource Corporation.

The company that became OmniSource began in 1943 when Irving Rifkin borrowed enough money to begin collecting and re-selling scrap out of the back of his truck. From there, his company continued to grow to form Superior Companies, owned by the Rifkin family. Today, OmniSource Corporation is owned and managed by Leonard Rifkin, chairman and CEO, and his sons—Danny, president and COO; Rick, president, Nonferrous Operating Group; and Marty, president, Nonferrous Specialty Group.

In the Toledo area, Kripke-Tuschman Industries Inc. began in the 1900s when Morris Tuschman started as a scrap peddler by purchasing ferrous and nonferrous scrap in the area. His route included a triangle between Toledo, Ohio; Monroe, Michigan; and Dundee, Michigan. From there, the business grew into the Tuschman Steel Company, formed in 1944. The Tuschman Steel Company, headed by Chester Tuschman, assumed a major role in the scrap processing industry. It was known as one of the industry's more progressive companies, having the forethought to install

modern baling, shearing, and containerized transportation equipment. In 1976, the Tuschman Steel Company merged with Linver-Kripke and Sherwin Metal Reclaiming, founded by Sherwin Kripke and his family, to form Kripke-Tuschman Industries Inc. In 1998, OmniSource further expanded its presence in Toledo by acquiring another long-time Toledo-owned scrap metal company, A. Edelstein and Sons Inc.

MAINTAINING QUALITY STANDARDS

As a scrap processing company, OmniSource helps turn obsolete products such as old automobiles and refrigerators, as well as the offal from manufacturing facilities, into products that can be remelted and formed into new steel coil, bars, and castings. Using state-of-the-art processing and sorting equipment, OmniSource is able to process and sort almost any scrap metal into the form, density, size, and chemistry specification steel mills and foundries require. OmniSource also has the capability to process and handle a variety of

▲ TED BACHO

▲ STEVE GARBER

nonferrous scrap through its granulating, shearing, baling, and precious metal refining operations.

Throughout all production processes, OmniSource and its staff of highly trained engineers maintain high product quality standards by employing a variety of chemical and quality analyses, as well as process control and testing procedures. Many OmniSource divisions are QS 9000, ISO 9002, and ISO 14001 registered.

OmniSource's most important asset is its people. To maintain its commitment to service, quality, continuous improvement, and on-time delivery at the lowest possible costs, the company provides customers with unmatched experience and expertise in the scrap metal industry. It is OmniSource's intellectual capital that truly differentiates the firm from the competition.

As a brokerage and metal trading company, OmniSource stands poised to lead the industry. Its brokerage offices are located throughout the United States and Canada, and keep a close eye on the national and international market. These offices stay abreast of both the metal producing and the consuming industries to provide clients with information on the most up-to-date pricing, strategies, and industry trends.

FORMING UNIQUE PARTNERSHIPS

OmniSource is known for monitoring, setting, and exceeding the standard for the scrap metal industry. For customers that produce a high volume of

scrap materials, OmniSource offers the option of on-site processing. Through a partnership between OmniSource and its customers, on-site scrap processing facilities are built to help streamline processing operations and reduce the customer's costs, while increasing net scrap revenue. By utilizing its expertise and firsthand knowledge of Scrap Management, OmniSource provides its customers with creative and innovative solutions. The company also provides partners, if required, with the financial capital necessary to secure the facilities and equipment necessary to make the agreement a success.

One of OmniSource's many partnering success stories is with DaimlerChrysler. When the automaker wanted to improve its scrap handling system at its Warren, Michigan, stamping plant, OmniSource provided a unique plan of action that included an on-site, off-line baling facility with state-of-the-art engineering and processing equipment, staffed by DaimlerChrysler employees and managed by OmniSource personnel. As a result of OmniSource's success at this stamping plant, the Scrap Management process has been expanded to numerous other Daimler-Chrysler facilities, including those in Sterling, Michigan, and Twinsburg, Ohio. OmniSource also has Scrap Management operations on-site at several of Ford Motor Companies' stamping plants and at AmeriSteel's steel mill in Jacksonville, Florida.

Through innovative partnerships and the development of Scrap Management, OmniSource has introduced

the industry to an entirely new way of managing the total scrap process. This approach, and pursuit of continuous improvement, has earned OmniSource the prestigious Daimler Chrysler Commodity Award for supply excellence (formally known as the Platinum Pentastar Award) for seven consecutive years.

OmniSource is always working to provide its customers with the flexibility and reliability they have come to expect. From large automakers to small machine shops, OmniSource provides a necessary service to its customers, while remaining mindful of quality, safety, and the environment.

Through innovative scrap processing, OmniSource Corporation helps divert materials from landfills, preserve natural resources for the future, and reduce the energy consumption required to make new steel products. With sound financial management and a dedicated and experienced management team, OmniSource is positioned to grow and remain a major force in the scrap processing, brokerage, metal trading, and Scrap Management industry.

UNIQUE EQUIPMENT, SUCH AS A MOBILE SHEAR, ALLOWS OMNISOURCE PERSONNEL TO PROCESS MANDREL-WOUND BUNDLES QUICKLY AND EFFECTIVELY (LEFT).

IN BALDWIN, FLORIDA, OMNISOURCE HAS A SCRAP MANAGEMENT SHREDDING OPERATION LOCATED AT THE AMERISTEEL MILL (RIGHT).

BY UTILIZING ITS EXPERTISE AND FIRSTHAND KNOWLEDGE OF SCRAP MANAGEMENT, OMNISOURCE PROVIDES ITS CUSTOMERS WITH CREATIVE AND INNOVATIVE SOLUTIONS.

▲ TED BACHO

▲ TED BACHO

Harold Jaffe Jewelers

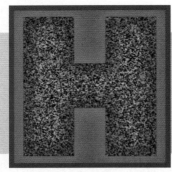

AROLD JAFFE JEWELERS IS AN INDEPENDENT, FAMILY-OWNED COMPANY, SERVING THE GREATER TOLEDO AREA SINCE 1946. ■ JAFFE WAS A WATCHMAKER, A TRADE LEARNED FROM HIS FATHER. HIS BACKGROUND WAS REPAIRING WATCHES FOR OTHER JEWELERS IN THE AREA, BUT THE BUSINESS RAPIDLY EXPANDED INTO FINE

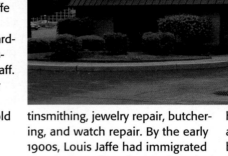

jewelry and diamonds. Today, Jaffe's sons carry on his legacy of quality and service. Guided by the spirit of Harold, his wife Shirley, and son Bruce, Jeff, and Ivan Jaffe have taken the business to a new level.

By following the simple philosophy of ultimate customer satisfaction instilled by their father, the Jaffe sons have created the foremost jewelry experience, including award-winning designers, master craftsmen, and a well-trained sales staff. Customers have learned to their great pleasure that there are no limits to the possibilities at Harold Jaffe Jewelers.

CREATING THE LEGACY

Harold Jaffe's father, Louis, traveled by foot and horse-drawn cart through his homeland of Latvia doing whatever was necessary to make his living. Among his many endeavors were tinsmithing, jewelry repair, butchering, and watch repair. By the early 1900s, Louis Jaffe had immigrated to America, where he continued working as a jack-of-all-trades to feed his growing family.

As a child, Harold Jaffe was drawn to watchmaking. Fascinated with the precision and intricacies of timepieces, Jaffe studied earnestly at his father's side. Soon, his reputation as a skilled tradesman grew, and he began repairing watches for other jewelers in the area and beyond. Known as the "watchmaker's watchmaker" to many, Jaffe was the individual more and more jewelers turned to when confronted with problem watches no one else could fix.

Emulating their father, Harold Jaffe's three sons eventually gravitated to the business, each finding his own niche: Jeff helped build the creative design aspects of jewelry manufacturing, as well as the advertising and marketing; Bruce, who died in 1985, learned his father's craft of watch repair; and Ivan became one of the most skilled and demanding gemologists in the industry. Working together as a family gave the Jaffes the ability to create one of the leading jewelry stores in the country.

AWARD-WINNING FAMILY JEWELER

Always ahead of the curve, the Jaffe family prides itself on identifying, and even creating, the latest trends in fine jewelry. The quality of their products and the uniqueness of their designs has evolved into a

SERVING THE GREATER TOLEDO AREA SINCE 1946, HAROLD JAFFE JEWELERS HAS THE AWARD-WINNING DESIGNERS, MASTER CRAFTSMEN, AND WELL-TRAINED STAFF TO ENSURE CUSTOMERS HAVE ULTIMATE SATISFACTION WITH THEIR EXPERIENCE.

distinctive "Harold Jaffe look," sought by customers from across the globe. Every custom design is developed from start to finish in the store's on-site studio, allowing each piece to be supervised totally by Jaffe craftsmen.

Winning awards is part of the family's legacy. Jaffe jewelry designs have been singled out for the highly prestigious DeBeers Diamonds International Award and Diamonds Today Award, both designed by Jodi Jaffe. At the same time, the company's advertising has won Addy awards for Best in its Class and Best of Show. In short, the store's creativity is recognized near and far.

AWARD-WINNING COMMUNITY SERVICE

As the owner of a Greater Toledo business for more than five decades, the Jaffe family also believes it is important to be involved in the community. "We make our living here," Jeff Jaffe explains. "We need to give back in any way we can."

This commitment is demonstrated by the number and variety of organizations that the family supports. Harold Jaffe was one of the founding fathers of the Toledo Jazz Society in 1980. Jeff Jaffe continues the family representation on the board today. Other family members have served on numerous other local boards as well.

As a result of its efforts, the Jaffe family has been honored twice by the Arts Commission of Greater Toledo for its participation and support of the Toledo-area arts community.

ULTIMATE CUSTOMER SATISFACTION

In the end, however, it is customer service that is the true hallmark of the business. Harold Jaffe instilled in his sons the philosophy of ultimate customer satisfaction, which dictates that they do whatever needs to be done to please the customer. This makes Harold Jaffe Jewelers a rare find in a world of self-serve shopping. Every member of the family and staff stands ready to assist with any need, from replacing a battery in a watch to designing a ring for an engagement. Using cutting-edge techniques, new designs are created, family heirlooms are preserved, and jewelry or watches are repaired by highly skilled, well-trained artisans.

In fact, training and technology are at the top of the list of prerequisites for the company's staff. The on-premises Gemological Laboratory is equipped with state-of-the-art equipment for the most sophisticated identification and grading of gemstones. The firm's laboratory features GEMPRINT, a laser gemstone fingerprinting system that is exclusive to Harold Jaffe Jewelers.

Still, it is the people who make the real difference in customer satisfaction. That is why at least one member of the Jaffe family can nearly always be found on the premises—"even though each one of our staff is part of our family, too," adds Jeff Jaffe. "We've even gone so far as to send them to school, just like our own children!"

This commitment to quality is part of the Jaffes' continual quest to educate and help each staff member become the best in his or her field, just like the company itself. As a member of the American Gem Society, Harold Jaffe Jewelers follows very strict rules of ethics that include strong educational programs, truthful advertising, and accurate presentation of product and value. Through their actions, members of the Harold Jaffe extended family have been living those ethics for more than 50 years.

EVERY CUSTOM DESIGN IS DEVELOPED FROM START TO FINISH IN THE STORE'S ON-SITE STUDIO, ALLOWING EACH PIECE TO BE SUPERVISED TOTALLY BY JAFFE CRAFTSMEN.

AS A MEMBER OF THE AMERICAN GEM SOCIETY, HAROLD JAFFE JEWELERS FOLLOWS VERY STRICT RULES OF ETHICS THAT INCLUDE STRONG EDUCATIONAL PROGRAMS, TRUTHFUL ADVERTISING, AND ACCURATE PRESENTATION OF PRODUCT AND VALUE.

The Andersons, Inc.

WHAT BEGAN PRIOR TO WORLD WAR II WITH A SINGLE GRAIN ELEVATOR AND ONE MAN'S DREAM HAS GROWN INTO A PUBLICLY TRADED CORPORATION THAT SERVES ITS COMMUNITY WHILE SERVING THE WORLD. IN 1947, THE ANDERSONS' FOUNDER HAROLD ANDERSON OPENED A

500,000 bushel grain elevator in Maumee, Ohio. That first year, 1.3 million bushels of grain were received. Today, with 14 state-of-the-art elevators in Ohio, Michigan, Indiana, and Illinois, The Andersons has 80 million bushels of storage space and handles more than 160 million bushels of grain annually.

Harold Anderson's family has remained committed to his dream. When he stepped down as CEO in 1968, his oldest son John took over, followed in 1986 by John's brother Dick. Today, Harold Anderson's grandson Mike is at the helm, backed by several other third-generation Andersons and more than 3,000 dedicated employees.

A CUSTOMER-FIRST PHILOSOPHY

Through the years, The Andersons has emphasized customer service. In the early years, Harold Anderson dealt directly with farmers within a 150-mile radius of Maumee. With the nine truck dumps in the first Maumee facility, trucks could be weighed in, unloaded, and weighed out in an average

of six minutes. Grain brought in by the farmers went directly to the large mills and processors throughout the United States and Canada.

The company's mission statement reflects the Golden Rule approach to customer service. Every effort is made to assure that all products and services offer value and serve a purpose. The Andersons also strives to treat its employees well, creating a family atmosphere in which diversity and individuality are valued.

GROWTH AND CHANGE

To keep up with customer demand and shifts in markets, the company has tackled changes head on and reaped the rewards. After more than a half century in business, The Andersons has been profitable in all but one year.

When the St. Lawrence Seaway opened in 1959, The Andersons saw a new opportunity for growth. This new navigation option linked the Great Lakes region to global markets. Then in 1968, a 12-million bushel grain elevator was built in Champaign, Illinois, the company's first location

outside northwest Ohio. The elevator was the first of its kind to load 100-car "unit trains" that were then sent to the East Coast, south to the Gulf of Mexico, and from there to ports around the globe.

The Andersons began formulating fertilizer for farmers in 1959. Today, it operates nine wholesale fertilizer operations with dry and liquid fertilizer in Ohio, Michigan, Indiana, and Illinois. The Andersons formulates and distributes nearly 1.5 million tons of dry and liquid agricultural fertilizer materials to a network of hundreds of dealers and distributors every year. In addition, nine farm centers in Ohio, Michigan, and Indiana sell agricultural fertilizer, chemicals, and seeds, and provide agronomic application services directly to farmers.

The Andersons' Processing Group is one of the top U.S. manufacturers of do-it-yourself turf care and lawn and garden products. It is also the leading supplier of premium professional turf products to golf courses, sports fields, lawn care operators, and other turf professionals coast to coast. The group's corncob milling business produces products for a wide variety of industrial and consumer markets, including industrial absorbents, pet bedding, and cat litter.

The Andersons has always depended heavily on the railroad system to deliver its grain. Since the company's beginning, it has managed, maintained, and repaired its own fleet of railcars. Today, The Andersons' Rail Group provides these same services to outside customers through its American Association of Railroads (ARA)-certified repair shop and a fleet of more than 4,800 rail cars rolling on tracks throughout the United States and Canada.

The Andersons also operates six large retail stores in Ohio—three in

BEGUN IN 1947 BY FOUNDER HAROLD ANDERSON, THE ANDERSONS TODAY BOASTS ONE OF THE NATION'S FINEST MANUFACTURING COMPLEXES, PROVIDING VALUE AND SERVICE TO NATIONAL, AS WELL AS INTERNATIONAL, AGRICULTURAL AND LAWN FERTILIZER MARKETS.

Toledo, two in Columbus, and one in Lima—featuring More For Your Home™, plus great value and extraordinary service. Customers can get everything they need to remodel a kitchen, finish the basement, fix a plumbing leak, take care of the lawn, care for a pet, fix the car, prepare dinner, landscape the home, pick up a gift, or throw a party.

As it has grown over the years, The Andersons has changed its ownership and corporate structure. An 11-member board of directors was also elected. In February of 1996, The Andersons went public, trading on the Nasdaq under the symbol ANDE.

SUPPORTING THE COMMUNITY

The Andersons has always generously donated a portion of profits to charitable causes. To better implement this goal, the Anderson Foundation was established in 1949 to distribute funds to local charities. In addition, full-time employees are offered a gift matching program through which the company matches individual contributions that meet established qualifications.

The Andersons' Agricultural Research Fund began with funding from an endowment to Ohio State University by the company in 1965. Since then, millions of dollars have been spent on grain quality research.

In an effort to partially endow future giving, The Andersons Fund Supporting Organization was established in 1995. Fifty-two acres of property were donated with the intent that the sale of the property would benefit local charities relating to human services, the arts, urban affairs, health, the environment, and education.

Perhaps the future of The Andersons is best summed up by current President and CEO Mike Anderson: "By building on the strong foundation of our past, our company has been built to last well into the future. The format, the structure, and the businesses which have evolved over more than 50 years will continue to change as we work hard to adjust to changing market and customer needs and to build on our capabilities."

Mosser Construction, Inc.

OSSER CONSTRUCTION, INC. WAS FOUNDED IN 1948, AND IS HEAD-QUARTERED IN FREMONT, OHIO, WITH A REGIONAL OFFICE IN TOLEDO. WITH MORE THAN 50 YEARS OF PROVEN EXPERIENCE, MOSSER HAS GAINED A REPUTATION OF QUALITY DESIGN AND BUILDING SERVICES.

With more than 500 field employees—including carpenters, millwrights, pile drivers, masons, bricklayers, ironworkers, operators, and laborers—providing an average total of 740,000 work hours per year, Mosser is one of the largest construction companies in Ohio. The company is one of very few considered to be self-performing, meaning that the firm employs tradesmen as full-time employees rather than subcontracting with workers on a job-to-job basis. This employment practice provides Mosser with greater control of its workforce. In addition, Mosser's workers know and understand the company and its philosophy.

Mosser's design and building ser-

ONE OF THE LARGEST CONSTRUCTION COMPANIES IN OHIO, MOSSER CONSTRUCTION, INC. HAS CULTIVATED A REPUTATION OF QUALITY DESIGN AND BUILDING SERVICES OVER THE COURSE OF MORE THAN 50 YEARS IN THE INDUSTRY.

BENTON PHOTOGRAPHY

vices include specialization in tilt-up and precast concrete construction, masonry construction, pre-engineered steel buildings, and renovation.

PROVIDING EXCELLENCE

As an employee-owned company, Mosser gives its employees stock in the company, and they treat the firm as if it were their own business. Employees have high values that are attributed to the empowerment by, and attitude of, top management. These values and company pride have contributed to Mosser's reputation for excellence.

The foundation of Mosser's strength is in the company's superintendents. Since the firm handles complicated jobs, superintendents must be highly skilled and knowledgeable. Each of these individuals brings more than 20 years of experience to the job, and knows how to get the most value for the customer with the least amount of money.

The direct contact by Mosser's supervisors with the company's workers and clients in the field fosters the firm's reputation of honesty and trustworthiness, commitment to follow-through, straightforwardness, and high-quality work. This integrity is a major strength for Mosser.

TOP-NOTCH CAPABILITIES

One of Mosser's most notable renovation projects, the Valentine Theatre, outshines the others in terms of complexity and notoriety. When Mosser signed on to perform the renovations on this Toledo landmark, the scope of the project focused on structural reinforcement. However, once the project was under way, workers discovered unforeseen structural issues, with extensive crumbling within the

walls and a roof that was being held up by the pressure of the building's outside walls. These findings presented new challenges for the work crew, but—in the Mosser spirit—the challenges were tackled head-on. The results are outstanding, with a fully renovated structure that is now enjoyed by thousands of community members each year.

Mosser's involvement in the Valentine Theatre won the company the coveted 1999 Build Ohio award, as well as the 2000 Build America award, given by the Associated General Contractors of America. These awards are presented to contractors for superior craftsmanship and quality.

Mosser also has completed several impressive building projects, including the University of Toledo's Wolfe Hall, which is home to the university's College of Pharmacy and life sciences and chemistry departments, and is considered to be one of the most advanced science facilities of its kind in the nation. This project was recognized by the International Masonry Institute, which gave Mosser Construction the 2001 Golden Trowel award for masonry excellence.

Oberlin College benefited from Mosser's expertise when the college decided to build a new environmental studies building on campus. Oberlin knew it didn't want just another teaching facility; instead, the school wanted a facility that was environmentally sound and demonstrated some of the environment-preserving systems, products, and techniques promoted in its environmental program. Mosser built a structure that contained state-of-the-art environmental systems and, rather than using traditional materials, coordinated the installation of pressed wheat soundboards in the auditorium and chemical-free carpets, as well as using PCB-free paints. Wood within the facility was taken only from certified forests, and even the wastewater system, which uses plants and fish to consume waste, is environmentally sound. Mosser's involvement at Oberlin College won the company the coveted 2000 Build Ohio award and the 2001 Build America award, given by the Associated General Contractors of America.

Mosser's excellence in design and building is supported by the company's commitment to safety. With one of the industry's best programs, the firm employs three full-time safety officers who are often more strict than safety agencies. Mosser's first-rate safety program has contributed to its ability to be self-insured by the Ohio Bureau of Workers' Compensation. This privilege is offered to fewer than 1 percent of all Ohio employers.

THE BENEFITS OF PARTNERING

The success of Mosser's projects can also be attributed to the company's commitment to a unique partnering program. Developed in the late 1980s by the Department of Transportation and

the Associated General Contractors of America, the partnering idea was born when these industry leaders became disenchanted with the finger-pointing and litigation associated with construction, and sought to develop a more beneficial, friendly, synergistic approach to doing business. Shortly after the idea was developed, Mosser embraced partnering as a way to create a team environment for the company's work.

Since 1993, Mosser has been encouraging dialogue between owners, architects, engineers, and con-

tractors to create a shared focus on doing jobs better. This shared focus has resulted in increased trust and respect and in greater productivity, with everyone working together toward a common goal.

Partnering, teamwork and brainstorming are used to come up with new solutions and to rectify errors. Utilizing this unique partnership approach, Mosser Construction, Inc. seeks to fulfill the changing needs of its quality clients, which has resulted in positive experiences for the company and its associates, as well as repeat business from its clients.

SSOE, Inc., Architects • Engineers

SSOE, INC.'S NEW HEADQUARTERS, WHICH WAS CREATED FROM A CANDIDATE FOR ADAPTIVE REUSE, DEMONSTRATES ITS COMMITMENT TO DOWNTOWN TOLEDO (RIGHT, TOP AND BOTTOM).

THOUGH JEEP HAS CALLED TOLEDO HOME FOR MORE THAN 50 YEARS, THE NEW PLANT—A 2.1 MILLION-SQUARE-FOOT, $1.2 BILLION INVESTMENT FOR ASSEMBLY BY DAIMLERCHRYSLER—REPRESENTS A NEW LEVEL OF COMMITMENT (LEFT, TOP AND BOTTOM).

the new Jeep plant, Medical College of Ohio, and The University of Toledo. Nationally, SSOE is one of *Engineering News Record* and *Building Design & Construction* magazines' top-ranked architectural and engineering firms.

SSOE serves its diverse customer base through distinct business units with team-oriented approaches. Each team specializes in key markets serving commercial, education, health care, and retail design. On the industrial side, SSOE serves the chemical, food, pharmaceutical, personal care, manufacturing, and automotive industries.

The first S in SSOE's name was derived from the company's original founder Alfred H. Samborn, a structural engineer who founded the firm in 1948. In the early years, company projects included heavy industry and structural detail design but later broadened into architecture, mechanical, and highway design. Through risk, hard work, and good fortune, Samborn's company experienced growth during its first decade and added the S (Jack Steketee), O (Burrie Otis), and E (John Evans) that would carry the name of Samborn, Steketee, Otis and Evans for the next 43 years.

Early on, Samborn instilled the importance of professional pride and integrity within his employees. This philosophy runs deep through the company today as SSOE employees are encouraged to be involved in the community and are led by example from within their own leadership. The company continually serves as a Pacesetter for its contributions to the United Way campaign and has sponsored exhibits at the Center of Science and Industry (COSI), Toledo Mud Hens, the Toledo Zoo, and continues its involvement in various philanthropic efforts.

In 1984, Samborn, Steketee, Otis and Evans honored its roots and officially changed the firm's name to SSOE, Inc. For the next decade, SSOE expanded on its reputation for service and integrity and further defined the company's future. In 1996, it was one of the first architectural and engineering firms in the country to receive the prestigious Q-1 rating by Ford Motor Company, and with the approach of the year 2000, it added the ISO 9001 quality certification.

Dedicated to downtown Toledo,

SSOE is a cornerstone on 10th and Madison and neighbor to the main library. A longtime downtown resident, SSOE saw roots in the Toledo Terminal Building and the LOF Building, and finally found a permanent home in the old Goodyear Tire Store. This was one of the first renovations of its kind in the downtown district and is a commitment from the firm that Toledo is home.

As the city's largest architectural and engineering firm, SSOE has provided many designing touches that have added to the skyline and character that are distinctly Toledo. Toledo's future is bright and SSOE, Inc. is full of hometown pride and excited about upcoming projects on the Maumee River Crossing Bridge, Crossroads of America, and the beautification of the Toledo area.

INCE 1950, WHEN COMPANY FOUNDER RICHARD K. RANSOM BEGAN SELLING FRESH CHEESE AT COUNTY FAIRS, AMERICANS HAVE ENJOYED HICKORY FARMS SPECIALTY FOOD PRODUCTS. RANSOM KNEW WHAT AMERICANS WANTED, AND HE PROVIDED IT. NOT ONLY DID HE MAKE HIS ROUNDS TO SHOWS, SETTING UP HIS SIX-FOOT BOOTH AND

offering samples, but he also supplemented these efforts with a mail-order business.

First, Ransom offered cheese, and then the famous Beef Stick®. His business was so successful, he decided to open a retail store in 1958. Located on North Reynolds Road in Toledo, the store was set up like an old country store with bins of products and complimentary sampling. By 1960, so many store visitors had inquired as to how to set up similar stores in their hometowns that Ransom began to franchise the stores.

From that basic concept, and a steadfast commitment to quality and customer service, grew the Hickory Farms of today—a business with more than 1,000 holiday seasonal kiosks in leading malls in the United States and Canada; eight food and food gift catalogs; a large and rapidly growing Web-based business; and a growing year-round presence in select supermarkets and mass merchandisers around the country. The company also operates an outlet

center in Maumee, Ohio, where some of Hickory Farms' most popular products, as well as discontinued items, are available year-round.

Current market research indicates that more than 90 percent of Americans are familiar with Hickory Farms, and more than 40 percent of all households have purchased the company's products. More important, of those consumers who have purchased the product, more than 85 percent rate "high quality" as the brand's distinguishing characteristic.

Hickory Farms is probably best known for its unique Beef Stick, the nation's leading brand of summer sausage, and Smokey Bar® Cheese. However, the company's product lines go beyond those to include specialty meats, seafood, fruits, gourmet foods, nuts, and candy. These items are sold under the brands Mission Orchards, Pinnacle Orchards, Pfaelzer Brothers, Almond Plaza, Ace Specialty Foods, and Squires Choice, as well as the Hickory Farms brand.

From its Maumee headquarters, Hickory Farms fulfills mail and

Internet orders for more than 3 million gifts each year, creates unique gift displays, and produces more than 4 million gift items annually. These gifts are assembled by hand and shipped to destinations throughout the United States and Canada. The firm hires thousands of seasonal associates to assist Hickory Farms' many holiday shoppers, who expect prompt, courteous attention and high-quality, beautifully designed products for gift giving.

Hickory Farms is proud of its Toledo-area heritage, and fortunate to be headquartered in a location rich with such talented people and resources.

THOUGH BEST KNOWN FOR ITS BEEF STICK, THE PRODUCTS OF HICKORY FARMS ALSO INCLUDE SPECIALTY MEATS, SEAFOOD, FRUITS, GOURMET FOODS, NUTS AND CANDY.

Master Chemical Corporation

LATE IN 1929, CLYDE SLUHAN LEFT THE ONLY HOME HE HAD EVER KNOWN, THE LUTHERAN ORPHANS' AND OLD FOLKS' HOME IN TOLEDO, TO STUDY CHEMISTRY AT OHIO WESLEYAN UNIVERSITY. TWENTY-TWO YEARS LATER, HE RETURNED WITH HIS WIFE MARIAN AND THEIR YOUNG FAMILY TO FULFILL HIS LIFELONG DREAM OF STARTING HIS OWN BUSINESS,

one that operated on the Golden Rule. On November 13, 1951, at the age of 40, Sluhan founded Master Chemical Corporation.

Sluhan graduated from Ohio Wesleyan in 1933 and during the next 18 years worked in chemical research and manufacturing, ultimately becoming involved with metalworking—one of the most basic of industries and yet central to most modern technology. He began research to develop a new generation of metalworking fluids, the first based on non-petroleum chemistry, to solve the traditional metalworking fluid problems and to dramatically improve metalworking productivity. Almost four years of research produced more than 3,500 formulations, which led to his development of TRIM®, the cutting fluid with which he launched his company.

NEW PRODUCT DEVELOPMENT

Originally located at 13 North Huron Street in Toledo, Master moved to Perrysburg in 1963. In the 50 years since its founding, Master has grown to become North America's largest independent developer, manufacturer, and marketer of high-quality metalworking fluids. From just one product in 1951, the TRIM product line has increased to more than 150 products, expanding from water-

miscible cutting and grinding fluids to aqueous parts and other industrial cleaners, corrosion inhibitors, tapping compounds, and specialty cutting and EDM oils.

Developing products with long, useful lives that reduce cost, disposal, and environmental impact has always been a research aim at Master. Increased public concern over the environment in the early 1970s led Master to develop equipment technology that enabled its customers to effectively manage and recycle fluids for extended life. Master's Systems Equipment Division is responsible for the development and manufacture of all its fluid management equipment and XYBEX® Recycling Systems.

NEW OPPORTUNITIES

Master has historically been involved in overseeing business and environmental resources as well as in reinvesting in the community's human and social resources. Financial and management support are provided to various civic organizations, such as Junior Achievement, select college programs, and the local Toledo and Perrysburg Symphonies. Tuition assistance is provided to company associates that want to further their education.

Today's global marketplace presents opportunities to the 190 Master Chemical associates around the globe. TRIM products are now not only developed and blended in Perrysburg, but are also produced in Texas, the United Kingdom, Indonesia, Thailand, and China. Master holds ISO 9001 and QS 9000 certifications for its quality management system, assuring customers of uniform product quality around the globe.

Additionally, customers receive sales and technical service support through an extensive network of highly trained domestic and international distributors that are supported by Master's district managers, service technicians, and technical service laboratories.

TRIM customers, whether in Cleveland or Coventry, St. Louis or Stuttgart, Topeka or Tokyo, can depend on Master's cutting-edge fluids and fluid management technology, uniformly high product quality, and service support, all aimed at increasing the customer's productivity and decreasing costs in an environmentally responsible manner. Unmatched products, conscientious service, and Christian business ethics distinguish Master Chemical Corporation as a company that is successful by making its customers and its employees successful.

WHETHER CHECKING CHEMICAL CONCENTRATION OF CUSTOMER SAMPLES WITH A REFRACTOMETER (LEFT) OR TESTING BACTERIA LEVELS IN COOLANT SAMPLES (RIGHT), MASTER CHEMICAL CORPORATION MAKES ITS CUSTOMERS SUCCESSFUL WITH HIGH PRODUCT QUALITY AND SERVICE SUPPORT.

THE COMPANY'S SYSTEMS EQUIPMENT DIVISION IS RESPONSIBLE FOR THE DEVELOPMENT AND MANUFACTURE OF ALL ITS FLUID MANAGEMENT EQUIPMENT (TOP).

MASTER'S HEADQUARTERS IS LOCATED IN PERRYSBURG (BOTTOM).

Brush Wellman Inc.

UST OUTSIDE THE VILLAGE OF ELMORE, OHIO, ALONG THE BANKS OF THE PORTAGE RIVER, LIES ONE OF THE REGION'S MOST SIGNIFICANT MANUFACTURING FACILITIES—ONE THAT BRINGS HIGH TECHNOLOGY AND INTERNATIONAL TRADE HOME TO NORTHWEST OHIO. THAT FACILITY BELONGS TO BRUSH WELLMAN INC. (BWI). ■ BWI'S ELMORE FACILITY IS A WORLD

leader in the production of high-performance engineered materials. The materials produced in Elmore play a critical role in the areas that are driving the modern economy: telecommunications, computers, medicine, aerospace, automotive electronic products, defense, and energy production. In every case, materials produced in Elmore are making life safer and better around the world—in fact, one-third of all of BWI's production is exported.

CREATING QUALITY

ndustries that use BWI products include the automotive industry for air bag sensors and other electronic devices; the medical industry for X-ray windows for mammography, lasers, and heart pacemakers; satellite components for severe weather forecasting; telecommunications, including cell phones and undersea fiber-optic cables; aerospace; national defense; computers; and fire sprinkler heads.

The facility in Elmore is the flagship of BWI's global manufacturing network. BWI is the largest wholly owned subsidiary of Brush Engineered Materials, which is a leader in a wide variety of engineered products.

More than 900 people work for BWI in Elmore, and their work is making a major economic contribution to their community and their region. Payroll at the Elmore facility is more than $46 million annually. Including purchasing, the company makes a $67 million economic impact each year in the local, five-county region. This economic impact is felt in every community in the region.

BWI also has a major impact on the provision of services by local governments. The company pays nearly $2 million annually in property taxes—money that goes to support local

schools, governments, and social services agencies. In addition, BWI is contributing another $2.5 million over 10 years to the Woodmore School District as part of the company's enterprise zone agreement.

DEDICATED TO THE COMMUNITY

n addition to being an economic leader, BWI is also committed to leading the way in being a good neighbor in Elmore. The company and its employees have been repeatedly named a Pillar of the Community by United Way, and provide support for numerous organizations in the community, including emergency response agencies and local charities. The spirit of service at BWI is found throughout the company. In fact, 80 percent of the employees at Elmore volunteer services on their own time in the community.

The company has created a nationally recognized, award-winning wildlife habitat. Northwest Ohio was, at one time, home to a large population of pheasants, but over the years the population has dwindled. BWI addressed this issue by providing more than 100 acres of protected

wildlife habitat stocked with native grasses, as well as pheasants, deer, and other wildlife.

Brush Wellman Inc. has enjoyed operating in northwest Ohio. The dedication and work ethic of the people who work at the company is unparalleled, and is the single most important reason why BWI has accomplished what it has. The economic contribution of BWI's Elmore facility dates back to 1953, when the plant began operations in the area. From that time until today, the company has been dedicated to producing quality products that improve lives around the world, while at the same time making the local region a better place to live.

FROM THE INITIAL OPERATIONS OF THE PLANT LOCATED JUST OUTSIDE ELMORE, OHIO, IN 1953 TO TODAY, BRUSH WELLMAN HAS BEEN DEDICATED TO PRODUCING QUALITY PRODUCTS THAT IMPROVE LIVES AROUND THE WORLD, WHILE AT THE SAME TIME MAKING THE LOCAL REGION A BETTER PLACE TO LIVE.

Sky Bank

STRONG ROOTS IN THE COMMUNITIES IN WHICH IT OPERATES AND A COMMITMENT TO PROVIDING FINANCIAL PRODUCTS AND SERVICES TO MEET INDIVIDUALS' NEEDS ARE THE CORNERSTONES OF SKY BANK'S BUSINESS PHILOSOPHY. SKY BANK HAS MAINTAINED THAT COMMITMENT, CONTINUING TO OFFER SMALL-TOWN, PERSONAL SERVICE

while taking full advantage of advances in technology. Sky Bank now has more than 200 banking centers and 150 ATM locations, as well as traditional banking products, Internet banking, home equity loans, and commercial cash management products to provide retail and commercial clients with a full range of products and services.

As a community-based company, Sky Bank is located in the cities, towns, and neighborhoods where clients work and live. By combining this convenience and accessibility with a full line of products and services, it is able to more effectively meet or exceed clients' financial needs. Sky Bank empowers employees to make decisions at the local level, so they're faster and in the best interests of clients.

Working to take care of local needs at all levels, Sky Bank provides specialized services in the areas of mortgages and small-business loans. Additional trust and cash management services are also offered. These services, coupled with the financial institution's commitment to the community, have helped to establish Sky Bank as a five-state community bank.

MORTGAGE EXPERTS

Providing a fast approval process for loans that is both efficient and convenient not only results in retention of current clients, but also in acquiring new clients by referral.

As a leader in home financing, Sky Bank understands the eagerness of potential home owners. To satisfy clients, the bank developed the 1/10 mortgage. This program promises credit approval in one hour or less, and closing within 10 days. The bank also offers a 24-hour-a-day, seven-day-a-week hot line staffed by qualified lenders with the authority to approve financing. Home buyers

will not reach an automated switchboard when calling Sky Bank. Instead, buyers can speak directly with a person who will answer questions and get the approval process under way as quickly as possible.

After mortgages are approved, contact with the client doesn't end. The bank offers the Watch 'N Save service, in which lenders notify clients if mortgage rates lower and refinancing is a cost-saving option. Mortgage loan clients are also eligible for a checking account with no monthly maintenance fee. These unique services have helped Sky Bank create a name for itself as a leader in the mortgage lending markets in Lucas, Williams, and Wood counties.

FOCUSING ON SMALL BUSINESSES

Sky Bank's reputation in the area of small business has earned it the distinction of being the number one Small Business Administration (SBA) lender in northwest Ohio for the SBA's last fiscal year. With a strong history of small-business-loan successes, the bank escalated its efforts and launched a major campaign focused on small-business lending in 2001.

The bank caters to clients by offering several different types of credit—

offering loans to existing small businesses or those that are just starting out. Loans are also available for equipment purchases, commercial building construction, development, and general business. Decisions for these loans are made locally, expediting the approval process.

EXTRAORDINARY SERVICE

"Our extraordinary service is what sets us apart," says Darlene Minnick, vice president, marketing/public relations. Not only does Sky Bank provide exceptional service to its clients, but it extends that spirit of service to its employees. The bank understands that in supporting its employees, clients will benefit from interacting with a well-trained staff member who has a positive attitude.

All Sky Bank employees receive intensive personal training on client service. Employees are trained to work as a partner with the client to assess their needs and help them achieve whatever financial goals they may have. This kind of commitment to employees—and, in turn, an employee's commitment to the client—has resulted in the bank's keeping long-tenured employees who have developed enduring relationships with the clients.

In the age of advanced technology, services are becoming less personalized, and striking the delicate balance between personal service and the technical advancements

necessary to meet clients' needs becomes more difficult. But at Sky Bank, local needs are met at the local level. The small-town culture allows the bank to provide faster, personalized service that is convenient and effective. Sky Bank understands some people still want to

deal directly with a person, while others prefer the more technological approach. The partnership between the bank and its clients is also supported by expanded, one-stop-shop banking centers that are staffed with commercial and mortgage lenders.

COMMUNITY FOCUS

Sky Bank is proud of its long-standing commitment to the communities it serves. Each year, bank employees donate thousands of volunteer hours to their communities to improve economic development and quality of life. This kind of involvement is a major priority at Sky Bank. Not only is employee participation in a wide range of organizations encouraged, it is expected.

The future is bright for this community-focused bank. Sky Bank will continue to provide superior service and support for its community in the coming years. Nurturing partnerships with current clients and forging partnerships with new clients will remain a top priority in the future, just as it has been for more than a half century.

Metal Forming & Coining Corporation

ETAL FORMING & COINING (MF&C) HAS BEEN A RECOGNIZED LEADER IN THE METALWORKING INDUSTRY SINCE 1953. THE COMPANY'S SUCCESS IS BASED ON THREE BASIC OBJECTIVES: SAFETY, QUALITY, AND PRODUCTIVITY. MF&C HAS BEEN EXCEEDING THESE GOALS WHILE

serving the demands of the automotive, commercial truck, off-highway, and industrial markets with the manufacture of high-quality net to near-net shaped cold formed and impact extruded components.

Whether providing automatic transmission components, diesel engine crossheads, disk brake caliper keys, or bearing retainers, MF&C's products are designed by highly qualified engineers and manufactured by using state-of-the-art equipment.

THE SUCCESS OF METAL FORMING & COINING CORPORATION (MF&C) IS BASED ON THREE BASIC OBJECTIVES: SAFETY, QUALITY, AND PRODUCTIVITY.

MF&C'S FACILITY IS EQUIPPED WITH MORE THAN 50 PRESSES WITH CAPACITIES FROM 50 TO 3,000 TONS.

RAISING THE BAR FOR QUALITY

Motivated by the demands of its customers, MF&C strives to provide the highest level of quality and productivity. As an established leader in the metalworking industry, MF&C must maintain high standards of quality along with associate training and development. In addition, safety and good corporate citizenship will enable the company to continue to achieve profitability and growth.

Since obtaining QS 9000 and ISO 9002 certifications, MF&C has achieved several coveted quality distinctions, including the Chrysler Quality Excellence Award, Chrysler

Pentastar Award, Chrysler Gold Pentastar Award, and Cummins Engine Continuous Improvement Award. Also, the company recently received the Ohio Award for Excellence.

MF&C is continuously raising the bar for meeting quality objectives. Recent goals to achieve ISO 14000 certification and the TS 16949 AIAG European Quality Standard have kept the MF&C team striving to achieve the highest standards possible.

A CARING COMPANY

To achieve the exacting goals the company sets for itself, MF&C relies on a dedicated team, and the firm's some 100 associates enjoy the environment they have endeavored to create. As a result of this dedication, the company has earned a reputation for being a large organization that is run like a small, family-owned business where caring, respect, and communication are the key.

MF&C's low turnover rate has been attributed to outstanding working conditions, high emphasis on safety, and excellent wages and benefits. Associates at all levels—from top management to operations personnel—share a mutual respect for each other. The company encourages

a self-direction environment and seeks suggestions for improvement. Utilizing the work team approach, MF&C's associates voluntarily participate with fellow associates in an effort to solve problems and offer new solutions.

As a manufacturing facility operating heavy equipment, MF&C considers safety a priority. To assure a safe working environment, the company takes a proactive approach, headed by a full-time safety director and supported by a safety committee made up of associates from all levels.

Continuous training supports the company's safety efforts, as well as its quest for quality and technology improvement. MF&C's extensive training program requires associates to participate in a minimum of 40 hours of training annually. Through a combination of in-house sessions and courses at the University of Toledo, MF&C provides opportunities for its employees to enhance their skills.

MANUFACTURING PROCESSES

MF&C performs a specialized manufacturing technique called cold forming, which involves shaping metals at room temperature using extreme

pressure. MF&C's facility is equipped with more than 50 presses with capacities from 50 to 3,000 tons.

One benefit of this specialized process is its ability to produce net or near-net shapes, meaning that the product is near completion following the cold forming process and, in most cases, does not require secondary operations such as machining. In addition, since the process does not require the material to be preheated, the molecular structure of the material is not broken; instead, the extreme pressure actually compacts the molecules, resulting in a stronger product. Other benefits include close tolerances, the ability to produce unique shapes, and the ability to provide a fine surface finish.

Another process employed by MF&C is flow forming, which involves placing a workpiece over a mandrel with the desired finished shape, and then using rollers to squeeze the workpiece into the desired shape. This process also creates net or near-net shapes at close tolerances with internal features such as splines. MF&C also offers laser welding, orbital forming, ring rolling, and swaging. The idea is to let the component design dictate the process selection.

NEW VENTURES

In 2001, MF&C launched a new direction for the company by establishing a new, wholly owned subsidiary called MFC NETFORM INC. Located in Sterling Heights, MFC NETFORM is based on a new philosophy, net-formed technology integration, which brings together the best metalworking processes to provide the ultimate net-formed components and assemblies.

As a research and development/technology center focused on new product development, MFC NETFORM is staffed with engineers who will review new processes and integrate traditional processes to create new products and solutions for the company's customers. The firm realizes that for this philosophy to be a success, customers must be willing to be a participant in the new product development, including early involvement in the design process. MFC NETFORM's customers will ultimately benefit from design flexibility, improved quality, and lower cost.

Since its beginning in 1953, Metal Forming & Coining Corporation has remained focused on three goals: safety, quality, and productivity. Through the years, the company has consistently focused on achieving these goals, and will do so for years to come with each new venture it undertakes.

AMONG THE MANY PRODUCTS THAT MF&C PROVIDES ARE DIESEL ENGINE CROSSHEADS, DISK BRAKE CALIPER KEYS, AND BEARING RETAINERS FOR LARGE SEMITRUCKS, HAY BALERS, AND FORKLIFTS.

MFC NETFORM INC., LOCATED IN STERLING HEIGHTS, IS BASED ON A NEW PHILOSOPHY, NET-FORMED TECHNOLOGY INTEGRATION, WHICH BRINGS TOGETHER THE BEST METALWORKING PROCESSES TO PROVIDE THE ULTIMATE NET-FORMED COMPONENTS AND ASSEMBLIES.

AS A MANUFACTURING FACILITY OPERATING HEAVY EQUIPMENT, MF&C CONSIDERS SAFETY A PRIORITY.

Teledyne Continental Motors-Turbine Engines

ELEDYNE CONTINENTAL MOTORS (TCM) INITIATED TURBINE ENGINES OPERATIONS IN TOLEDO IN 1955 WHEN CONTINENTAL MOTORS CORPORATION (CMC) TOOK OVER THE LEASE OF U.S. AIR FORCE PLANT #27. WITHIN A FEW YEARS, THE DETROIT-BASED CONTINENTAL AVIATION AND ENGINEERING (CAE) UNIT OF CMC MOVED ITS ENTIRE

business from Detroit to Toledo. In 1965, Continental Motors Corporation and its Continental Aviation and Engineering unit were purchased by Ryan Aeronautical, who was subsequently purchased by Teledyne, Inc. in 1970.

Today, Teledyne Continental Motors-Turbine Engines (TCM-TE) is a productive business segment of Teledyne Technologies, Inc., a worldwide designer and manufacturer of electronic and communication products, aerospace engines, and systems engineering solutions.

ADVANCED PROPULSION PRODUCTS

TCM-TE provides advanced small turbine engines to a variety of customers around the world. These services include aerospace prime contractors and government agencies. Within TCM's 350,000-square-foot Toledo facility, a number of small, but very well known, turbine engines are manufactured.

One of the products Teledyne is best known for is the J69-T25 turbojet engine, which powers the U.S. Air Force (USAF) T-37 trainer aircraft. This engine has been in active service for more than 40 years. It is the only manned engine that the Turbine Engines unit produces, and

one of the most dependable turbine engines in the USAF's active inventory. The J69-T41 derivative powers the Firebee high-performance aerial target and reconnaissance systems that pioneered unmanned aerial vehicles (UAVs) in the early 1960s, and were used extensively during the Vietnam conflict.

In an effort to help the T-37 meet the demand for pilot training in the late 1990s, Teledyne accelerated manufacture of spare parts for the J69-T25. This accomplishment was recently recognized by the USAF, which presented Teledyne with a Green Status Award and thanked the company for its hard work in getting the aircraft back to full mission readiness capability.

Another of Teledyne's products is the J402 turbojet engine. Developed in the 1970s and in production for more than 25 years, this gas turbine engine was the first of its kind to power a modern, high-technology, antiship cruise missile—the U.S. Navy's Harpoon weapon system. The J402 is the first U.S. gas turbine engine to be managed by an electronic fuel control. In addition, the engine does not require any overhaul, and has demonstrated more than 20 years of storage life without maintenance.

A derivative of the J402 has been developed for the USAF's Joint Air-to-Surface Standoff Missile (JASSM) weapon system. The engine for this missile will enter production in 2002

THE GREEN STATUS AWARD IS PRESENTED BY COLONEL SCOTT LYON FOR HELPING RETURN THE T-37 AIRCRAFT AND ITS J69 ENGINE TO FULL MISSION CAPABILITY.

for the U.S. Air Force and Navy, as well as for eventual sale to allied nations. This focus on expendable, unmanned turbine engines has made TCM a recognized leader in the development and production of unmanned air vehicle propulsion systems.

Whether the engine is manned or unmanned, TCM prides itself on its ability to conduct all aspects of its business—from design and development through qualification testing and production—within its Toledo facility. The company's ability to conduct high-technology testing within its development and production facility is unique within the industry in its size class. While TCM's competitors work with outside testing facilities, Teledyne can test its products within its Toledo facility with the capability of supersonic speeds up to Mach 2—twice the speed of sound at an altitude of 90,000 feet.

TCM-TE has been known for its low-cost development and manufacture of small gas turbine engines for unmanned military aircraft, including missiles and UAVs, since the early 1960s. Today, TCM-TE is driven by its objective to become the premier supplier of small turbine engines for both military and commercial customers. Teledyne continues to emphasize research and development in order to provide its customers the most technologically advanced products available.

COMMITTED TO SAFETY, QUALITY, AND THE COMMUNITY

Teledyne's Toledo plant employs approximately 200 local workers, many of whom have advanced degrees in business, finance, engineering, physics, mathematics, and computer science. Reflecting back to its roots in Detroit, the company's hourly employees are represented by the UAW Local 12. These dedicated employees work together to maintain a safe, productive environment, which has resulted in Teledyne's reputation as a low-injury workplace.

TCM is ISO 9001 registered. This third-party international certificate of registration was issued by the British Standards Institution (BSI) following assessment of quality standards in engineering development, manufacturing, purchasing, and quality management, including customer service. Teledyne is working toward AS 9100 certification, a new distinction that recognizes quality, development, and technology advancement within the aerospace industry.

Teledyne is also committed to the community by striving to be a considerate neighbor and an environmentally friendly business that maintains the safety of the surrounding area. To this end, the company takes careful measures to properly dispose of cutting fluids, scrap material, cutting chips, and jet fuels used in the manufacturing and development of its products. These award-winning efforts have been recognized by the State of Ohio through its Green Buckeye award in 1997 and 1998.

Workers in the TCM's Toledo plant are involved in the community and participate in the annual United Way campaign. Teledyne also sponsors high school seniors interested in getting experience in the workforce before graduation, offering co-ops and internships with the University of Toledo and Bowling Green State University. Further, the company seeks to assist local commerce by working with area suppliers and subcontracting various parts to be manufactured by other companies in Toledo. With a commitment to its employees and the environment, Teledyne Continental Motors-Turbine Engines remains dedicated to supporting the Toledo area.

Toledo-Lucas County Port Authority

ITH A MOTTO THAT VIRTUALLY GUARANTEES EFFICIENCY AND SERVICE—FOUR LINES, NO WAITING—THE TOLEDO-LUCAS COUNTY PORT AUTHORITY PROMISES GREAT THINGS. THIS QUASI-GOVERNMENT ENTITY IS DEDICATED TO PROMOTING THE TOLEDO AREA AS

the region's premier international transportation center. Organized as the first port authority in the state, founders of the Toledo-Lucas County Port Authority were instrumental in the passage the Ohio Port Authority Act. When construction began on the St. Lawrence Seaway, community leaders in Toledo led a statewide effort to pass this act. The Ohio Port Authority Act, which went into effect in 1955, stated that a government organization, separate from the city or county, was needed to maximize international trade efforts in the Great Lakes.

Over the years, laws governing port authorities have changed to now include activities that encour-

age, foster, aid, or promote air or water transportation, economic development, or residential facilities. In step with those changes, the Toledo-Lucas County Port Authority expanded its focus. In 1973, it took over management of the Toledo Express and Metcalf airports, and, in 1988, added finance programs. Then, in 1994, the port authority acquired

Central Union Terminal, organized a comprehensive renovation and refurbishing campaign, and re-opened the facility in 1996, bearing the name Central Union Plaza.

EXPANDING ITS MISSION

Today, it is the mission of the port authority to assure that the Toledo area's water, air, rail, and surface transportation assets are developed and operated in

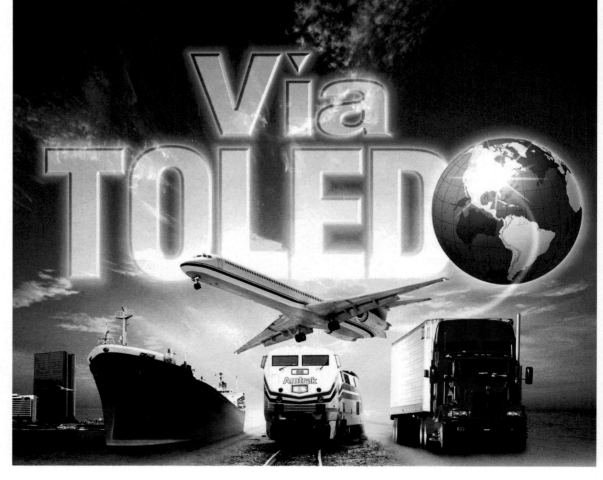

THE MISSION OF THE TOLEDO-LUCAS COUNTY PORT AUTHORITY IS TO ASSURE THAT THE TOLEDO AREA'S WATER, AIR, RAIL, AND SURFACE TRANSPORTATION ASSETS ARE DEVELOPED AND OPERATED IN A COHESIVE, COORDINATED, AND SAFE MANNER, AND TO PROVIDE MAXIMUM EFFICIENCIES AND BENEFITS TO SHIPPERS, RECEIVERS, AND PASSENGERS, AS WELL AS TO PROMOTE AREA JOB RETENTION AND CREATION.

a cohesive, coordinated, and safe manner, and to provide maximum efficiencies and benefits to shippers, receivers, and passengers, as well as to promote area job retention and creation. To achieve these goals, the port authority promotes Toledo as a link to the world via a comprehensive transportation network that includes air, highway, rail, pipeline, and water.

In addition to managing and developing Toledo's transportation assets, the port authority administers various finance programs to help local companies with expansion efforts and the purchase of equipment. Through four financing programs—the Northwest Ohio Bond Fund Program, SBA 504 Loan Program, Stand-Alone Bond Issues, and Ohio 166 Direct Loan Program—the Toledo-Lucas County Port Authority has offered nearly $500 million and retained or created nearly 10,000 local jobs since the program's inception. The Northwest Ohio Bond Fund Program alone accounts for more than $102 million, as well as the retention and creation of more than 4,300 jobs.

OHIO'S LINK TO THE WORLD

Within a day's drive, Toledo has access to more than half of the North American market. Utilizing the Port of Toledo, the area has access to foreign markets through the Great Lakes/St. Lawrence Seaway System. Additional access to the world is also obtainable through Toledo Express Airport. Toledo is home to one of the five largest passenger rail hubs in the nation, and is located directly on the intersection of two of the country's busiest interstate highways—I-75 and I-80/90.

The Port of Toledo is situated on the Maumee River. Located on the

riverfront and accessible by rail and truck, the Port of Toledo Grain Complex contains three grain terminals with the capacity to store up to 22 million bushels of grain, including corn, soybeans, and wheat. In addition, Toledo is one of the largest coal and iron ore ports in the world, with facilities at the confluence of Lake Erie and the Maumee River.

Home to air cargo industry leaders BAX Global and Grand Aire, Toledo Express Airport is one of the busiest airports for cargo in the United States. It was recently ranked by the Boyd Group, an aviation consulting firm, as one of the fastest-growing airports in the country. In fact, Toledo Express was ranked number 11 in the nation for potential growth. Commercial airlines such as USAir, Air Tran, Northwest, Comair, and ASA Delta Connection operate out of Toledo Express, linking northwest Ohio to travel destinations around the globe. Toledo's other

air transportation venue, Metcalf Airport, is a general aviation facility used by corporate and private planes.

Since its rededication in 1996, Central Union Plaza has been home to the Toledo Metropolitan Area Council of Governments (TMACOG) and the Lucas County Educational Services Center. Central Union Plaza is also home to Ohio's busiest passenger rail terminal, with six Amtrak departures daily linking northwest Ohio to Chicago and major destinations in the eastern United States, including New York, Philadelphia, and Washington.

Focusing on both transportation and economic development, the Toledo-Lucas County Port Authority and its staff of more than 70 employees are dedicated to showcasing Toledo as Ohio's World Transportation Center. The port authority will help the area thrive for years to come.

Cavista Corporation

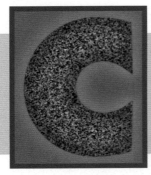

AVISTA CORPORATION IS SET APART FROM OTHER REAL ESTATE COMPANIES BY PROVIDING A COMPLETELY INTEGRATED, ONE-STOP SERVICE FOR ITS CLIENTS. THE FIRM OFFERS RESIDENTIAL BROKERAGE THROUGH CAVALEAR REALTY COMPANY; COMMERCIAL AND INDUSTRIAL BROKERAGE AND PROPERTY MANAGEMENT THROUGH

Zyndorf-Serchuk Incorporated; real estate development through Cavalear Corporation; construction through Cavalear Construction; and financing through Vista Mortgage, Vista Capital, and Vista Funding Corporation.

By providing a complete line of real estate services to the Toledo area, Cavista Corporation has become a company whose reputation speaks volumes locally and in the industry as a whole.

LEADING THE WAY

Cavista Corporation was founded by Edwin M. Bergsmark, its chairman and chief executive officer. David A. Boston is president and chief operating officer.

In 1989, Bergsmark launched Vista Capital Group, a commercial mortgage banking firm, where he made a reputation for himself by finding financing for difficult projects that were otherwise rejected by more traditional lenders.

Vista Capital acquired Cavalear Realty Company and Cavalear Development in 1996, and created a vertically integrated real estate firm named Cavista Corporation.

One of the most recognized names within the Cavista organization is Cavalear Realty Company. Cavalear Realty has evolved to become one of the top 100 real estate firms in the country. With 14 offices and more than 450 agents serving northwest Ohio and southeast Michigan, Cavalear prides itself on employing a staff with a wide variety of backgrounds and extensive knowledge to better serve the prospective home owner.

Cavalear has recently partnered with Coldwell Banker, and as a Coldwell Banker franchisee, will leverage Cavalear Realty, now known as Coldwell Banker Cavalear Realty, locally and nationally. However, Coldwell Banker Cavalear Realty remains locally owned and operated. Cavalear's comprehensive Web site contains a substantial database of residential properties, which provides clients with an easy way to begin the search for the perfect home.

In addition, Coldwell Banker

CAVISTA CORPORATION OFFERS RESIDENTIAL BROKERAGE THROUGH CAVALEAR REALTY COMPANY; COMMERCIAL AND INDUSTRIAL BROKERAGE AND PROPERTY MANAGEMENT THROUGH ZYNDORF-SERCHUK INCORPORATED; REAL ESTATE DEVELOPMENT THROUGH CAVALEAR CORPORATION; CONSTRUCTION THROUGH CAVALEAR CONSTRUCTION; AND FINANCING THROUGH VISTA MORTGAGE, VISTA CAPITAL, AND VISTA FUNDING CORPORATION.

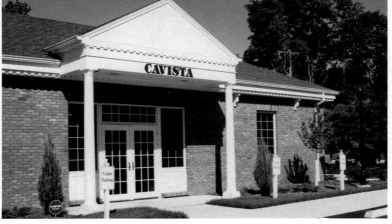

Cavalear Realty offers full-service realty relocation, serving more than 15,000 communities in the United States, and providing services that include personal tours of neighborhoods, assistance with temporary housing, and home market analysis.

EXPANDING THE AREA

Zyndorf-Serchuk Incorporated, a leader in commercial real estate in northwest Ohio, was acquired by Cavista in 1999, and is another highly visible and successful arm of Cavista. In addition to selling and leasing office, retail, and industrial space, Zyndorf-Serchuk also offers assistance with development details, including zoning and government approvals; site selection and assemblage; and real estate inspections. In addition, Zyndorf-Serchuk provides residential and commercial property management.

Cavista Corporation's financial service companies are on hand to assist clients: Vista Mortgage Company provides mortgage financing at the most competitive rates and acceptable programs; Vista Capital, one of the country's top commercial-mortgage banking firms, has more than $2 billion in loan originations; and Vista Funding Corporation has issued more than $200 million in bonds and notes.

Residential housing communities developed by Cavalear Corporation include the Hamlet, Stone Oak, the Quarry, and The Homestead. These and numerous other developments have expanded the Toledo area's residential landscape beyond the metropolitan area. Cavalear Construction builds premier homes and villas, as well as commercial structures, throughout northwest Ohio.

Other Cavalear subsidiaries include Cavalear Leasing, involved in business equipment leasing; Cavalear Kentucky, owner of Lexington's Marriott Griffin Gate Resort and developer of the bluegrass area's Windsor Farms Golf community; and Cavista Technologies Inc.

FACING THE FUTURE

According to Bergsmark, "On-line listings, mortgage loans, relocation services, and assistance in preparing a property for market—all this and more is available through one company. There should be no need for a home buyer or seller to go anywhere else."

Cavista Corporation can promise its customers better resources and technology for the best service possible. This integration of services has helped Cavista earn its place as the largest company of its kind in the Greater Toledo area.

Cavista Corporation's plan for the future is simple: continue to provide the same first-rate services to Toledo and its surrounding areas. This vision for the future is an indicator of Cavista Corporation's commitment to real estate services in northwest Ohio, and its success will certainly continue in the coming years.

CAVISTA CORPORATION CAN PROMISE ITS CUSTOMERS BETTER RESOURCES AND TECHNOLOGY FOR THE BEST SERVICE POSSIBLE. THIS INTEGRATION OF SERVICES HAS HELPED CAVISTA EARN ITS PLACE AS THE LARGEST COMPANY OF ITS KIND IN THE GREATER TOLEDO AREA.

Northwestern Ohio Building and Construction Trades Council

OR NEARLY A HALF CENTURY, MEMBERS OF THE NORTHWESTERN OHIO BUILDING AND CONSTRUCTION TRADES COUNCIL HAVE CONTRIBUTED TO THE INDUSTRIAL EXPANSION OF THE TOLEDO AREA. FROM THE DAVIS BESSE NUCLEAR PLANT TO THE NEW DAIMLERCHRYSLER TOLEDO JEEP PLANT, MEMBERS OF THE COUNCIL HAVE MADE THEIR MARK IN THE AREA.

As an umbrella organization, the council represents nearly 11,000 members from 26 local craft unions representing 14 international unions. These highly skilled workers cover a multitude of trades, including asbestos workers, boilermakers, bricklayers, carpenters, cement finishers, electricians, elevator constructors, glaziers, ironworkers, laborers, operating engineers, painters, plasterers, plumbers, roofers, and sheet metal workers.

CHANGING WITH THE TIMES

Formerly known as the Toledo Building Congress, the Northwestern Ohio Building and Construction Trades Council was chartered in 1958. Then and now, its mission has been to use its financial resources to aid, maintain, develop, harmonize, and advance the interests of the affiliated local unions and their memberships through research, legislative and public relations, and community involvement activities.

Since its inception, the organization has had to change with the times. As new industry standards have been set, the council has offered new and upgraded current training programs. And, as the building trades industry has expanded, the council has entered new areas, including renovation, restoration, and building maintenance.

Perhaps the greatest change the council has faced and continues to address is the need for constant recruitment. Currently, the need for workers is great. In fact, building trades comprise the nation's second-largest industry, exceeded only by manufacturing. But industry needs are not being met. Although the rewards of construction work are great and the earning potential is high, the industry as a whole struggles to fight the stereotypes of construction work.

SIGNIFICANT COMMUNITY IMPACT

It is estimated that some 70 percent of the jobs available today require technical training of some sort. Building tradesmen fall into this large category, and the services that workers in the building trades provide actually make a significant impact on the community. In northwest Ohio alone, more than 12 million hours of unionized construction work are performed annually, generating earnings in excess of $525 million. These earnings are then turned back to the community by creating spending opportunities for the housing, transportation, and retail markets.

As part of its mission, the Northwestern Ohio Building and Construction Trades Council impacts the

FROM THE DAVIS BESSE NUCLEAR PLANT TO THE NEW DAIMLERCHRYSLER TOLEDO JEEP PLANT, MEMBERS OF THE NORTHWESTERN OHIO BUILDING AND CONSTRUCTION TRADES COUNCIL HAVE MADE THEIR MARK IN THE AREA SINCE 1958.

▼ COURTESY OF FIRST ENERGY CORP.

T O L E D O

at the junior or senior level who live in Defiance, Fulton, Hancock, Henry, Lucas, Ottawa, Paulding, Putnam, Sandusky, Williams, or Wood counties are eligible for enrollment.

Academy instructors and administrators admit the curriculum is challenging. Instructors from Northwest State Community College in Archbold offer courses that focus on math and communication skills. Students in their junior year supplement classroom learning with weekly construction site visits, which introduce them to a variety of trades. The summer internship program allows students to participate in on-the-job training in their field of choice. During the students' senior year, they must declare a major and are employed in their desired field. Classroom and work-site training alternate weekly.

Tough academics and on-the-job training are only part of the challenges students face. The academy operates on a 100 percent attendance policy that requires students to use Saturdays to make up any and all classes they may have missed during the week. These stringent standards help to prepare the students for a successful transition from school to work.

Striving to infuse the profession with high-quality workers illustrates the Northwestern Ohio Building and Construction Trades Council members' strong belief in and dedication to their fields. Local workers take pride in their trades and in the structures throughout the area that they have helped to create.

THE MISSION OF THE COUNCIL IS TO USE ITS FINANCIAL RESOURCES TO AID, MAINTAIN, DEVELOP, HARMONIZE, AND ADVANCE THE INTERESTS OF THE AFFILIATED LOCAL UNIONS AND THEIR MEMBERSHIPS THROUGH RESEARCH, LEGISLATIVE AND PUBLIC RELATIONS, AND COMMUNITY INVOLVEMENT ACTIVITIES.

community through a variety of charitable efforts. For example, the council is the third-largest contributor to the Old Newsboys through collections. The Northwestern Ohio Building and Construction Trades Council is ranked within the top 10 donors in the country for Dollars Against Diabetes (DADS). Further support toward the treatment and cure for diabetes has been shown through the donation of a hospital in Florida for diabetes patients. Locally, thousands of hours of work are donated each year by the various trades.

WORKING TOGETHER TO SUPPORT THE FUTURE

The future of the building trades is solely dependent on new workers entering the industry and receiving the proper training to meet high industry standards. To support the future, members of the building trades have developed partnerships to meet recruitment and training goals.

A joint effort between labor and management groups in northwest Ohio, the Alliance of Construction Professionals' (ACP) purpose is to inform potential workers of industry opportunities and recruit new workers for the trades. By combining funds to advertise, the ACP is able to get its message to a larger audience.

Recruitment and retention efforts are further supported by the Construction Opportunity Center (COC), which operates as a one-stop center for information and referral for all the building and construction trade ap-

prenticeship programs. The building trades fund the center, which also facilitates informational workshops for member contractors, unions, tradesmen, and the community. The COC also recruits and aids in retention of minorities and females.

The Building Trades Academy (BTA) represents another joint effort. Created in 1999 out of a school-to-work program founded by the International Brotherhood of Electrical Workers Local 8 and the Toledo chapter of the National Electrical Contractors Association, BTA is a joint partnership between education, business and industry, organized labor, community-based organizations, parents, and students.

BTA is one of few such schools in the country, and is the only school of its kind operating as a charter school where students can earn college credits. High school students

FOR NEARLY A HALF CENTURY, MEMBERS OF THE NORTHWESTERN OHIO BUILDING AND CONSTRUCTION TRADES COUNCIL HAVE CONTRIBUTED TO THE INDUSTRIAL EXPANSION OF THE TOLEDO AREA.

Calphalon Corporation

FOUNDED BY RONALD M. KASPERZAK, CALPHALON CORPORATION—FIRST KNOWN AS COMMERCIAL ALUMINUM COOKWARE COMPANY—WAS LAUNCHED IN 1963. THE COMPANY NOW LEADS THE INDUSTRY IN THE PRODUCTION OF PREMIUM QUALITY COOKWARE AND KITCHEN ACCESSORIES FOR COOKING ENTHUSIASTS. ■ ORIGINALLY, THE COMPANY

supplied raw aluminum cookware to the food service industry. Then, in the late 1960s, Kasperzak incorporated an electrochemical process of treating aluminum, hard anodization, into his manufacturing process, which improved both aluminum's durability and its performance in the kitchen. Kasperzak called his hard-anodized aluminum cookware Calphalon and continued marketing it to the trade.

But soon, nonprofessionals—at-home gourmets who appreciated the exceptional performance of Calphalon—began to seek it out. The product became hot, so to speak. So hot in fact, that by the mid-1970s, Commercial Aluminum Cookware had closed its food service division and had begun to focus exclusively on marketing professional-quality products to home chefs.

Commercial Aluminum Cookware Company was officially renamed Calphalon Corporation in April 1997, and was acquired by Newell-Rubbermaid, Inc., in 1998. Newell-Rubbermaid is headquartered in Freeport, Illinois, and is a $7 billion, global marketer of such well-known consumer brands as Sharpie®, Paper Mate®, Parker®, Waterman®, Rubbermaid®, Calphalon®, Little Tikes®, Graco®, and Levolor®.

CULTIVATING A PASSION

Eating may be a basic human need, but for many, the process of preparing, serving, and enjoying food is a personal passion. Calphalon encourages that passion by bringing a wide range of high-performance products to market. Offering consumers a choice of countless vessel shapes and three different cooking surfaces—hard-anodized, nonstick, and stainless steel—the company prides itself on making the perfect pan for virtually any recipe. Other Calphalon products—like bakeware, cooking utensils, tabletop accessories, and kitchen textiles—also enhance the cooking and entertaining lifestyle that so many Calphalon consumers enjoy.

Calphalon works hard to help consumers enjoy an optimum cooking experience. The company has always made consumer education

LEADING THE INDUSTRY IN THE PRODUCTION OF PREMIUM QUALITY COOKWARE AND KITCHEN ACCESSORIES, CALPHALON CORPORATION WORKS HARD TO HELP CONSUMERS ENJOY AN OPTIMUM COOKING EXPERIENCE.

a priority, offering in-depth training for retail personnel, in-store demonstrations and videos, expert telephone help for consumers, Calphalon cookbooks, and more.

The company's interactive Web site offers exciting recipes, a detailed description of all Calphalon products, cookbook and restaurant recommendations, live chats with celebrity chefs, and other unique features. Visitors can even find out—by taking a simple, interactive questionnaire—which Calphalon cookware best suits their lifestyle.

The Calphalon Culinary Discovery Tour is another educational program the company undertakes each year—one that benefits both consumers and professional cooking schools. The tour is actually a traveling cooking school, featuring some of the best-known chefs in the country as its faculty. Consumers are invited to attend lectures, demonstrations, and hands-on cooking classes led by these culinary luminaries. Classes are held in the kitchens of local host cooking schools. In conjunction with the Calphalon Culinary Discovery Tour, the company endows nearly $100,000 in academic scholarships and cookware gifts each year to the schools that host the tour.

Calphalon's newest consumer education venue, the Calphalon Culinary Center, opened its doors in Chicago in fall 2001. The center continues the company's tradition of providing top-quality education to consumers, and will also offer instruction and professional certification programs for the restaurant trade. Intertwined with the instruction of techniques, the center will help instill a greater appreciation of food from cultural, economic, and historic perspectives.

Courses at the center will range from evening workshops on topics like chocolate or pairing wine and cheese to more in-depth, one- and two-week-long classes covering topics ranging from basic bread baking

to knife skills. The courses will include lectures, demonstrations, and hands-on activities facilitated by staff instructors and guest authors, chefs, and other culinary experts.

CALPHALON CULTURE

As involved as the company is in the preparation and enjoyment of food, it is only natural that Calphalon should also support programs whose goal is to provide hunger relief. In cooperation with Share our Strength, one of the nation's foremost hunger relief organizations, Calphalon was instrumental in bringing the popular fund-raiser Taste of the Nation to Toledo.

For more than 40 years, Calphalon Corporation's employees have taken pride in manufacturing cookware that meets the very highest performance standards. The success of the Calphalon brand in the marketplace is due, in no small measure, to these dedicated craftsmen. This long-standing commitment to quality, combined with a cultural emphasis on innovation, will continue to distinguish Calphalon as a company and as a brand.

OFFERING CONSUMERS A CHOICE OF COUNTLESS VESSEL SHAPES AND THREE DIFFERENT COOKING SURFACES—HARD-ANODIZED, NON-STICK, AND STAINLESS STEEL—THE COMPANY PRIDES ITSELF ON MAKING THE PERFECT PAN FOR VIRTUALLY ANY RECIPE.

Columbia Gas of Ohio

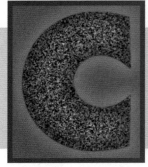

OLUMBIA GAS OF OHIO, A NISOURCE COMPANY, IS AN INVESTOR-OWNED PUBLIC UTILITY THAT SELLS NATURAL GAS AND PROVIDES NATURAL GAS TRANSPORTATION SERVICES. IN TOTAL, COLUMBIA GAS SERVES MORE THAN ONE-THIRD OF OHIO'S NATURAL GAS CUSTOMERS. ■ NATURAL GAS—A CLEAN, COMFORTABLE, CONVENIENT,

and affordable energy source—is provided by Columbia through its reliable delivery system by courteous, attentive, expert customer service representatives.

CUSTOMER RESPECT AND LOYALTY

Maintaining customers' respect and loyalty is a high priority for Columbia Gas. In addition to delivering premier customer service, Columbia offers a variety of programs and partnerships designed to provide the greatest customer and community benefit.

Customer CHOICE℠ was developed in conjunction with the Public Utilities Commission of Ohio (PUCO) and the Ohio Consumers' Counsel (OCC). The largest voluntary program of its kind in the country, Customer CHOICE℠ offers several options for natural gas consumers. While Columbia continues to deliver natural gas safely and reliably—as well as providing local services, including meter reading, emergency response, and pipeline maintenance—customers have the opportunity to reduce their energy costs by purchasing their natural gas from a variety of nonutility suppliers. This competition, which gives customers the opportunity to shop for energy the way they do for other goods and services, has resulted in lower prices.

Further, Columbia continually seeks partnerships with nonprofit organizations that provide families with food, clothing, and shelter. Through a partnership with the Salvation Army, for example, Columbia participates in HeatShare, an emergency fund that assists low-income families in paying their heating bills in order to help them avoid termination of service.

COMMITMENT TO THE COMMUNITY

Senior members of the community are also a priority for Columbia. Through the company's Service for a Lifetime Program, customers aged 60 and older can benefit from special bill payment options, home weatherization services, and other assistance. Service for a Lifetime helps the company learn more about customer needs and expectations so that Columbia can offer the appropriate services. In addition, the firm works to train its employees to recognize issues that are important to older customers, while giving them the authority to respond quickly. Ultimately, Service for a Lifetime helps Columbia provide its aged-60-plus customers with information and resources that support their lifestyles.

Specific benefits of the Service for a Lifetime Program include WarmChoice, which provides free weatherization services for customers who meet income requirements, as well as weatherization tips and referrals. Service Plus also offers customers the options of having an easy-to-read thermostat installed or their existing thermostat modified, as well as having modified appliance controls installed to make setting temperatures easier.

In an attempt to make its services affordable to a wider constituency, Columbia also offers its WarmChoice program to other qualified low-income customers. Serving some 1,600 people each year, the program offers services such as a home energy inspection, space and water heating system repair and replacement, attic and wall insulation, sealing of major air leaks, and safety checks on appliances. For most participants, this program reduces bills by an average of 30 percent. And for Columbia, making sure customers have safe gas heating

SERVING MORE THAN ONE-THIRD OF OHIO'S NATURAL GAS CUSTOMERS, COLUMBIA GAS OF OHIO DELIVERS PREMIER CUSTOMER SERVICE AND OFFERS A VARIETY OF PROGRAMS AND PARTNERSHIPS DESIGNED TO PROVIDE THE GREATEST CUSTOMER AND COMMUNITY BENEFIT.

equipment and a more comfortable home makes sense.

Columbia has developed an education campaign for children with a friendly mascot named Cozy Cat™. Through brightly colored posters, coloring books, and other tools, as well as an interactive Web site, Cozy Cat teaches young people about safety and what to do if they smell natural gas. While inhaling natural gas fumes is not harmful, Cozy Cat explains that natural gas is combustible and can be dangerous if used improperly. Children are taught to get out of the house if there is a gas odor, and to ask a grown-up to call the gas company.

OPTIONS FOR CUSTOMERS
Special payment plans associated with Service for a Lifetime include the Extra Protection Plan, which ensures that Columbia will work with the customer to avoid winter service disconnections. Recovery First offers a 30-day bill deferment if the customer is hospitalized, and Adjusted Due Date allows monthly gas bills to coincide with Social Security or pension checks.

All Columbia Gas customers can benefit from payment options, including the Budget Payment Plan, ZipCheck automatic payment, and E-bills, or electronic bill payment.

Commitment to its customers is also evident in the company's community investment philosophy, which states that Columbia is dedi-

cated to improving the quality of life, diversity, and fullness of opportunity in the communities served by the firm. Locally, Columbia is an active participant in the United Way program, reaching the $100,000 giving level in 1999.

Columbia's philosophy of Better Together encourages employee volunteerism with various organizations, including participation in the March of Dimes Walk-a-Thon, tutoring and mentoring in schools, and Junior Achievement. Columbia also participates in a matching gift pro-

gram where every dollar an employee donates to a major college or university is matched by the company. In total, the firm donates more than $1 million of its profits to various programs.

With special attention to customer service and a focus on community involvement, Columbia Gas of Ohio intends to remain an active corporate citizen. Customers with a diverse array of needs will continue to find options and assistance through the company's many services, programs, and partnerships.

THROUGH BRIGHTLY COLORED POSTERS, COLORING BOOKS, AND OTHER TOOLS, AS WELL AS AN INTERACTIVE WEB SITE, COZY CAT TEACHES YOUNG PEOPLE ABOUT SAFETY.

Medical College of Ohio

THE MEDICAL COLLEGE OF OHIO (MCO) WAS CREATED BY THE OHIO GENERAL ASSEMBLY IN 1964, AND IS TODAY CONSIDERED ONE OF THE CORNERSTONES OF THE TOLEDO COMMUNITY. WHEN THE FIRST CLASS OF 32 MEDICAL STUDENTS BEGAN STUDIES IN 1969, MCO HAD APPROXIMATELY 150 EMPLOYEES, INCLUDING FACULTY

CLOCKWISE FROM TOP:
THE 475-ACRE MEDICAL COLLEGE OF OHIO (MCO) CAMPUS INCLUDES 11 BUILDINGS, WITH THREE ON-CAMPUS HOSPITALS, A MEDICAL LIBRARY, AND STATE-OF-THE-ART RESEARCH LABORATORIES.

SINCE ITS FIRST GRADUATING CLASS IN 1972, MCO HAS PROVIDED EDUCATION TO MORE THAN 10,000 HEALTH CARE PROFESSIONALS. EIGHTY PERCENT OF THE PHYSICIANS PRACTICING IN NORTHWEST OHIO HAVE GRADUATED OR RECEIVED TRAINING FROM MCO.

MCO IS TEACHING THE NEXT GENERATION OF HEALTH CARE PROVIDERS THROUGH ITS FOUR SPECIALIZED SCHOOLS: THE SCHOOL OF MEDICINE, SCHOOL OF NURSING, GRADUATE SCHOOL, AND SCHOOL OF ALLIED HEALTH.

members and administrators. Area physicians also volunteered their services as teachers to provide students with a comprehensive curriculum. MCO was the fourth medical school in Ohio and the 100th in the country.

Since its first class of medical student graduates, MCO has conferred more than 3,100 doctor of medicine degrees, more than 280 doctor of philosophy in medical sciences degrees, and more than 900 master's degrees in nursing, biomedical sciences, occupational health, occupational therapy, physical therapy, public health, and physician assistant studies.

In addition to its teaching accomplishments, MCO established itself in the research community by performing northwest Ohio's first kidney transplant operation in 1972. Currently, MCO ranks third in extramural grant/contract support of biomedical research among Ohio's public colleges and universities.

Through the years, MCO has built its reputation on successfully integrating teaching and research with health care delivery, providing the patient with cutting-edge, comprehensive care delivered in a caring, compassionate environment. MCO's

four schools—the School of Medicine, School of Nursing, Graduate School, and School of Allied Health—help the college accomplish its education, research, and service missions. Today, faculty members train upwards of 2,000 students each year for a profession in health care.

HIGH-QUALITY MEDICAL FACILITIES

Occupying 475 acres in south Toledo, MCO is home to three teaching hospitals, each with accreditation by the Joint Commission on Accreditation of Healthcare Organizations.

The Medical College of Ohio Hospital is a 258-bed facility offering transplants and Level I trauma care, as well as clinical programs and services that feature the latest advances in medicine and technology. The hospital provides highly specialized medical and surgical care in a professional and caring environment.

MCO/Mercy Rehabilitation Hospital, the campus' second hospital, is a joint operation agreement between MCO and Mercy Health Partners. The hospital, which is licensed for

36 beds, offers a full range of inpatient and outpatient services.

The Lenore W. and Marvin S. Kobacker Center, MCO's third teaching hospital, treats children through 18 years of age who have severe behavioral and emotional problems. It is licensed for 25 beds. As the only hospital of its kind in the area, the center provides a daily school program operated in conjunction with the Toledo Board of Education and the MCO Department of Psychiatry. A team of board-certified psychiatrists, clinical child psychologists, social workers, therapists, nurses, teachers, and residents is on call 24 hours a day.

The Center for Creative Instruction is another vital component of MCO's commitment to innovative educational methods. Teams of medical illustrators and software engineers collaborate to facilitate the learning process with technology—a genuine model of ingenuity. In addition, the Advanced Technology Park of Northwest Ohio provides fertile ground for biomedical research and start-up ventures. A 133-acre environment near the MCO campus,

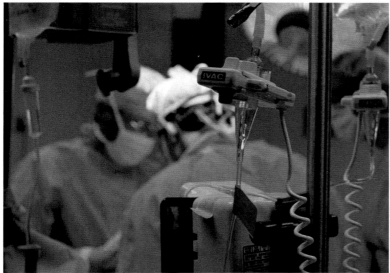

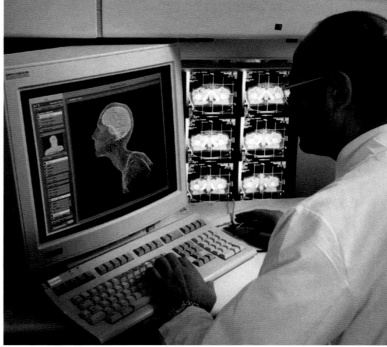

it is the fulcrum of the high-technology industry meeting research efforts, university resources, and commerce.

A CORNERSTONE OF THE COMMUNITY

MCO remains a strong asset to the Toledo community—both medically and economically. With three facilities and hundreds of faculty members, the college provides Toledo residents with a wide range of services. In addition, MCO is the eighth-largest employer in Toledo and the 10th largest in northwest Ohio, providing an annual economic impact estimated at $471 million.

The college includes the MCO Cancer Institute, a facility that is staffed with experts from many specialties, and is devoted to cancer research, education, and treatment. Offering patients local access to a high level of cancer care, the institute provides clinical assessment, treatment, and support. Through research initiatives, MCO's cancer experts seek to understand the disease at the molecular, cellular, and physiological levels, as well as to educate health care professionals and the public. The Comprehensive Breast Center, within the institute, and its nationally recognized staff of health care providers offer a full range of patient care services, including clinical trials, psychological support, and research information. As a significant member of the Toledo community, MCO seeks to continuously provide outreach programs that improve the health of local families. Using education as its tool, MCO launched a Mini Med School in 2001. Open to the public, the six-week classroom experience shares accurate, up-to-date health and science information in a fun, and often interactive, atmosphere. Topics include kidney and heart function, women's health, infection and the immune system, cancer, and what it takes to become a doctor.

SECURING THE FUTURE

Academic medical centers such as MCO rely on contributions from alumni, friends, corporations, and foundations to provide the resources crucial to student and faculty excellence in the college's classroom, laboratory, and clinical settings. The MCO Foundation has provided more than $19 million in financial support to MCO and its facilities since 1990.

The future of the Toledo community is brighter thanks to the services the Medical College of Ohio provides. Securing the future of MCO essentially secures the future of the region.

MCO HAS A LONG-STANDING REPUTATION FOR PROVIDING CUTTING-EDGE SURGICAL CARE OF COMPLICATED TRAUMA, NEUROLOGICAL, CARDIAC, ORTHOPEDIC, AND SURGICAL ONCOLOGY CASES (LEFT).

MCO RESEARCHERS RECEIVE MILLIONS OF DOLLARS IN RESEARCH GRANTS AND CONTRACTS EACH YEAR (RIGHT).

MCO IS THE ONLY HEALTH CARE INSTITUTION IN NORTHWEST OHIO COMBINING EDUCATION, RESEARCH, AND PATIENT CARE.

Buckeye CableSystem

UCKEYE CABLESYSTEM HAS BEEN A PIONEER IN THE CABLE SERVICE INDUSTRY FOR TOLEDO SINCE ITS INCEPTION IN 1965. WHEN OTHER CITIES LIKE DETROIT AND CLEVELAND WERE JUST TALKING ABOUT CABLE, TOLEDO WAS CONNECTED. NOW, ALMOST FOUR DECADES LATER, BUCKEYE CABLESYSTEM CONTINUES TO SERVE THE

Greater Toledo area with the best in cable entertainment, excellent customer service, and the latest in high-tech fiber optics.

Cable entertainment has changed a lot over the years, and Buckeye CableSystem has been considered an early pioneer in the industry. In the mid-1970s, for example, Buckeye CableSystem began rebuilding dual cable to offer its customers 24 channels instead of 12. Today, the company offers more than 60 standard channels, as well as a host of premium channels and options.

In 1987, after an evaluation of its customer service, Buckeye Cable-System decided to offer customer service access 24 hours a day, seven days a week. This bold, new move was one of the first of its kind in the industry. Today, Buckeye Cable-System, which operates a call center staffed with caring customer service representatives, is distinguished by its commitment to service. Qualified technicians will even conduct home visits to train customers on new cable technologies.

NEW TECHNOLOGY

In 1999, a high-speed cable modem service called Buckeye Express was launched. This service eliminates the need for a telephone line to access the Internet,

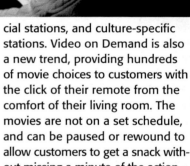

and offers high-speed access—at the click of a mouse—up to 20 times faster than through a dial-up phone line. With customer service always a top priority, Buckeye maintains the service locally, ensuring more control and faster response if glitches should occur.

Another Internet access option is offered through Buckeye World-Gate, which provides access through a customer's television. Telephone lines and a PC are not needed, and the Internet is accessible with a wireless keyboard, offering twice the speed of a typical telephone modem.

Some of the latest technology—including digital service—will offer customers more channels and option packages, as well as many niche programs like sports, in-depth finan-

cial stations, and culture-specific stations. Video on Demand is also a new trend, providing hundreds of movie choices to customers with the click of their remote from the comfort of their living room. The movies are not on a set schedule, and can be paused or rewound to allow customers to get a snack without missing a minute of the action—just as if they were using their VCR.

MORE TO THE COMMUNITY

As a vital part of the community, Buckeye Cable-System is actively involved in local organizations. Through the donation of time, money, and services, Buckeye CableSystem does its part to help Toledo with its commitment to education, Buckeye's top priority. The company provides grants to elementary school teachers; free cable service and commercial-free educational programming to schools; various scholarships; and free sports coverage for many high school football and basketball games.

Throughout its history, Buckeye CableSystem has provided quality choices for viewers and support for the growth and development of the Toledo area. Doubtless, the company will continue this commitment to quality in the coming years.

THROUGHOUT ITS HISTORY, BUCKEYE CABLESYSTEM HAS PROVIDED QUALITY CHOICES FOR VIEWERS AND SUPPORT FOR THE GROWTH AND DEVELOPMENT OF THE TOLEDO AREA.

Poggemeyer Design Group

THOUGH IT IS BASED IN A SMALL-TOWN, COLLEGE COMMUNITY, POGGEMEYER DESIGN GROUP'S (PDG) REACH IS NATIONWIDE IN SCOPE. HEADQUARTERED IN BOWLING GREEN, OHIO, PDG HAS OFFICES AND RESOURCES THROUGHOUT OHIO, AS WELL AS IN INDIANA, KENTUCKY, NEVADA, AND WASHINGTON, TO MEET THE NEEDS OF ITS

broad client base. Founded as an engineering and surveying company, PDG opened its doors in 1968 with just two employees. Since then, the firm has expanded its services and its employee base now exceeds 240. Today, PDG provides clients with single-source responsibility providing superior architecture, engineering, surveying, and planning services all coordinated as one team.

MULTIDISCIPLINED SERVICES

PDG works for both the private and the government sectors. With its multidisciplined team, PDG oversees projects from inception all the way through to completion. In addition, one of the company's unique services is its ability to help secure funding for clients. PDG is one of only a limited number of consulting firms in the state that operate a specific division to seek grant funding and other financial assistance. From 1995 to 2000, PDG was able to secure more than $183 million in grants and low-interest loans for its clients. This service is one of the primary reasons PDG has such a strong working relationship with more than 200 governmental entities resulting in a significant amount of annual repeat business.

By taking such a thorough approach, PDG can assure its clients an attention to detail that is second to none. Each PDG project is handled by an experienced project manager who carries the project through all phases, including client relations, regulatory agency approvals, contracting agency reviews, and design coordination. The close working relationship that develops from this process helps keep clients informed every step of the way. PDG's affiliate firm, Industrial Fluid Management, Inc. (IFM), is located in Defiance, Ohio, and serves clients in Ohio,

Kentucky, Michigan, and Indiana. This environmental services company provides maintenance services, technical consultation, bio-augmentation, plant operations, and laboratory testing and pilot study capabilities, as well as myriad other services to small and medium-sized towns and villages throughout the region. IFM also assists industrial, municipal, and institutional concerns with their water and wastewater management needs. In addition, the company specializes in ultra pure water systems serving the needs of industry and institutions in the midwestern region.

BUILDING A REPUTATION OF INTEGRITY

Providing services that surpass customer expectations is what PDG does best. Because of its ability to deliver innovative design, technical superiority, and outstanding quality, PDG has built a reputation of integrity with various government entities, businesses, and individuals. Proof of the company's respected name has been repeatedly confirmed by its ranking

as one of the top 500 firms in the nation by *Engineering News-Record*. PDG has been listed in this prestigious magazine every year since 1993.

It is clear that Poggemeyer Design Group's dedication to quality work and its expanding expertise have prompted the company's current success. And with a growing list of satisfied clients and the referrals that often follow, PDG's continuing success is a certainty.

OFFERING SERVICES IN ARCHITECTURE, ENGINEERING, SURVEYING AND PLANNING, POGGEMEYER DESIGN GROUP HAS DEMONSTRATED ITS EXPERTISE IN (CLOCKWISE FROM RIGHT) THE CITY OF BOWLING GREEN MUNICIPAL COURT, TOLEDO CORRECTIONAL INSTITUTION, AND THE BOARDROOM OF AMP-OHIO, INC.

FEINKNOPF PHOTOGRAPHY

MARTIN M. MATYAS GREAT LAKES AEROCAM

PROFILES IN EXCELLENCE

1971 - 2001

TARTA

in the area. Whether the passengers are school children, commuters, or just local citizens needing affordable, reliable transportation, TARTA is there.

TARTA is a political subdivision of the state and answers to a 17-member Board of Directors, with each member representing one of the communities TARTA serves. In addition to the city of Toledo, TARTA serves Maumee, Ottawa Hills, Perrysburg, Rossford, Spencer Township, Sylvania, Sylvania Township, and Waterville.

TARTA is meeting its goal "to provide safe, reliable, efficient, affordable, and courteous service to each rider," with annual ridership numbers increasing steadily through the years. Recent totals have reached some 10 million passengers per year, with school children accounting for more than half of TARTA's riders.

AN EMPHASIS ON SAFETY

TARTA drivers are responsible for some very precious cargo. That places a great emphasis on safety and accident prevention. TARTA conducts regular safety meetings with all drivers and provides intensive training to new drivers. This training includes three weeks of

The Toledo Area Regional Paratransit Service (TARPS) is available for persons whose physical or mental disabilities prevent them from using regular TARTA service.

classroom and on-the-road training. Once behind the wheel, drivers are in constant radio communication with the dispatcher should any emergency arise.

TARTA also sponsors a student safety campaign for junior high students that stresses "Let the bus go…then you go." This reminds students that city buses are not like school buses—they do not have flashing lights to stop traffic and alert drivers someone may be crossing. Young people learn the importance of waiting until the bus has pulled away completely and the roadway is clear before crossing the street. In recognition for all of its efforts,

TARTA was the recipient of six national safety awards in the 1990s.

TARPS

The Toledo Area Regional Paratransit Service (TARPS) is a specially designed system of vehicles that serve special needs patrons whose mental or physical impairments prevent them from using the traditional TARTA service. Riders must submit an application to be eligible for the service, but once approved, TARPS riders need only call ahead to reserve their place on the bus. TARPS offers curb-to-curb service with its 30 mini-buses and vans in operation from 6 a.m. to 11 p.m. daily. Each vehicle is equipped with lifts, wheelchair tie-downs, and standard seats.

A dramatic increase in usage was seen from 1999 to 2000 when ridership jumped 35 percent. As usage increases, so can the potential for problems with service operation. To keep the system running smoothly, a TARPS users committee meets regularly to address needs of passengers and work through any problems. Thanks to its help, TARPS has been able to fine tune its operation and work with no denials of service since February 2000.

Government Station is one of five transit stations in downtown Toledo where passengers may either pick up or transfer buses.

THE TARTA TROLLEY

TARTA currently owns six, 1800s streetcar-style trolleys that operate weekdays as noontime shuttles around the downtown area. For a nominal fare, patrons can travel from the downtown loop to additional locations including the Farmers' Market and the Center of Science and Industry (COSI).

In addition, the trolleys are available for charter. Popular for weddings, group outings, progressive dinners, and parades, the trolleys can accommodate up to 22 passengers each and are available throughout the year. During the holidays, the trolleys are decked out in lights and are often rented by groups wishing to tour local holiday light displays.

The Holiday Trolley Sleigh also operates on weekends during the holiday season. It runs on a set schedule between Westgate and the Franklin Park Mall. The Holiday Trolley Sleigh allows riders to sit back and relax while avoiding the hectic holiday traffic.

SERVING THE COMMUNITY

TARTA derives its funding from local taxes, state and federal funds, and fare boxes, as well as from the advertising companies place on the buses. The people of Toledo and surrounding communities renewed a 1 mill levy in November 2000, which provides more than half of TARTA's total annual operating budget. Capital expenses such as purchasing new buses are covered by federal, state, and local grants.

To thank the communities that support it, TARTA supports many area community activities. It works with local events like the Jamie Farr Ladies' Professional Golf Association (LPGA) Tournament and conventions to coordinate transportation. In support of the new Mud Hens stadium, TARTA will be building two stations within the ballpark structure.

Further, TARTA has developed many additional services to add convenience to the lives of its riders. To assist in efforts to keep the Toledo area in compliance with EPA air quality standards, TARTA provides free bus service on Ozone Action Days. Bike racks have been installed on the front of all buses to facilitate usage by bicycle riders. TARTA's Park and Ride service is offered from 12 parking lots throughout the metropolitan area. Commuters can reduce wear and tear on their cars; save money on gas, maintenance, and parking; and relax while someone else does the driving.

TARTA will continue to provide these services and much more in the years to come. Plans to purchase additional buses with global positioning system technology to announce stops and major intersections along the route are in the works. Upgrading of the downtown stations and rehabilitation of maintenance facility are also planned. And, as the population fluctuates, TARTA will adjust routes and expand its service area to meet the needs of the community.

With a tradition of running the buses regardless of the weather, and with a fare below the country's average, TARTA remains the most reliable, affordable ride in town.

TARTA'S ENTIRE FLEET IS NOW EQUIPPED WITH BIKE RACKS.

SIX TROLLEYS CAN BE CHARTERED FOR SPECIAL OCCASIONS. THEY ARE ALSO DECORATED DURING THE HOLIDAYS AND OPERATE SPECIAL HOLIDAY SHOPPING SHUTTLES BETWEEN WESTGATE AND FRANKLIN PARK MALLS.

The Spieker Company

HE SPIEKER COMPANY IS A GENERAL CONTRACTING FIRM CREDITED WITH THE BUILD-ING AND REFURBISHING OF MANY WELL-KNOWN STRUCTURES IN THE TOLEDO AREA, SUCH AS THE PUT-IN-BAY'S PERRY'S MONUMENT. SPIEKER IS ALSO THE COMPANY THAT PERFORMED THE RESTORATION OF THE MAIN LIBRARY DOWNTOWN AND THE TOLEDO

Museum of Art. Spieker has done multiple renovations inside the walls of the Toledo Hospital, as well as revitalized many of the buildings for Toledo Public Schools.

Quietly located off three major highways, Spieker lets its reputation speak for itself and finds that word-of-mouth recommendation allows the company to attract more business. By providing quality work at competitive pricing, The Spieker Company has found that customers will return with additional projects and share their experiences with others in the industry, thus introducing new clients to Spieker.

The next time someone picks up a telephone they may think of The Spieker Company. Spieker has been involved with many of the major communication companies, building and upgrading facilities for AT&T, Ameritech, GTE/Verizon, WorldCom, ALS, MCI, and SBC. These facilities are located in Ohio, Michigan, Pennsylvania, Indiana, Kentucky, Illinois, and West Virginia.

The Spieker Company was created in 1977 when the Henry J. Spieker Company eliminated its general contracting operations. At that time, two of the company's employees, Dale Kuehnle and Norm White, saw an opportunity to start The Spieker Company. Both Kuehnle and White led the company until Kuehnle's retirement in 1987. Today, White, along with Andy Keller, continues to lead the company into the future.

The Spieker name is associated with quality building in northwest Ohio. The Henry J. Spieker Company was founded in 1888, and was hired to construct hundreds of buildings, many of which are considered landmarks of the area today. Structures that include the Toledo Blade, Toledo Museum of Art, Commodore Perry

Hotel, Toledo Club, University Hall at the University of Toledo, and numerous area schools are all the handiwork of the Henry J. Spieker Company.

The Spieker Company continues to construct and refurbish some of the area's landmarks. Some of its most recent projects include BGSU football stadium, Northwest Ohio Cardiology Consultants, Farmers' Market, National Air Guard facilities at Toledo Express, Josina Lott Activity Center, Fort Meigs Museum, and Dillard's (formerly Lion Department Stores).

When Kuehnle and White created The Spieker Company, they operated out of a 2,000-square-foot facility in Holland, Ohio. At that time, only five office personnel and 20 field workers made up the company's staff. Within three years, the company had moved into larger quarters, increased the number of office workers to eight, and doubled the number of field workers. Today, The Spieker Company's present home constitutes 20,000 square feet, and the company employs some 12 office and 100 field workers.

The steady growth The Spieker Company has experienced in terms of office space and employees is overshadowed by its tremendous growth in business volume. In 1977,

OVER THE YEARS, THE SPIEKER NAME HAS BE-COME SYNONYMOUS WITH QUALITY BUILDING IN NORTHWEST OHIO. THE SPIEKER COMPANY IS CREDITED WITH THE BUILDING AND REFUR-BISHING OF MANY WELL-KNOWN STRUCTURES IN THE TOLEDO AREA.

the company saw revenue totaling $250,000; in 2000, final numbers show revenue reaching the $30 million mark.

Acquiring the company's current location was a strategic move looking toward the future. Access to the major highways within that area makes serving customers more convenient. With the flexibility to reach major destinations, Spieker can easily serve its clients throughout Ohio and the surrounding states.

Many of the clients The Spieker Company serves today are clients that have been with the company since the early years. Ninety percent of the work the company is contracted to perform is with repeat customers.

This kind of loyalty is a direct result of the way The Spieker Company does business. With Spieker, clients are handled on a single-person-responsibility system. In other words, one person handles a project from the estimate phase through construction completion. This individualized attention illustrates The Spieker Company's commitment to customer service and satisfaction.

The company's versatility is another attribute that keeps clients coming back. Spieker has always been willing to handle unusual or complex projects, regardless of size. The company works to offer innovative and creative solutions and methods specific to each project. Serving clients in Ohio and surrounding states, The Spieker Company seeks out unique projects, and strives to give its clients what they want, at a competitive price and in a timely manner.

With its organizational structure and financial health, The Spieker Company has the ability to handle a project from a $500 door replacement to a $9 million facility. Operating under the motto of Spieker/Stability/Satisfaction, The Spieker Company has established its name as a high-quality general contracting firm. Workers at The Spieker Company know that if they exceed their clients' expectations, the clients will return as customers again and again.

Great Lakes Window, Inc.

REAT LAKES WINDOW, INC. (GLW) IS NOT ABOUT BUILDING WINDOWS. IT IS ABOUT BUILDING RELATIONSHIPS—WITH ITS EMPLOYEES, CUSTOMERS, AND VENDORS. IT IS ABOUT BUILDING RELATIONSHIPS THAT HELP ENSURE THE SUCCESS OF EVERYONE IN THE GLW FAMILY. ■ SINCE 1981, GLW HAS GROWN

from an entrepreneurial, five-person company to one of the largest manufacturers of vinyl windows and patio doors in North America. The firm offers a complete line of single-hung, double-hung, casement, picture, sliding, awning, bay, bow, and garden windows, as well as sliding and hinged patio doors. GLW is committed to providing home owners with beautiful, energy efficient, and easy maintenance products.

Today, GLW employs more than 700 people at its six-acre headquarters and manufacturing facility in suburban Perrysburg Township. These workers, including assembly operators, mechanics, truck drivers, engineers, customer service representatives, and a host of others, are all dedicated to the manufacturing and marketing of one of the highest-

CREATING PREMIUM PRODUCTS—PRODUCTS MADE USING STATE-OF-THE ART TECHNOLOGY, MODERN EQUIPMENT, AND CUTTING-EDGE OPERATIONAL TECHNIQUES—GREAT LAKES WINDOW, INC. HAS BECOME ONE OF THE LARGEST MANUFACTURERS OF VINYL WINDOWS AND PATIO DOORS IN NORTH AMERICA.

quality vinyl windows made today. GLW is supported by the strength of its parent company, Nortek, Inc.— a $2 billion company headquartered in Providence—that is a leading international designer, manufacturer, and marketer of building products for residential and commercial markets.

PRODUCTS, PROCESS, PEOPLE

GLW's history of industry success is built around its leadership in three key areas: products, process, and people. The company is best known within its industry as the trendsetter with

firsts that have set industry standards. GLW was the first company to offer vinyl windows with an argon gas insulator, and the first to construct a vinyl frame with patented R-Core® insulation. The company was also the first of its kind to offer decorative glass options, solid brass hardware, a three-point patio door locking system, and recessed tilt latches. With a strong focus on customer service, GLW was the first company to offer a transferable, entire-window warranty.

These types of innovations have resulted in numerous awards for

GLW, including being a four-time winner of the Diamond Crystal Industry Achievement Award given by *Window & Door* magazine.

GLW's windows and doors are set apart from the competition as premium products—products made using state-of-the art technology, modern equipment, and cutting-edge operational techniques. GLW utilizes a manufacturing process known as Demand Flow Technology, which ensures a consistent, high-quality product while manufacturing the most diverse product offering in the industry. Virtually each and every window and door manufactured at GLW is ordered by a specific dealer for a specific home owner, a process enhanced by DFT.

People are a key ingredient of GLW's success. A primary goal of the company is to attract and motivate a team of talented individuals, creating a work environment that fosters personal development, mutual respect, innovation, and accomplishment. In an environment of trust and cooperation, GLW's employees work together supporting the needs of each other and the business. Company management is committed to making GLW an "employer of choice".

CUSTOMER CARE

GLW's primary customer is its extensive network of dealers. An in-house customer care department is available to take orders and provide support to dealers. GLW also provides its customers with a variety of resources, including superb sales and marketing support tools. In short, GLW helps its customers take care of their customers.

The home owners not only benefit directly from GLW's customer support to dealers, but also reap the rewards of the company's lifetime warranty on its products, offering home owners peace of mind.

INTEGRITY AND EXCELLENCE

GLW is a company that meets challenges head on. Employees take pride in their work and strive to build the best product in the industry, as well as deliver the most consistent service possible to their customers. In all facets of the business, GLW employees focus on exceeding customer expectations each and every day. This commitment to customer care is a key element in GLW's culture.

The individuals who design and build GLW windows and doors are committed to fulfilling custom orders to exact customer specifications. They are dedicated to the details that make the product unique; they seek to provide the product with breadth in design, along with custom options that cannot be found at just any window manufacturer. GLW employees complete the finishing touches, with attractive options like beveled-leaded glass, designer grid

options, and natural-looking wood-grain laminates. To these workers, making windows and doors is not just a job, but a commitment to the customer.

LOOKING FORWARD

GLW has been providing high-quality products for nearly a quarter century. The company's commitment to quality and customer service will continue in the years to come, as it continues to hold on to the vision to be innovative and to meet the challenge to achieve high quality without sacrificing style. And the firm will continue to maintain those long-standing relationships with its customers, vendors, and employees, as well as develop and nurture new relationships.

There is a slogan that circulates around Great Lakes Window, Inc. that probably best summarizes what GLW is all about: "Great Lakes Window offers many options—second best isn't one of them."

To GLW WORKERS, MAKING WINDOWS AND DOORS IS NOT JUST A JOB, IT IS A COMMITMENT TO THE CUSTOMER.

GREAT LAKES WINDOW OFFERS A COMPLETE LINE OF SINGLE-HUNG, DOUBLE-HUNG, CASEMENT, PICTURE, SLIDING, AWNING, BAY, BOW, AND GARDEN WINDOWS, AS WELL AS SLIDING AND HINGED PATIO DOORS.

Children's Discovery Center/Discovery Express

N 1982, WITH AN EXTENSIVE BACKGROUND IN EARLY CHILDHOOD EDUCATION, A LOVE FOR CHILDREN, AND A FEW INNOVATIVE IDEAS, LOIS MITTEN FOUNDED CHILDREN'S DISCOVERY CENTER (CDC). DETERMINED TO BECOME A LEADER IN CHILD CARE, MITTEN BEGAN TO EXPLORE NEW TRENDS IN THE INDUSTRY. SHE NETWORKED WITH OTHER CHILD CARE PROFESSIONALS

to discuss ways to make her child care program unique. She also traveled to the most innovative child care facilities and children's museums around the country and abroad, and returned to Toledo to offer the most exciting ideas she could find to the community. These award-winning child development centers, with six northwest Ohio locations, help children to explore their interests and reach their highest potential.

A REPUTATION OF EXCELLENCE

CDCs have four distinct qualities that set them apart from other child care centers: the children's museum concept, the project-based curriculum, the spiritual component, and the program's national recognition.

At CDC, children are encouraged to see, touch, and do. The centers have various museum-like exhibits to stimulate the children's minds. At Discovery Express, CDC's sister company, children can view X-rays at the Discovery Clinic, captain the Discovery Ship, explore the depths of the ocean from the controls of a submarine, prepare tortillas in the Mexican restaurant, or travel to new

frontiers from the helm of a computer keyboard. Children can also run, climb, garden, and explore on the award-winning playground.

Combined with the children's museum concept is a child-centered, project-based curriculum. Developed in Reggio Emilia and hailed as an exemplary model of early childhood education by *Newsweek* in 1991, this approach utilizes a curriculum that promotes creativity, collaboration, imagination, and self-expression through various activities—including art, music, and drama—with the goal of helping the child develop his or her self-confidence and self-image. Children learn that they are part of God's creation, and that it is important to love and care for one another.

Despite the fact that hers is a local company, Mitten has won several awards, including Entrepreneur of the Year, Small Business Person of the Year, Manager of the Year, Ohio Child Care Administrator of the Year, and the Athena Award. CDC has achieved accreditation through the National Academy of Early Childhood Programs and the National Association of Child Care Providers. Mitten's

child development centers have also been featured in several national publications, including *Inc.*, *Early Childhood News*, *Executive Female*, *Polaroid Newsletter*, *Business Start-Ups*, *Entrepreneur Magazine*, and *Child Care Information Exchange*.

A CAPABLE, LOVING STAFF

An award-winning program like CDC's would be impossible without its staff of dedicated teachers and administrators. Center administrators hold degrees in early childhood education or related fields. Most CDC teachers hold education degrees and have in-depth experience working with young children. Since ongoing professional development is key to a high-quality program, CDC provides extensive opportunities for additional training.

Children's Discovery Center/Discovery Express is proud of its honors and national accreditation, but the company is prouder still of the day-to-day operations of its centers and of the many happy, healthy children who have learned, developed, and grown under their guidance and care.

LOIS MITTEN, FOUNDER OF CHILDREN'S DISCOVERY CENTER (CDC)/DISCOVERY EXPRESS, DEMONSTRATES HER LOVE FOR CHILDREN.

JESSICA DEVINEY ENCOURAGES THE CHILDREN'S CREATIVITY THROUGH THE MEDIUM OF ART (LEFT).

CHILDREN AT CDCS LEARN THROUGH HANDS-ON EXPERIENCES (RIGHT).

Midwest Environmental Control, Inc.

STABLISHED IN TOLEDO IN 1983, MIDWEST ENVIRONMENTAL CONTROL, INC. FIRST PROVIDED SERVICES RELATED TO THE ASBESTOS ABATEMENT INDUSTRY. SINCE THEN, THE COMPANY HAS GROWN AND EVOLVED TO OFFER A GREATER RANGE OF SERVICES TO CUSTOMERS ALL ACROSS THE COUNTRY. ■ BASED IN TOLEDO SINCE ITS INCEPTION,

Midwest Environmental Control has been providing cost-effective, high-quality environmental services in the tristate area and to clients throughout the nation. Since the mid-1990s, the company has operated two offices in southern California, serving customers in Arizona, Nevada, and California. Those clients include the U.S. Army Corps of Engineers, U.S. Air Force, NASA, and U.S. Bureau of Prisons.

From the Toledo office, the company provides environmental services to customers ranging from individual home owners to large manufacturers, hospitals, banks, institutions, and commercial establishments. Midwest's continuing commitment to its customers is a promise of reliability, integrity, and complete customer satisfaction.

EXTENSIVE CAPABILITIES

Spanning some two decades, the company has performed thousands of projects in virtually every setting and degree of complexity. Midwest Environmental Control has demonstrated capability in a wide range of environmental services, including asbestos, lead paint, mercury and PCB remediation, Phase I and II environmental surveys,

asbestos and lead surveys, underground storage tank removal and replacement, and hazardous waste cleanup and disposal.

The company showcased its expertise in an asbestos and lead removal project for the U.S. Air Force in South Carolina, which required that the building, a 6 million-cubic-foot aircraft hangar, be completely enclosed and under negative air pressure. Lasting more than a year, the work was accomplished through the efforts of experienced, committed workers and the most advanced specialized equipment.

Another challenging project—performed for NASA on a rocket engine test pad once used for the Saturn rocket that launched the first men to the Moon—required workers to be suspended more than 500

feet above the desert floor at Edwards Air Force Base in California.

SOLVING PROBLEMS

Whether working for the U.S. Defense Department in a top-secret setting or for the locally owned gas station in Toledo, Midwest Environmental Control is interested in helping people solve their environmental problems.

The ever changing environmental laws and regulations present challenges for companies of all sizes. For the owner of a gas station or trucking company, it may be a leaking underground storage tank or a highway accident spill. For a manufacturing facility, it could be handling hazardous waste or an emergency hazardous substance release. For other companies or individuals, it may be knowing the environmental condition of a particular property before buying or selling.

Keeping up with federal, state, and local laws pertaining to the many facets of environmental issues is a complex and time-consuming task. Midwest Environmental Control strives to stay abreast of new legislation affecting environmental regulations that could impact customers. Ultimately, the company's charge is to listen to customers, to see their problems as its problems, and to offer common sense, cost-effective solutions.

REMOVING ASBESTOS INSULATION FROM PIPING SYSTEM AT AN OHIO FACTORY

PERFORMING ASBESTOS REMOVAL AT ROCKET ENGINE TEST PAD, EDWARDS AIR FORCE BASE (LEFT)

OBTAINING SOIL SAMPLES USING OUR ADVANCED 4 WHEEL DRIVE HYDRAULIC DIRECT-PUSH UNIT (RIGHT)

A PRACTICAL APPROACH

Most business owners have heard the stories of companies spending exorbitant amounts of money on a seemingly small problem. Complex regulatory requirements, fear of liability, lost production, and runaway costs often leave businesses frustrated when facing environmental mandates and the threat of fines and legal fees. Sensitive to these issues, the company has attained its leadership status by taking an intelligent, practical, customer-centered approach to solving environmental problems.

The company brings to each client not only years of technical expertise, but also personal dedication to find the right fix for that customer. Not every environmental problem requires an extensive—or even expensive—solution. Hundreds of clients, disappointed by higher estimates of other firms, have been pleasantly surprised when they obtained a second opinion.

Midwest Environmental Control is committed to offering clients timely, responsive, professional services and providing innovative, cost-effective solutions to the complex environmental problems facing businesses today. A combination of the company's reputation and services has resulted in strong customer trust and loyalty.

INNOVATIVE SOLUTIONS

The development of new products and equipment is constantly reinventing the environmental services industry. So, to best serve its customers, the company maintains the best people, products, and equipment.

For example, customers requiring groundwater or soil samples can save time and money with the firm's hydraulic, direct-push sampling technology. More borings can be placed in less time, resulting in a more accurate picture of site conditions at less cost. In contrast to conventional drilling rigs, this system provides rapid mobilization, minimal site disturbance, reduced wastes, better access to restricted areas, and more samples in less time. It all translates into cost and time savings for the customer.

In the field of lead paint removal, the company owns and operates the latest lead abatement equipment, which includes mobile and trailer-mounted recyclable steel shot blasting systems accommodating up to five blaster nozzles simultaneously. An advantage of recyclable steel shot blasting is minimization of waste, as the steel shot is used many times. Only the dislodged lead-contaminated material is separated and contained for disposal.

A Midwest Environmental Control customer needed several miles of airport runway and taxiway striping removed under strict conditions. First, the material was classified as hazardous. Second, any debris left behind during removal could be sucked into air intakes of multimillion-dollar experimental aircraft. The task was to provide runway stripe removal and to capture all of the material at the source.

Midwest Environmental Control developed a HEPA filtered vacuum removal system meeting the specifications of the customer at a competitive price.

GOAL ORIENTED

Customer satisfaction is paramount at Midwest Environmental Control. This sole objective is key to the continued success and successful completion of projects, large and small, for valued clients. The philosophy is quite simple: If the customer has relied on the firm to perform a service, then Midwest Environmental Control will accomplish that task by delivering the most timely, economical, and quality service possible.

Every project entrusted to the company becomes a personal challenge to succeed and satisfy the customer. To see the customer's needs and problems become the company's needs and challenges is the motivation to find solutions and meet or exceed the customer's expectations. Quality of workmanship, materials, and the finished product are what customers remember long after a project is completed.

Every member of Midwest Environmental Control, Inc. understands the importance of quality people and quality service. At every level, the company is committed to delivering quality services and products.

ProMedica Health System

INCE 1986, PROMEDICA HEALTH SYSTEM HAS GROWN TO BECOME THE LARGEST, MOST COMPREHENSIVE INTEGRATED HEALTH SYSTEM IN NORTHWEST OHIO AND SOUTHEAST MICHIGAN. THE COMPANY SERVES 23 COUNTIES STRETCHING FROM MICHIGAN'S LENAWEE COUNTY IN THE NORTH, LIMA IN THE SOUTH, THE OHIO STATE

border in the west, and Sandusky in the east.

Striving to be the best of the best in health care, ProMedica Health System seeks to improve the health of the people in the communities it serves through its five divisions: ProMedica Ambulatory and Acute Care; ProMedica Physicians Corporation; ProMedica Health, Education, and Research Corporation; ProMedica Continuing Care Services; and ProMedica Insurance.

The foundation for all of ProMedica's services is its mission and values, which appear in all of the company's facilities, including medical office buildings, hospitals, and continuing care facilities. ProMedica's six major values—collaboration, community-based, compassion, excellence, integrity, and stewardship—are the driving force behind the company's nationally recognized success. In fact, *Modern Health Care* magazine ranked ProMedica one of the country's top 100 health systems,

based on performance, integration, physician participation, and ability to offer a full spectrum of services.

AN INTEGRATED HEALTH SYSTEM

ProMedica is called an integrated health system because it cares about—and provides services for—people in any type of

health care situation. ProMedica Ambulatory and Acute Care operates 80 outpatient facilities and 11 hospitals within five geographic regions in northwest Ohio and southern Michigan. Through the Lake Erie Health Alliance, a coalition of hospitals in northwest Ohio and southeast Michigan, participating health care facilities reap the benefits and

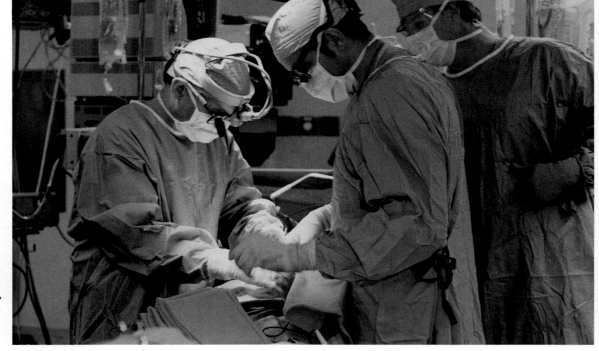

WITH A NETWORK OF HOSPITALS KNOWN FOR SUPERIOR CARE IN THE AREAS OF CARDIOLOGY, CARDIOVASCULAR SURGERY, VASCULAR SURGERY, ONCOLOGY, ORTHOPEDICS, AND NEUROSCIENCES, PROMEDICA HEALTH SYSTEM OPERATES 11 HOSPITALS WITHIN NORTHWEST OHIO AND SOUTHEAST MICHIGAN.

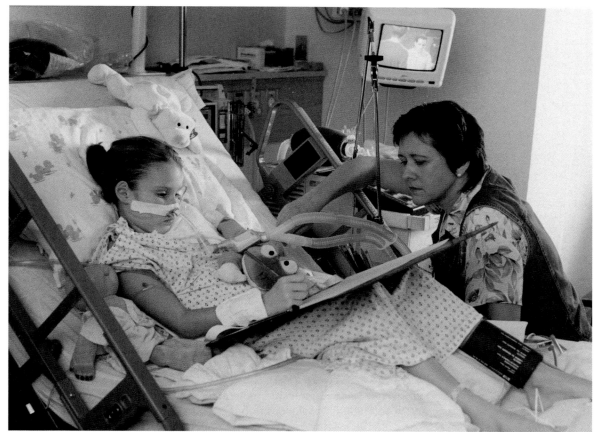

cost advantages of coordinated purchasing, distribution, and other support functions.

ProMedica Physicians Corporation includes 120 primary care physicians specializing in family practice, internal medicine, obstetrics and gynecology, and pediatrics, and providing care from 40 convenient locations in the metro Toledo area. ProMedica also includes 550 affiliated physicians.

ProMedica Continuing Care Services includes senior, rehabilitative, and transportation services. Senior services include Lake Park, a Sylvania skilled nursing facility specializing in rehabilitation services; the Goerlich Center for Alzheimer's Care; St. Francis Health Care Centre, a long-term care and rehabilitation hospital located in Green Springs, Ohio; Charlotte Stevenson House in Adrian; and Charles Fay and Provincial House in Michigan.

In 2001, ProMedica formed a partnership with Visiting Nurse Corporation, which includes Visiting Nurse Service, Visiting Nurse Health Care, and Visiting Nurse and Health Care. Combining the strengths of ProMedica's Caring Home Health Services will only enhance the organization's ability to care for those in need. Visiting Nurse Corporation, along with Caring Home Health Ser-

vices, provides patients with in-home IV therapy; chemotherapy; wound care; physical, speech, and occupational therapy; and medical equipment supply. Home health aides are also available to help with patients' day-to-day needs, including meal preparation and nutritional guidance, shopping, personal care, and maintaining a safe living environment.

Rehabilitative services are located

throughout all five regions in northwest Ohio and southern Michigan.

ProMedica Air & Mobile Transportation Network is also part of ProMedica Continuing Care Services. It includes a medical helicopter service for communities in northwest Ohio, in addition to eight state-of-the-art mobile intensive care vehicles. These vehicles and the transport teams who operate them provide medical care comparable to an inten-

sive care unit, with specialization in the critical care of adult, maternal, pediatric, and neonatal patients. The network is based at the Toledo Hospital and operates from two satellite facilities—Mercy Hospital in Monroe, Michigan, and Defiance Hospital.

To most people, ProMedica Insurance is known as Paramount Health Care. As a locally owned and operated insurance provider since 1988, Paramount focuses on quality, service, and wellness. Through offices in Maumee, Ohio, and Monroe, Michigan, Paramount serves as the region's largest HMO, with more than 210,000 members. It was the first organization in northwest Ohio to be accredited by the National Committee for Quality Assurance, the recognized standard of quality in the field. Paramount has received further recognition for its efforts from *U.S. News & World Report* and *Newsweek*, who ranked it as one of the top HMOs in the country. *Modern Health Care* magazine has continually ranked Paramount as one of the top 10 fastest-growing, provider-owned health care plans in the country.

As the company's newest business area, ProMedica Health, Education, and Research Corporation concentrates on family practice residency programs at Flower and the Toledo hospitals, research programs, research affiliations, and medical/surgical fellowships.

ProMedica currently has more than 40 academic affiliations throughout the country.

A REGIONAL HEALTH CARE LEADER

With a network of hospitals known for superior care in the areas of cardiology, cardiovascular surgery, vascular surgery, oncology, orthopedics, and neurosciences, ProMedica Health System operates 11 hospitals within northwest Ohio and southeast Michigan. The central region consists of the Toledo Hospital, Flower Hospital, and Children's Medical Center.

Built in 1874, the Toledo Hospital offers 646 acute care beds and is the largest hospital in northwest Ohio. It includes the Toledo Hospital Heart Institute—an advanced technology center for the prevention, diagnosis, and treatment of heart disease—and the Center for Women's Health, which focuses on obstetrics, education, and care for women of all ages. The Toledo Hospital has received Consumer Choice awards five years in a row from the National Research Corporation, the national leader in health care performance measurement.

Toledo Children's Hospital opened its doors as a hospital within the Toledo Hospital in 1994. With "to help create an environment in which all children are treated with

respect, compassion, dignity and love" as its stated goal, Toledo Children's Hospital recognizes that children are unique and require different types of care from adults. Care at Toledo Children's Hospital—which has 150 beds, including newborn intensive care, pediatric intensive care, hematology/oncology, pediatric cardiology and cardiac surgery, pediatric surgery, and general surgery—takes place in a child-friendly environment, where play and art therapy are incorporated into medical treatment plans to help kids get through their hospital stays as comfortably as possible.

Located in Sylvania, Flower Hospital is best known for its Cancer Care Center, which boasts a 20-year history of quality cancer care. The hospital provides a comprehensive diagnostic and treatment center. Affiliated with Flower Hospital is the Flower Rehabilitation Center, which contains 45 beds for patients who are undergoing rigorous rehabilitation treatments.

ProMedica's north region is served by Lenawee Health Alliance (LHA), which includes Bixby Medical Center and Herrick Memorial Hospital. LHA is committed to providing quality care to the citizens of Lenawee County.

The organization's south region includes Fostoria Community Hospital and Lima Memorial Health System, through a joint operating

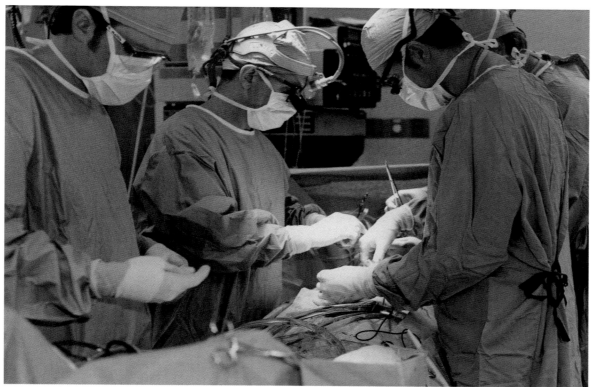

company with Lima Memorial Hospital and Blanchard Valley Health Association.

Defiance Hospital is located in ProMedica's west region. The hospital offers psychiatric care, intensive care, medical/surgical, obstetrics, emergency room, outpatient radiology, and laboratory services in its 80-bed facility. Defiance is currently building a new regional medical center. The new facility will have larger, all private inpatient rooms; a more private emergency room setting; and a women's and children's center, among other amenities.

ProMedica's newest facility, Bay Park Community Hospital, is located in the east region. This 70-bed facility opened in fall 2001 in Oregon, Ohio. The hospital provides its community with quality obstetrics, medical/surgical, intensive care, and emergency room services. Bay Park's campus also includes a professional office building with physician offices, a rehabilitation center, and a diagnostic center.

COMMUNITY FOCUS

As ProMedica is one of the region's largest employers, its presence in the communities it serves is great. The company and its employees significantly impact their communities through high-quality care, financial contributions, free health screenings, community partnerships with other not-for-profit health-care-related

agencies, and hundreds of hours of volunteer time.

The company as a whole is aware that its communities rely on it for people and financial resources, and it is happy to provide those resources. ProMedica Health System donates approximately $41.5 million annually through financial contributions and educational programs. Toledo Children's Hospital, for example, is involved with advocacy programs to reduce alcohol and tobacco use among children; teach teenage mothers how to cope with their pregnancies, and then raise, nurture, and provide for their babies; promote immunization programs to keep kids healthy; and teach effective ways to deal with negative peer pressure.

A BRIGHT FUTURE

ProMedica's support of its communities will continue well into the future. Supported by its unwavering commitment to service and a strong system of corporate values, ProMedica will continue to bring the best hospitals, physicians, health plans, and special services to northwest Ohio and southeast Michigan. In short, ProMedica Health System will remain an award-winning company that focuses on the patient and works to exceed the expectations of those it serves.

EISC, Inc.

ORTHWEST OHIO IS ENJOYING A TECHNOLOGICAL RENAISSANCE. TRACE THE ORIGIN OF EXCITING NEW DEVELOPMENTS IN INFORMATION TECHNOLOGY (IT), ADVANCED MANUFACTURING, LIFE SCIENCES, OR TECHNOLOGY COMMERCIALIZATION, AND IT LIKELY WILL LEAD TO ONE SOURCE: EISC, INC. AS ONE OF THE

region's recognized technology leaders, EISC has been a catalyst for technology-based economic development, and is directly accountable for millions of dollars of positive economic impact on the area's economy.

Formed in 1987 as one of Ohio's seven Thomas Edison Program technology centers, EISC was originally conceived as a resource for manufacturers to enhance their global competitiveness by improving quality, productivity, and profitability. Indeed, in fiscal year 2000, EISC helped nearly 600 companies in such sectors as automotive, glass, plastics, and food processing to advance their technical competency and market strength. The technology center reported that its clients enjoyed approximately $22.5 million in cost savings and increased sales of more than $51 million from 1995 through 2000. During that same period, EISC helped to create or retain more than 800 jobs in northwest Ohio.

EISC's clients have traditionally been small to medium-sized manufacturers who have chosen the cen-

ter as a preferred, objective resource for adopting breakthrough practices to make them high-performance firms. With its thumb on the pulse of industry's needs, EISC has responded with a suite of services designed to provide enterprise-wide solutions, like lean manufacturing concepts, E-business strategy development, Six Sigma methodology, international quality and environmental standards implementation, new product development, strategic thinking, and more.

BLAZING TRAILS TO THE FUTURE

As the information-focused economy has spawned whole new markets and channels, as well as mandated changes in the ways companies approach customers, EISC has been the conduit for the establishment of relevant, contemporary technology resources in northwest Ohio. The center's strategic plan, beginning fiscal year 2002, shows a strong alignment with science and technology policy at the highest state level. Parallel goals relate to aiding the formation and growth of new technology companies and fostering an entrepreneurial climate.

With these objectives in mind, EISC has been instrumental in several key regional initiatives. Early in 2000, the center directed the formation of the Regional Technology Alliance (RTA), in conjunction with the City of Toledo, to attract and nurture technology-based businesses and the people who work for them. Within a year of RTA's creation, EISC worked with its partners, including the Regional Growth Partnership, to hire an executive director and set up office space for this private/public consortium. Julian Gravino, EISC president and CEO, serves as vice chairman of RTA's governing board. RTA works to support local businesses, educational and health care systems, and the IT industry to help diversify the regional economy into the technology sector.

Another key element in building the area's needed technology infrastructure is the creation of the Information Technology Alliance of Northwest Ohio (ITANO). Before the creation of this alliance, many perceived that there was no IT industry in the region. However, EISC knew that in order for IT to become a key driver in northwest Ohio, the center needed a professional orga-

WITH HEADQUARTERS IN TOLEDO, AND THROUGH THREE NORTHWEST OHIO LOCATIONS, EISC, INC. SERVES THE GREAT LAKES REGION AND CERTAIN NATIONAL AND INTERNATIONAL SECTORS (TOP).

THE 36,000-SQUARE-FOOT EISC FACILITY HOUSES A LARGE COMPUTER AIDED DESIGN/ COMPUTER AIDED MANUFACTURING (CAD/ CAM) AREA WITH ADVANCED WORKSTATIONS AND SOFTWARE, A HIGH BAY SHOP AREA EQUIPPED WITH A VARIETY OF COMPUTER NUMERICAL CONTROL (CNC) EQUIPMENT, AS WELL AS TRAINING AND CONFERENCE ROOMS (BOTTOM).

EISC PROVIDED AFFORDABLE ACCESS TO ENGINEERING AND DESIGN SERVICES FOR A MANUFACTURER OF SECURITY MECHANISMS FOR HANDGUN HOLSTERS. THE COLLABORATION RESULTED IN A VIABLE PROTOTYPE OF A LOCKING MECHANISM THAT OFFERS SAFETY AND A QUICK DRAW FOR LAW ENFORCEMENT OFFICERS.

nization to support it. By assisting with the development of its business strategy and by appointing its first president, EISC launched ITANO during spring 2000. As part of its sister Edison center, Ohio's IT Alliance, ITANO represents hundreds of members of software development, hardware creation, programming, Web development, IT education, and government/nonprofit/corporate IT departments, who come together to collaborate and exchange ideas. With EISC's president and CEO as its chairman of the board, ITANO's goal is to help the IT professional get whatever they need to grow, including business assistance, joint venture contracts, networking forums, and

educational seminars.

When EISC is not paving the way for necessary improvements to advance the IT industry in the region, its Center for Innovative Food Technology (CIFT) program leverages its large USDA contract with special funds from the State of Ohio to help develop a totally new industry in the state: nutraceuticals. Also known as functional foods, nutraceuticals are food products with health benefits beyond simple nutrition. Genetically modified potatoes that inhibit hepatitis B, fortified cereals that lower cholesterol, snack foods that diminish the risks of heart disease or osteoporosis—all are examples of disease-fighting, nutraceutical

food products. CIFT's winning proposal, *Foods of the Future: Commercialization in the Nutraceutical Industry*, submitted and awarded in 2001, provides for scientific, technical, and business support to develop, validate, commercialize, and market new, functional food products.

Helping smaller manufacturing companies thrive in a global marketplace. Blazing trails for the new economy in the northwest corner of Ohio. Pioneering advances in food processing to serve a nation. EISC stands by its mission to nurture and deliver breakthrough technologies and solutions to its customers in Toledo, in the Great Lakes area, and beyond.

KRIS EGGLESTON, PRO-PAK QUALITY MANAGER, CAME TO EISC FOR LEAN MANUFACTURING AND PROBLEM SOLVING TRAINING FOR 12 OF THE COMPANY'S CREWMEMBERS. THE RESULT: PRODUCTION DOUBLED FOR THIS MAUMEE, OHIO, MANUFACTURER OF CORRUGATED BOXES (LEFT).

TODD KRIEGEL, SENIOR VICE PRESIDENT OF ACME MACHINE AUTOMATICS, TURNED TO EISC FOR HELP WITH BECOMING CERTIFIED IN QS 9000, THE INTERNATIONAL QUALITY STANDARD PERTAINING TO AUTOMOTIVE SUPPLIERS. THE PARTNERSHIP SAVED THE OTTOVILLE, OHIO, MANUFACTURER AS MUCH AS $12,000 (RIGHT).

The Radisson Hotel-Toledo

INCE IT WAS BUILT IN 1987, A STAY AT THE RADISSON HOTEL-TOLEDO HAS GIVEN GUESTS A TOTAL EXPERIENCE WITH THE OPPORTUNITY FOR A GOOD NIGHT'S SLEEP AND A HOST OF AMENITIES. GUESTS HAVE EASY ACCESS TO MANY OF TOLEDO'S HOT SPOTS THANKS TO BOTH THE HOTEL'S DOWNTOWN LOCATION AND ITS CONVENIENT SHUTTLE SERVICE.

And most important, the Radisson provides a caring staff whose goal it is to exceed guests' expectations.

The hotel management is proud of the stability of the facility and of its employees. The staff sees working at the Radisson as a lifestyle, not just a job, and is committed to its work. That commitment is recognized and mirrored by the management, who can be seen picking up a room service tray that had been left in the hall or stopping to chat with a guest. Together, the staff and management work as a team to assure complete guest satisfaction.

Guests come to appreciate the personal attention from the staff with its trademark Yes I Can® service philosophy, which ensures that the Radisson will provide caring, cour-

teous, and responsive staff members who are willing to go above and beyond to satisfy guests.

This personal attention to detail includes developing a rapport with guests and knowing the history of repeat guests. It may mean remembering who likes decaffeinated tea with a lemon wedge along with his morning muffin, or who prefers the *Wall Street Journal* with her glass of chilled orange juice.

With high-quality service and attention to detail, business travelers and convention attendees alike will feel at home in one of the 400 guest rooms, including the impressive two story Presidential Suite, which features a breathtaking view of Toledo's riverfront. The hotel also offers 52 business-class rooms on two floors with

private key entry; two executive board rooms; and 11 meeting rooms, which include audiovisual equipment.

A vast 5,478-square-foot ballroom complete with large, glass chandeliers and a wall of windows also overlooks the streets of downtown Toledo and its riverfront. At the end of a busy day, the Summit Street Grille features American cuisine and is perfect for a relaxing, sit-down meal. Or, the Ballpark Lounge and Lobby Bar are suitable locations for cocktails and conversation.

A CORPORATE HOTEL

The Radisson's close proximity to many of the area's attractions makes this city an easy sell. The award-winning Toledo Zoo and Toledo Museum of Art are

THE RADISSON HOTEL-TOLEDO'S DOWNTOWN LOCATION AND ITS CARING STAFF WHOSE GOAL IT IS TO EXCEED GUESTS' EXPECTATIONS MAKE IT A TOP CHOICE FOR BUSINESS TRAVELERS OR GROUPS OF VARIOUS SIZES.

SINCE IT WAS BUILT IN 1987, A STAY AT THE RADISSON HOTEL-TOLEDO HAS GIVEN GUESTS A TOTAL EXPERIENCE WITH THE OPPORTUNITY FOR A GOOD NIGHT'S SLEEP AND A HOST OF AMENITIES.

within a short distance of the hotel. And, located just down the street is the Center Of Science and Industry (COSI), ready to provide a day packed full of family fun. Across the river are restaurants to suit any taste and the Sports Arena & Exhibit Hall with a varied list of events to entertain everyone—from the sports enthusiast to hobbyists of all kinds.

Specific to the convention market, the 75,000 square feet of floor space available at the SeaGate Centre is yet another selling point for many companies seeking a suitable convention site. In addition, opposite the Radisson is another hotel property that offers an additional 200 guest rooms. Combining the convention facility with 600 total guest rooms and local restaurants and attractions makes it a one-stop-shop site.

The Radisson prides itself on its flexibility and willingness to adapt to any size or type of group regardless of the age of its attendees, backgrounds, or purposes. Whether it's 500 teenagers in town for a church retreat, or a trade show featuring hundreds of exhibitors from across the country, the Radisson and its partners are committed to the success of the event. This commitment to quality and service has earned the Radisson Hotel-Toledo a favorable reputation with many new and repeat customers who have booked the facility now and will continue to do so for years to come.

WITH HIGH-QUALITY SERVICE AND ATTENTION TO DETAIL, GUESTS AT THE RADISSON HOTEL-TOLEDO WILL FEEL AT HOME IN ONE OF THE 400 GUEST ROOMS.

Hilton Hotel and Dana Conference Center

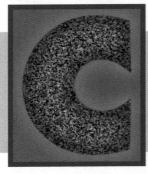

ENTRALLY LOCATED IN THE TOLEDO AREA, THE HILTON HOTEL AND DANA CONFERENCE CENTER RESTS ON THE 350-ACRE CAMPUS OF THE MEDICAL COLLEGE OF OHIO (MCO), OFFERING ITS GUESTS THE HILTON TRADEMARK OF A HIGHER LEVEL OF SERVICE. CATERING TO BOTH THE LEISURE AND THE BUSINESS TRAVELER, HILTON

makes its guests feel at home by providing comfortable guest rooms, complete banquet and meeting facilities, and a variety of amenities.

For the business portion of the visit, Hilton includes the attached Eleanor N. Dana Conference Center for business meetings, training sessions, banquets, and conferences. The attached hotel makes the combined facilities ideal for hosting out-of-town meeting attendees.

On a larger scale, the Hilton is well equipped to handle special events of all sizes. With 213 guest rooms and two ballrooms with banquet capacity for up to 500 people, the hotel is often reserved for company parties, weddings, and other celebrations. Keeping in mind the importance of customer satisfaction, a banquet manager is on-site for all events to assure that everything goes smoothly.

THE SERVICE TRADEMARK

As one of 270 Doral International properties, the Hilton is part of the largest independently owned hotel management company in the country. Coupled with the prestige of its parent company, the Hilton Toledo bears the name of one of the world's finest hotels. Through the years, the Hilton name has become synonymous with quality service and customer satisfaction. The Hilton Toledo is no exception.

In addition to the Hilton's customer-first philosophy, guests can expect an enjoyable dining experience and a number of extras.

CONVENIENTLY LOCATED IN SOUTH TOLEDO ON THE 350-ACRE CAMPUS OF THE MEDICAL COLLEGE OF OHIO, THE HILTON HOTEL OFFERS ITS TRADEMARK SERVICE ON EVERY OCCASION AND AT EVERY OPPORTUNITY.

Whether guests are dining in the Iris Restaurant or privately in their rooms, they can enjoy daily breakfast and lunch buffets as well as daily dinner specials. With a courteous staff available to serve guests for breakfast, lunch, and dinner, the Iris offers a variety of entrées in an elegant setting.

Whispers Lounge is tucked away to provide a comfortable atmosphere. It offers a wide array of beverages and specialty drinks, and is perfect for a relaxing conversation or a chance to catch the latest news and scores on the big-screen television or a friendly game of pool.

For the convenience of guests, the hotel also has a gift shop and ATMs available. The hotel's business center—open 24 hours a day, seven days a week—provides an excellent work environment. Recreational facilities such as a large indoor pool, sauna, and whirlpool allow visitors other ways to enjoy their stay.

Hilton guests also receive complimentary access to the Henry L. Morse fitness center. The center is located at the Medical College building, and

WITH 213 GUEST ROOMS AND TWO BALLROOMS WITH BANQUET CAPACITY FOR UP TO 500 PEOPLE, THE HOTEL IS OFTEN RESERVED FOR COMPANY PARTIES, WEDDINGS, AND OTHER CELEBRATIONS.

is accessible via an indoor walkway from the hotel and conference center. Within the fitness center's 33,000-square-foot facility, visitors may utilize the indoor running track, basketball court, racquetball courts, aerobic space, state-of-the-art fitness machines, and free weights.

Yet another attraction of the Hilton and Dana Conference Center property is the Bryan Academic Commons located outside the facilities. The commons includes three acres of pathways and quiet sitting areas on beautifully landscaped grounds that feature waterfalls, sculptures, and flowering trees and plants. Many guests choose to hold outdoor receptions in this relaxing area.

THE ELEANOR N. DANA CONFERENCE CENTER

The Hilton is the only hotel in northwest Ohio with a conference center that is accredited by the International Association of Conference Centers (IACC). The

Eleanor N. Dana Conference Center was opened in 1983, and received IACC accreditation in part because it offers both breakout and large meeting capabilities, as well as an on-site conference planner.

Within the center's two-story structure is 12,000 square feet of meeting space in 17 rooms. Most meeting rooms are equipped with a slide projector, an overhead projector, an audio system, a flip chart, and video playback capabilities. For all other needs, a wide variety of state-of-the-art audiovisual equipment is available.

The center's Lucas Auditorium houses an oversized projection screen, a stage, and a full-service projection booth. The booth is set up above the meeting area and comprises two high-intensity slide projectors, a liquid crystal diode (LCD) video projector, and various sound and lighting controls.

The Dana Center provides most of its technical and audiovisual

equipment from its in-house inventory, but will arrange for specific equipment to meet customer demands if necessary. The center is also equipped with two satellite reception dishes for C-band or Ku-band video teleconferences.

THE IDEAL LOCATION

By offering such an array of services, the Hilton Toledo, along with the Dana Conference Center, has become the ideal location for several local companies to hold business meetings, trade shows, product rollouts, reunions, conferences, and training sessions. Some of the many local businesses that have utilized the Hilton and Dana Conference Center include Dana Corporation, Bax Global, Libbey, Owens-Illinois, University of Toledo, and Spartan Chemical.

The Hilton is conveniently located in south Toledo with easy access to downtown attractions. The Toledo Zoo, Toledo Museum of Art, and two large shopping malls are within 15 minutes of the hotel. Out-of-town guests are offered a complimentary shuttle service to and from the Toledo Express Airport, which is less than 20 minutes away.

For business or relaxation, travelers and guests discover that the Hilton Toledo offers its trademark service on every occasion and at every opportunity. Hilton lives up to its promises and enjoys the chance to cater to visitors and old friends.

CATERING TO BOTH THE LEISURE AND THE BUSINESS TRAVELER, HILTON MAKES ITS GUESTS FEEL AT HOME BY PROVIDING COMFORTABLE GUEST ROOMS, COMPLETE BANQUET AND MEETING FACILITIES, AND A VARIETY OF AMENITIES.

BAX Global Inc.

LTHOUGH TOLEDO'S HUB SERVICES AUSTRALIA, CANADA, MEXICO, AND THE UNITED STATES, BAX GLOBAL INC. HAS A VAST NETWORK OF DESTINATIONS AROUND THE WORLD. AS ONE OF THE LARGEST HEAVY-CARGO TRANSPORT COMPANIES IN THE WORLD—INCLUDING CARGO FOR THE ELECTRONICS,

computer, fashion, retail, automotive, and aerospace industries, among others—BAX services large industrial clients who demand fast, reliable service.

In fact, the company prides itself on its ability to provide fast, door-to-door, customs-cleared shipping services with few size and weight limitations. From Australia to Azerbaijan, Uganda to Ukraine, and countries in between, BAX Global

lives up to its name as a business that truly serves the entire globe.

THE TOLEDO HUB

BAX Global is a $2.1 billion, global transportation and supply chain management company, based in Irvine, that offers a full line of cargo transportation services to business-to-business shippers worldwide. The company's roots date back to 1972, when Burlington

Northern Air Freight began operation. The Pittston Company—BAX Global's parent company—made air freight history in 1982 when it made the largest acquisition ever in Burlington Northern Air Freight. The company diversified into air transport, and purchased a fleet of airplanes in 1985 to operate out of Fort Wayne. Then, in 1991, Burlington Air Express moved its North American HUB to the new, state-of-the-art Toledo facility.

Operating as BAX's main HUB, Toledo is home to the company's largest facility—a 279,000-square-foot building situated on 65 acres. Fifty acres are utilized as an aircraft parking apron, while the HUB structure occupies the remaining 15 acres. The building measures three football fields long and one football field wide, and features a state-of-the-art material handling system especially designed for heavy freight and oversized cargo. With the capacity to sort some 4 million pounds of cargo per day, the Toledo HUB offers its customers tremendous time and cost savings.

GOING THE EXTRA MILE

Able to handle packages weighing as little as 10 pounds, as well as shipments weighing thousands of pounds, BAX works hard to serve its customers. The company has the ability to combine land, air, and sea services to meet its customers' transportation needs, and is willing to go the extra mile to ensure on-time delivery.

To meet customer demands, BAX offers a suite of services to accommodate varied shipment parameters. Guaranteed services such as Guaranteed First Arrival, Guaranteed Overnight, and Guaranteed Second Day offer a 100 percent money-back

BAX GLOBAL INC.—ONE OF THE LARGEST HEAVY-CARGO COMPANIES IN THE WORLD—SERVICES LARGE INDUSTRIAL CLIENTS WHO DEMAND FAST, RELIABLE SERVICE.

guarantee if the shipment is not delivered on time.

BAX's Standard services—including Standard Overnight and Standard Second Day—offer a lower-cost alternative for the customers. For even greater savings, customers can utilize BAXSaver, which assures that delivery will be made within one to three business days, but offers no additional guarantees or refunds.

Included in BAX's diversified services are strategically located logistics management centers. As globalization persists, customs brokerage and dealing with foreign currencies can become overwhelming. To address this issue, BAX provides highly trained customer service representatives who are experts in global logistics strategies. In addition to Toledo's logistics center, other BAX centers are located in Australia, France, India, London, Malaysia, and Singapore.

Toledo's location is of further benefit to BAX customers. From BAX's facility at the crossroads of I-80/90 and I-75, cargo can easily be transported economically by truck to a large area of the country and Canada.

BAX GLOBAL IS A $2.1 BILLION, GLOBAL TRANSPORTATION AND SUPPLY CHAIN MANAGEMENT COMPANY, BASED IN IRVINE, THAT OFFERS A FULL LINE OF CARGO TRANSPORTATION SERVICES TO BUSINESS-TO-BUSINESS SHIPPERS WORLDWIDE.

BAX IS ITS PEOPLE

The people at BAX are the company's single biggest asset," says Steve Grier, vice president of HUB Operations. Grier describes BAX employees as hard-working, dependable people who do their jobs at all hours of the day regardless of the climate. "They are the engine that makes everything work," says Grier.

With such a strong emphasis on its employees, BAX makes a substantial investment in training, and has pioneered training in the air freight carrier field. New employees at the Toledo HUB go through orientation, basic training, technical training, and then practical, hands-on training. Basic training includes numerous hours of learning each individual component involved in an air freight business. The practical training employees receive depends on the individual job. Load planners, tug and forklift operators, aircraft marshalers, and k-loader operators, for example, receive additional hours of hands-on training.

Training doesn't stop with the newly hired employee. BAX offers regular, ongoing training and requires the involvement of all its employees. Grier estimates that of the nearly 1,000 employees at the Toledo HUB, from 400 to 500 people are in some type of training each month.

Another tribute to BAX's people is the longevity of the company's management team. In total, the 11 individuals who make up the senior group represent some 150 years of experience. BAX typically promotes from within, so managers have experienced the jobs their employees do.

BAX Global Inc. is a union-free company that focuses on its employees and strives to create a desirable working environment. On a whole, the company realizes, as its motto states, that "it's the people—not the planes—who deliver."

WITH THE CAPACITY TO SORT SOME 4 MILLION POUNDS OF CARGO PER DAY, THE TOLEDO HUB OFFERS ITS CUSTOMERS TREMENDOUS TIME AND COST SAVINGS.

HCR Manor Care

A S THE LEADING OWNER AND OPERATOR OF LONG-TERM CARE CENTERS IN THE UNITED STATES, HCR MANOR CARE HAS CARVED OUT A DISTINCTIVE POSITION IN THE HEALTH CARE INDUSTRY. ITS RESPECTED HEARTLAND, MANORCARE, AND ARDEN COURTS FACILITIES FOCUS ON PROVIDING QUALITY

care—and quality caring—for patients with diverse needs. This quality of caring is a tribute to the more than 54,000 employees who put smiles on patients' faces and provide the personal touch that is a critical part of the treatment process.

High-quality care for patients and residents is provided across the country through a network of more than 500 long-term care centers, assisted living facilities, outpatient rehabilitation clinics, and home health care offices. Partnerships and other ventures supply high-quality pharmaceutical products and management services to physician practices. The company's services span 33 states. HCR Manor Care is a New York Stock Exchange company (symbol: HCR) and part of the S&P 500 Index.

Locally, more than 1,000 people are employed by HCR Manor Care. Nursing centers in the Toledo area include Heartland of Perrysburg, Heartland—Holly Glen, Heartland of Wauseon, Heartland of Oregon, and Heartland of Browning in Waterville.

HCR MANOR CARE'S HEARTLAND SKILLED NURSING CENTERS IN TOLEDO, PERRYSBURG, OREGON, WATERVILLE, AND WAUSEON PROVIDE PHYSICIAN-PRESCRIBED NURSING CARE AROUND THE CLOCK.

Perrysburg Commons offers homelike living with assistance. Ancillary and outpatient physical therapy businesses include Heartland Rehabilitation Services, Heartland Home Health Care and Hospice, Maumee

Urgent Medical Care Center, Alexis Industrial Medical Clinic, and Retina Vitreous Associates. Heartland Medical Information Systems, a medical transcription business, is also headquartered in Toledo.

A BROAD SPECTRUM OF CARE

HCR Manor Care's commitment to excellence provides high-quality care along the entire spectrum of patients' needs, including skilled nursing care, subacute medical/ rehabilitation care, Alzheimer's care, rehabilitation, ancillary care, and assisted living.

In the company's skilled nursing centers, experienced professionals provide physician-prescribed, comprehensive health care around the clock. High-quality medical care through registered and licensed practical nurses; certified nursing assistants; and physical, occupational, and speech therapists is

HEARTLAND REHABILITATION SERVICES PROVIDES THERAPY IN A VARIETY OF LOCATIONS IN ADDITION TO ITS CLINICS, INCLUDING SCHOOLS, WORK SITES, HOSPITALS, AND PEOPLE'S HOMES.

complemented by social services; therapeutic recreational activities; and dietary, housekeeping, and laundry services. Programs are designed to give the highest level of functional independence to residents.

HCR Manor Care's subacute programs offer cost-effective, short-term alternatives to hospital stays. Hospital stays are shortened or eliminated by providing medical and rehabilitation programs for patients recovering from major surgery or severe illness or injury. In this way, patients are able to recover in a supportive environment that is specifically designed to speed the recovery process.

HCR Manor Care is an industry leader in providing care for those with Alzheimer's disease and other forms of dementia. A consistent, planned, and sequenced daily schedule is delivered to residents in a protected, low-stress, success-oriented environment. Alzheimer's patients in all stages of the disease receive specialized care and programs from highly trained staff.

Rehabilitation services are provided in each of HCR Manor Care's skilled nursing centers; outpatient clinics; and work sites, schools, homes, hospitals, and other off-site locations. Licensed therapists provide physical, speech, respiratory, and occupational therapy for patients recovering from major surgery; strokes; heart attacks; workplace and sports injuries; neurological and

PERRYSBURG COMMONS, AN UPSCALE RETIREMENT CENTER, OFFERS A HOMELIKE, RESIDENTIAL SETTING FOR THOSE WHO NO LONGER WANT THE HEADACHES OF RUNNING A HOUSEHOLD.

orthopedic conditions; and other illnesses, injuries, and disabilities.

Patients and residents in the company's skilled nursing and assisted living centers receive personalized physician medical services. Oftentimes, patients do not require the level of care offered by a hospital or skilled nursing center. HCR Manor Care provides a spectrum of ancillary services to assist patients who want to remain in their homes and receive the medical and related care they need to function. In addition, it provides hospice services in people's homes and in its skilled nursing centers.

Dedicated units within many of HCR Manor Care's skilled nursing centers, as well as stand-alone assisted living centers, provide a home-like, residential setting. Residents live independently while receiving personal care assistance as needed. A broad spectrum of social/recreational activities is also part of the assisted living experience.

CIRCLE OF CARE®

What makes HCR Manor Care's commitment to caring different from other health care providers is its comprehensive training, launched in 1988, to bring out the helping, respectful, and responsive nature that is within each one of its employees. Over this span, more than 80,000 employees have completed the company's Circle of Care program. More than just a work program, Circle of Care is a philosophy focusing on how people should treat one another.

Because it is a philosophy, the Circle of Care principles extend to how someone interacts with friends, family members, and even the clerk at the grocery store. Its principles are constantly being reinforced throughout the day. This philosophy is what drives HCR Manor Care's commitment to excellence and will be the glue in the company's growth strategies and commitment to caring for patients and residents.

HEARTLAND HOME HEALTH CARE AND HOSPICE CAN PROVIDE THE MEDICAL AND RELATED PROFESSIONAL CARE AND ASSISTANCE NEEDED BY THOSE WISHING TO REMAIN IN THEIR HOMES.

Anderzack-Pitzen Construction, Inc.

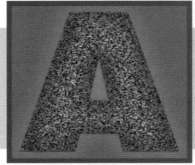

smaller jobs that larger, established companies had passed over. In 1996, founder Mike Anderzack teamed up with Jim Pitzen to form Anderzack-Pitzen Construction, Inc.

Today, the concrete construction company that got its start from the founder's garage has evolved into a successful heavy/civil contractor. Anderzack-Pitzen specializes in grading, earthwork, underground sewer and waterline utilities, heavy highways and roadways, structural concrete, bridges and structures, cold milling, asphalt and concrete paving, and building renovation projects. Working primarily on government-funded projects throughout Ohio and Michigan, the company maintains a focus on hiring and buying locally to help support and develop the Toledo area.

ANDERZACK-PITZEN CONSTRUCTION, INC. SHOWCASED ITS VERSATILITY AND CREATIVITY IN ITS RENOVATION OF THE MAPLEWOOD MARKETPLACE FOR THE CITY OF SYLVANIA, OHIO, MAINTAINING THE BUILDING'S HISTORICAL INTEGRITY AND MAKING ROOM FOR SHOPS, OFFICES, AND A RESTAURANT (TOP).

THE COMPANY'S TEAM OF PROFESSIONALS FOCUSES ON FINDING CREATIVE SOLUTIONS, AS EVIDENCED BY THE WORK DONE ON THIS FUEL UNLOADING STATION FOR A TOLEDO TURBINE ENGINE MANFACTURER (BOTTOM).

PROVIDING INNOVATIVE SOLUTIONS

Anderzack-Pitzen is a modest company located in Metamora, Ohio. By no means, though, does it consider itself a typical construction company. With headquarters located in a renovated turn-of-the-century barn, it prides itself on its versatility and ability to diversify to meet—and sometimes even anticipate—market demand. Its team of professionals focuses on finding creative solutions and carrying through to completion a job well done.

A recently completed project for the City of Sylvania, Ohio, is testament to the company's hallmark versatility and creativity. The historic Maplewood building, formerly an auto dealership, was slated for demolition. A group of concerned community members organized an effort to save the structure. Anderzack-Pitzen was contracted to gut the building without tearing it down and restore the structure to maintain its historical integrity. Today, the building is home to several specialty shops, offices, and a restaurant.

A Toledo turbine engine manufacturer also benefited from Anderzack-

Pitzen's unique expertise on a project that involved installing a large fuel separator tank. The excavation area needed to be large enough to accommodate the tank's size. In addition, the conditions of the ground were unstable, so determining an effective shoring method was a crucial element. Typical trench-shielding methods were either ruled out as ineffective or too costly. But Anderzack-Pitzen was up for the challenge. Mike Anderzack worked with a specialty equipment company to set up a slide rail system that saved time and material costs and delivered to the owner a specified product as well.

In addition, the company has a long record of collaboration with public works of local municipalities to handle a variety of environmental projects, including sewer separations. In many older neighborhoods throughout Toledo and surrounding areas, sanitary sewer systems are connected with storm systems. Anderzack-Pitzen has the capabilities to remove the old system and install new systems, then install new sidewalks, curbs, and driveways that may have been disrupted during the sewer replacement process.

QUALITY PEOPLE, QUALITY PERFORMANCE

Anderzack-Pitzen is as versatile with its approach to its work as it is in its relationship with employees. As a union contractor, the company employs local union workers and proven professionals affiliated with the Associated General Contractors of Northwest Ohio, Inc. "We hand pick our employees to meet our specific needs," Anderzack says, "and acquire people whose skills are versatile. Our success is determined by the way that we complete a job, and the diverse strengths of our employees are a major part of that."

"We pride ourselves on the expertise of our office and field staff at all levels," adds Pitzen. The firm's expert staff relies on teamwork for getting the job done. Crews work together for safety and production on all projects, with safety ranking as the number-one priority.

Over the years and through many projects, a team of quality people with a track record of top-notch performance has steadily built the company's reputation. Principals Anderzack and Pitzen credit the company's success to its solid reputation in the area. A good working relationship with the communities and companies it works with has created a growing list of excellent

referrals from past clients.

As it continues to be a niche player providing quality performance with quality workers to communities within an approximate 100-mile radius of Toledo, the future of Anderzack-Pitzen is clear. It will continue to support

Toledo's economy by hiring locally, buying locally, and financing locally. "Toledo is on the move," Pitzen says, "and we're going to be part of it. The Toledo area is truly coming of age and Anderzack-Pitzen wants to be in the middle of it all."

CARRYING THROUGH TO COMPLETION ON A TRANSMISSION MAIN AND PUMP STATION, ANDERZACK-PITZEN CREWS PROVED THEIR DILIGENCE AND EXPERTISE. OVER THE YEARS AND THROUGH MANY PROJECTS, A TEAM OF QUALITY PEOPLE WITH A TRACK RECORD OF TOP-NOTCH PERFORMANCE HAS STEADILY BUILT THE COMPANY'S REPUTATION.

ANDERZACK-PITZEN SPECIALIZES IN GRADING, EARTHWORK, UNDERGROUND SEWER AND WATER-LINE UTILITIES, HEAVY HIGHWAYS AND ROADWAYS, STRUCTURAL CONCRETE, BRIDGES AND STRUCTURES, COLD MILLING, ASPHALT AND CONCRETE PAVING, AND BUILDING RENOVATION PROJECTS.

MedCorp, Inc.

F THERE IS AN AMBULANCE RACING DOWN THE STREETS OF TOLEDO WITH ITS LIGHTS FLASHING AND SIRENS WAILING, CHANCES ARE IT'S ONE OF MEDCORP, INC.'S VEHICLES RESPONDING TO AN EMERGENCY. WITH A FLEET OF MORE THAN 100 EMERGENCY MEDICAL SERVICES (EMS) AND TRANSPORT VEHICLES, MEDCORP CURRENTLY SERVICES 80 TO 90 PERCENT OF THE TOLEDO AREA.

MedCorp has more than 350 employees in 13 offices in Ohio, and is considered the largest EMS company in the state.

Owned by Richard and Laurie Bage, MedCorp was founded in 1992 in Toledo. In an effort to further service Toledo and its surrounding areas with his expertise, Richard Bage formed MedCorp. The couple not only brings years of experience to the company, but also a strong commitment to education, quality, service, and a high work ethic—the combination of which has resulted in countless successes for MedCorp.

FOUNDED IN 1992, MEDCORP, INC. IS ONE OF THE AREA'S LEADING SUPPLIERS OF MEDICAL TRANSPORT SERVICE.

STATE-OF-THE-ART EQUIPMENT

With a 1,600 percent growth rate since 1993, MedCorp plans to continue its expansion in Toledo and the surrounding areas. MedCorp currently makes approximately 10,000 patient contacts a month, and with each call its vision is simple: to be the best provider of ambulette, emergency medical, and mobile diagnostic services in Ohio. By providing superior quality, service, and value to its clients, MedCorp's mission is to meet the needs of more and more

communities, as the company continues to expand its growth throughout the state of Ohio.

As the area's leading supplier of medical transport services, MedCorp provides 24-hour-a-day, seven-day-a-week coverage of emergency and nonemergency requests. As first responders to medical emergencies, MedCorp's highly trained EMS crews are able to perform specialized services on the scene and during transport. MedCorp also provides cardiac, ventilator, and neonatal

patients with critical care transportation, as well as nonemergency medical transfers.

MedCorp's vehicles carry the most up-to-date equipment to service those in need. Advance Life Support (ALS) vehicles are staffed by only the most highly trained emergency medical technicians. In addition, MedCorp has a fleet of nonemergency ambulettes, equipped with wheelchair lifts to provide transportation for mobility impaired and special-needs children. In step with the company's

AT MEDCORP HEADQUARTERS COMMUNICATION CENTER, IT PROVIDES SUPERIOR QUALITY, SERVICE, AND VALUE TO ITS CLIENTS (LEFT).

THE MEDCORP EMERGENCY DISPATCH CENTER RECEIVES AN AVERAGE OF 3,000 CALLS EACH DAY (RIGHT).

commitment to quality and service, MedCorp's ambulette drivers are CPR-certified, and the service is approved by Medicaid.

MedCorp's Mobile Diagnostics division provides the community with a broad range of diagnostic services on wheels. Focused primarily on homebound patients and those in extended care facilities, these vehicles are staffed with a registered and certified staff that is able to bring general radiology and ultrasonography, cardiac-related testing and imaging, and Doppler studies right to the patient's door.

Of course, all of these services would not be possible without MedCorp's highly computerized dispatch center, which receives an average of 3,000 calls each day. With seven emergency medical dispatching (EMD)-certified employees on duty at all times, the center is tied to many county 911 systems, which often require the assistance of MedCorp to handle many or most of their service requests. Local citizens and representatives from long-term care facilities, hospitals, and other medical facilities are able to dial directly into MedCorp's dispatch center to request assistance.

WITH A FLEET OF MORE THAN 100 EMERGENCY MEDICAL SERVICES AND TRANSPORT VEHICLES, MEDCORP SERVES 80 TO 90 PERCENT OF THE TOLEDO AREA.

A VITAL COMMUNITY LINK

MedCorp is committed to the community in which it serves not only with top-notch medical transportation and mobile diagnostics, but also with quality employees. Med-Corp works to stay up to date with technology, and provides ongoing, in-house training for its workers. Ambulette drivers are required to have 20 hours of training, as well as first aid and drivers training. EMS technicians are required by the state to take 80 hours of continuing education every three years. New EMS workers go through eight hours of training before setting foot in an ambulance; they must have more than 100 hours of supervised, on-the-job training before they are permitted to go on a call alone. All of this training is provided by MedCorp.

MedCorp also extends its training to the community by providing CPR classes to nurses in long-term-care facilities. In addition, the company sponsors safety days at local schools, complete with ambulance tours and coloring books to familiarize children with its services. MedCorp also staffs the Toledo Zoo's first aid booth each summer, and participates in other programs that offer free transportation for terminally ill patients.

Beyond its medical-related contributions, MedCorp participates in the Toys-4-Tots program, filling up trucks for children in need during the Christmas season. The company also supplies items for food banks and other charitable organizations.

As a Toledo-based business, MedCorp is proud of its ability to offer the same quality care as larger companies, provided by the firm's staff of employees who share a vested interest in their community.

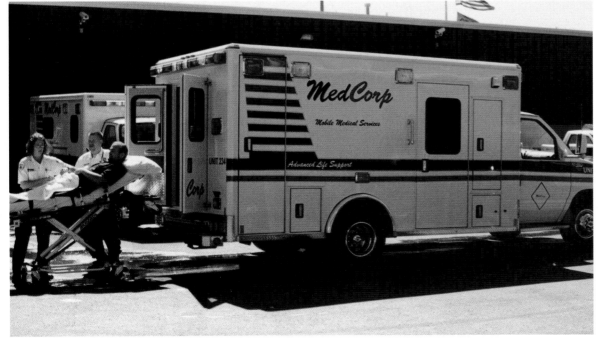

MEDCORP'S MISSION IS TO MEET THE NEEDS OF MORE AND MORE COMMUNITIES, AS THE COMPANY CONTINUES TO EXPAND ITS GROWTH THROUGHOUT THE STATE OF OHIO.

The Clarion Hotel Westgate

WHEN KEN MACLAREN, OWNER OF THE CLARION HOTEL WESTGATE, LEFT THE EDUCATION FIELD IN 1977 TO PURSUE HIS OWN COMMERCIAL REAL ESTATE BUSINESS, HE NEVER IMAGINED HE WOULD BE BUYING A 10-ACRE COMPLEX IN 1993 THAT INCLUDED TWO HOTELS; A 300-car, covered parking garage; and an office building. But, when the property came up for sale, the price was right, and MacLaren saw an opportunity for success.

When MacLaren purchased this complex, he converted one of the hotel buildings—which was built in 1973, and needed some cosmetic and structural attention—into a Clarion Hotel. Today, the Clarion Hotel Westgate is the largest locally owned hotel in the area. The Clarion is also the largest full-service union hotel in Toledo, with the entire food and beverage and housekeeping staff affiliated with the union.

The other hotel on the property was updated by MacLaren as well. The 70-room Secor Inn, as it had been known since it was built in 1986, was renamed Comfort Inn. As a benefit to guests at the Comfort Inn, all amenities at the Clarion are made available for their use, including the pool areas and restaurant.

QUALITY GUARANTEE

The Clarion contains 305 guest rooms, a full-service restaurant, and the Brasserie, the hotel lounge. The hotel has 20,000 square feet of banquet and meeting facilities that focus on the Atrium, a beautiful, open-air space commonly used for receptions and luncheons.

The Atrium and Crystals are only a few of the Clarion's first-class offerings. The hotel staff are so committed to making sure that guests enjoy their stay that they offer a 100 percent money-back guarantee. With safety and security as the staff's principal concern, cleanliness and prompt, courteous customer service are top priorities as well. John Logsdon, general manager, expects his staff to keep these goals in mind at all

THE CLARION HOTEL WESTGATE CONTAINS 305 GUEST ROOMS, A FULL-SERVICE RESTAURANT, AND THE BRASSERIE, THE HOTEL LOUNGE.

times. "We want to be the exemplary hotel in Toledo for service and quality," Logsdon says.

That the Clarion lives up to these expectations is obvious from its busy lobby, which is always bustling with the comings and goings of guests or visitors. Numerous events are held throughout the year in the meeting areas, and wedding receptions and other festivities fill the banquet halls. The Clarion's reputation for a comfortable stay and exemplary service has attracted such notable guests as former President Bill Clinton, Jesse Jackson, and Jamie Farr.

CENTRAL LOCATION

The Clarion's central location is one of the hotel's most appealing attributes. The complex's driveway is only yards away from both east and west access to I-475. With such convenient access to one of Toledo's major thoroughfares, many of the city's attractions are within 10 minutes of the hotel. The University of Toledo, for example, is only two miles away. Downtown is approximately six miles away. And out-of-town travelers will find the Clarion Hotel within 16 miles of the Toledo Express Airport. The hotel even offers a convenient

transportation service to its guests for travel to and from the airport.

Guests can enjoy many leisure activities within walking distance, including a large, six-screen cinema; the Westgate Shopping Center; and nationally known chain and local eateries. Additional restaurants and the Franklin Park Mall, one of Toledo's largest and finest indoor shopping malls, are located within a few miles of the complex.

A NEW ATTITUDE

Although the Clarion Hotel has seen its share of successes, the current management is not content to rest on its laurels. Plans are already under way to implement major cosmetic changes in guest room decor, including the installation of new carpet and the remodeling of the bathrooms.

In an effort to attract a new generation of clients, the marble and brass of the present-day lobby will be replaced with a trendier look. A portion of the Atrium will be con-

verted into a bistro-style restaurant and a gaming area, and the restaurant and lounge will be given a bar-and-grill-type concept. With the new look of the restaurant and lounge areas, the hotel hopes to attract more guests, who will visit the area's attractions and choose to stay at the Clarion during their travels.

MacLaren, as property owner, has new things in store as well. He is currently developing a resort facility at the Legacy Golf Club in Ottawa Lake, Michigan, as well as properties in Sylvania Township and Florida. With these kinds of growth avenues open for exploration, the Clarion Hotel Westgate expects to continue to please its guests and to count on their repeat business.

Buckeye TeleSystem

UCKEYE TELESYSTEM, BUCKEYE CABLESYSTEM'S AFFILIATE COMPANY, PROVIDES LOCAL TOLEDO-AREA BUSINESSES AN ALTERNATIVE CHOICE FOR LOCAL AND LONG-DISTANCE TELECOMMUNICATIONS SERVICES. THANKS TO THE EARLY INTRODUCTION OF FIBER-OPTIC TECHNOLOGY INTO ITS CABLE DISTRIBUTION NETWORK, BUCKEYE

CableSystem has set a firm foundation for Buckeye TeleSystem to utilize its knowledge of and experience with fiber-optic technology to provide the northwest Ohio area with lower-cost telecommunications supported by high-quality service.

TeleSystem's service offerings—which include local phone, long distance, data, and video—are suited for customers ranging from local Fortune 500 companies to education facilities. Government agencies and hospitals also are prime customers for the company's services.

THE HOMETOWN ADVANTAGE

Buckeye TeleSystem is the only locally owned and operated provider of business telecommunications in the Greater Toledo area; therefore, Buckeye TeleSystem is able to serve the area better than its competitors. The company calls this its hometown advantage.

Buckeye TeleSystem has been certified by the Public Utilities Commission of Ohio (PUCO) as a competitive local exchange center (CLEC), so it is able to compete with other, more traditional telecommunications companies. TeleSystem offers com-

petitive pricing and a direct sales staff headquartered locally. Most companies have a tech support center far from customers, but TeleSystem is ready with local representatives who provide solutions tailored to the customer's specific needs.

HIGH STANDARDS FOR CUSTOMER SERVICE

TeleSystem upholds high standards for customer service through effective billing that is timely, accurate, and understandable; customer support by trained experts; responsive repair by locally headquartered field technicians; quality installation with minimal interruption of day-to-day operations; and superior product knowledge. Members of the TeleSystem team work together to establish a personal relationship with each customer the company serves.

This personal relationship is sparked by the consultative sales approach used when meeting with clients. Buckeye TeleSystem understands that customers know better than anyone how their businesses work and what their businesses need to be successful. Therefore, Buckeye TeleSystem provides cus-

tomers with the latest information on telecommunication technology and recommends solutions that best fit the customer's needs, goals, and budget.

Buckeye TeleSystem's advanced network and cutting-edge technology allow the company to provide its customers with one connection for all of the client's telecommunication needs. Once that connection is made, Buckeye TeleSystem takes a proactive approach to system operation by utilizing its network operations center (NOC). This center houses a network monitoring system that operates 24 hours a day, seven days a week. This system is equipped with a fully trained engineering staff, and an uninterruptible power supply that restores power within seconds of an outage and guards against electrical spikes.

Thanks to Buckeye TeleSystem, Toledo is one of the top 25 cities in the country for its telecommunication network capability. "We're doing what everyone else is just talking about," explains Suzanne Garza, supervisor of marketing. And Buckeye TeleSystem is doing it with the support of premier customer service.

BUCKEYE TELESYSTEM'S ADVANCED NETWORK AND CUTTING-EDGE TECHNOLOGY ALLOW THE COMPANY TO PROVIDE ITS CUSTOMERS WITH ONE CONNECTION FOR ALL OF THE CLIENT'S TELECOMMUNICATION NEEDS.

BUCKEYE TELESYSTEM IS THE ONLY LOCALLY OWNED AND OPERATED PROVIDER OF BUSINESS TELECOMMUNICATIONS IN THE GREATER TOLEDO AREA; THEREFORE, BUCKEYE TELESYSTEM IS ABLE TO SERVE THE AREA BETTER THAN ITS COMPETITORS.

Egional Growth Partnership (RGP) is a public/private economic development organization that helps northwest Ohio compete for new business and retain current companies. Since its inception in 1994, the RGP's focus has been the economic development of the counties that

make up the northwest Ohio region. The organization works with area manufacturing, industrial, and technology companies to promote expansion and retention, as well as focusing on attracting new businesses to the area.

The RGP works to promote northwest Ohio's strategic location; efficient, convenient, and effective transportation network; trained workforce; and variety of financing opportunities. It provides various industry-based economic data to interested entities, and acts as a facilitator for new business opportunities by keeping up with information regarding workforce preparedness, technology, and the overall business climate.

The results of the RGP's efforts, in conjunction with its regional partners, are visible in the success it has achieved. Within its first six years, the organization and its partners have created 27,029 new jobs, retained 44,754 jobs, and generated approximately $8.4 billion in new capital investments for northwest Ohio. Recently, in recognition of its efforts to boost international trade, the RGP received the Governor's Excellence in Exporting Award, or Governor's E Award.

COMMUNITIES WORKING TOGETHER

Northwest Ohio has become a dominant global player, efficiently working as a powerful alliance of 11 counties. The Northwest Ohio Regional Economic Development (NORED) association is made up of regional development experts and representatives of each county, local governments, and area businesses.

Members of NORED work with RGP for the benefit of all of northwest Ohio, with the common goal

of boosting business activity in the region. This is accomplished through joint efforts in trade shows and advertising; a big-picture view of economic development and legislation; and a shared, comprehensive database with information on industrial sites and buildings, demographics, and economic information for the entire region.

A NETWORK OF FUNDING PARTNERS

The RGP acts as a facilitator for a variety of services, including low-interest loans and other creative financing alternatives and incentives, grant writing, marketing support, and legislative advocacy. For companies interested in expanding into northwest Ohio, the RGP is a one-stop shop for site selection needs. By bringing the necessary resources together, the RGP offers these companies significant savings of time and a staff with more than 130 years' combined professional experience in the economic development field.

The RGP's partners include the Toledo-Lucas County Port Authority, Toledo Area Chamber of Commerce, Associated General Contractors (AGC) of Northwest Ohio, NORED, Regional

Technology Alliance (RTA), and Northwest Ohio Mayors and Managers Association (NOMMA).

The future for northwest Ohio is full of possibilities. The Regional Growth Partnership will continue to work toward its mission: to be globally recognized as a leading region for high-performance manufacturing and business development with sustained growth in employment, income, and tax base. This will be accomplished through training the region's workforce in technology, according to the latest industry trends, and continuing to push international trade as an increasingly important factor in northwest Ohio's economic future.

REGIONAL GROWTH PARTNERSHIP, A PUBLIC/ PRIVATE ECONOMIC DEVELOPMENT ORGANIZATION, WORKS WITH AREA MANUFACTURING, INDUSTRIAL, AND TECHNOLOGY COMPANIES TO PROMOTE EXPANSION AND RETENTION, AND TO ATTRACT NEW BUSINESSES TO THE AREA.

LLTEL IS ONE OF THE NATION'S LEADING TELECOMMUNICATIONS AND INFORMATION SERVICES COMPANIES, SERVING MORE THAN 10 MILLION COMMUNICATIONS CUSTOMERS IN 24 STATES, AND PROVIDING INFORMATION SERVICES TO TELECOMMUNICATIONS, FINANCIAL, AND MORTGAGE

clients in 55 countries and territories.

In recent years, ALLTEL has participated in a series of major acquisitions and a revolutionary integration of its wireless and wire line operations, creating the nation's sixth-largest wireless communications company and sixth-largest local telephone company. ALLTEL has annual revenues in excess of $7 billion.

A FULL-SERVICE PROVIDER

LLTEL is a national leader in providing customers with bundled communications services, including local telephone, wireless, long-distance, paging, and Internet access. The company has successfully implemented a strategy of combining the scale and presence of a large telecommunications provider with newly deployed digital technology, capable of serving a customer's complete communications needs. For example, ALLTEL has used its wireless presence to launch competitive local telephone service in more than 40 cities nationally, including Toledo.

As an integrated communications provider, ALLTEL is in a position of immense competitive strength. In addition to providing bundled services to geographically clustered markets, the company has a roaming partnership that has created the nation's largest standardized digital wireless network, covering 95 percent of the United States' population.

ALLTEL INFORMATION SERVICES

key to ALLTEL's bundled communications strategy is its billing system, which allows the company to deliver multiple service charges on a single bill. This billing system, Virtuoso II, was developed by ALLTEL Information Services, the company's information technology business unit.

In addition to serving the telecommunications industry, ALLTEL Information Services serves financial and mortgage clients in 55 countries and territories, including 48 of the top 50 U.S. banks. ALLTEL provides loan-servicing automation for more than 20 million mortgage loans, with balances exceeding $2 trillion. Additionally, more than 34 percent of the total dollar volume of outstanding U.S. consumer loans, including mortgages, is processed on ALLTEL Information Services' software.

In 2001, ALLTEL Information Services announced it would provide data processing services for Ford Financial's 8 million North American loan/lease accounts, strengthening ALLTEL's position as a worldwide leader in lending automation. The two companies had worked together for two years to develop and implement a model automotive receivables financial lease and lending system.

ROOTED IN INNOVATION

LLTEL can trace some of its corporate roots back to five small Ohio telephone companies, which came together as part of Mid-Continent Telephone Corp. of Hudson, Ohio, in 1960. Mid-Continent founder Weldon Case, who began his career at Hudson-based Western Reserve Telephone Co., shaped Mid-Continent into one of the largest independent telephone companies in the country.

In 1983, Mid-Continent merged with Allied Telephone Co. of Little Rock to form ALLTEL, which is today headquartered in Little Rock. Following the merger, Case served as ALLTEL's chairman until he retired in 1991.

In 1998, ALLTEL completed its largest acquisition to date with the purchase of 360° Communications,

ALLTEL IS A CUSTOMER-FOCUSED COMPANY DEDICATED TO PROVIDING HIGH-QUALITY, STATE-OF-THE-ART TECHNOLOGY AND SERVICES TO MEET CUSTOMERS' INDIVIDUAL NEEDS AND LIFESTYLES.

which included the Toledo wireless market. As a result of the $6 billion merger, ALLTEL gained 2.6 million wireless customers in 15 states. ALLTEL continued its expansion in 2000 by entering new markets such as Phoenix, Tampa, and Cleveland, increasing its wireless customer base by more than 15 percent through a wireless property exchange with Bell Atlantic and GTE.

COMMITMENT TO SERVICE AND TECHNOLOGY

ALLTEL is a customer-focused company dedicated to providing high-quality, state-of-the-art technology and services to meet customers' individual needs and lifestyles.

In Toledo, ALLTEL has a call center that is open around the clock to simplify the lives of the company's more than 720,000 customers. The ALLTEL center has been recognized for excellent customer service. In fact, in a 2000 year-end customer satisfaction survey, the center scored the highest marks in categories that included helpful representatives and representative knowledge.

Commitment to technology is also a focus for ALLTEL. In the wireless industry, the company has upgraded from analog to digital technology. In Toledo, ALLTEL uses code division multiple access (CDMA) wireless technology. The firm is on the cutting edge of the convergence of Internet and wireless applications;

ALLTEL now sells many wireless digital phones that are manufactured with built-in Web browsers so that wireless customers can navigate the Internet with ALLTEL's Web-Unwired product.

COMMITMENT TO TOLEDO

ALLTEL prides itself on playing an active role in supporting the Toledo community through various sponsorships and support of philanthropic efforts. For example, the company plays an important role in the Jamie Farr Kroger Classic LPGA Tournament, which raises funds for numerous northwest Ohio children's charities. From 1985 to 2000, the tournament generated $3.2 million for more

than 50 local children's charities.

Additional community support is provided by ALLTEL's Toledo employees, who participate in the March of Dimes and Toledo Humane Society yearly walkathons, and through corporate sponsorships to various sports programs at the University of Toledo.

ALLTEL plans to continue its tradition of excellence in technology, customer service, and community involvement. With rapid changes in technology, the company will continually search for new ways to simplify the lives of its customers. In addition, ALLTEL will remain a good corporate citizen by seeking opportunities to give back to the communities it serves.

ALLTEL HAS USED ITS WIRELESS PRESENCE TO LAUNCH COMPETITIVE LOCAL TELEPHONE SERVICE IN MORE THAN 40 CITIES NATIONALLY, INCLUDING TOLEDO.

ALLTEL NOW SELLS MANY WIRELESS DIGITAL PHONES THAT ARE MANUFACTURED WITH BUILT-IN WEB BROWSERS SO THAT WIRELESS CUSTOMERS CAN NAVIGATE THE INTERNET WITH ALLTEL'S WEB-UNWIRED PRODUCT.

Towery Publishing, Inc.

BEGINNING AS A SMALL PUBLISHER OF LOCAL NEWSPAPERS IN 1935, TOWERY PUBLISHING, INC. TODAY HAS BECOME A GLOBAL PUBLISHER OF A DIVERSE RANGE OF COMMUNITY-BASED MATERIALS FROM SAN DIEGO TO SYDNEY. ITS PRODUCTS— SUCH AS THE COMPANY'S AWARD-WINNING URBAN TAPESTRY SERIES, BUSINESS

directories, magazines, and Internet sites—continue to build on Towery's distinguished heritage of excellence, making its name synonymous with service, utility, and quality.

COMMUNITY PUBLISHING AT ITS BEST

Towery Publishing has long been the industry leader in community-based publications. In 1972, current President and CEO J. Robert Towery succeeded his parents in managing the printing and publishing business they had founded four decades earlier. "One of the more impressive traits of my family's publishing business was its dedication to presenting only the highest-quality products available— whatever our market might be," says Towery. "Since taking over the company, I've continued our fight for the high ground in maintaining this tradition."

During the 1970s and 1980s, Towery expanded the scope of the company's published materials to include *Memphis* magazine and other successful regional and national publications, such as *Memphis Shopper's Guide*, *Racquetball* magazine, *Huddle/FastBreak*, *Real Estate News*, and *Satellite Dish* magazine. In 1985, after selling its locally focused assets, the company began the trajectory on which it continues today, creating community-oriented materials that are often produced in conjunction with chambers of commerce and other business organizations.

All of Towery Publishing's efforts, represented on the Internet at www.towery.com, are marked by a careful, innovative design phi-losophy that has become a hallmark of the company's reputation for quality and service. Boasting a nationwide sales force, proven editorial depth, cutting-edge graphics capabilities, ample marketing resources, and extensive data management expertise, the company has assembled the intellectual and capital resources necessary to produce quality products and services.

URBAN TAPESTRY SERIES

Towery Publishing launched its popular Urban Tapestry Series in 1990. Each of the nearly 100 oversized, hardbound photojournals details the people, history, culture, environment, and commerce of a featured metropolitan area. These colorful coffee-table books spotlight communities through an introductory essay authored by a noted local individual, an exquisite collection of photographs, and in-depth profiles of select companies and organizations that form each area's business core.

From New York to Vancouver to Los Angeles, national and international authors have graced the pages of the books' introductory essays. The celebrated list of contributors includes two former U.S. presidents— Gerald Ford (Grand Rapids) and Jimmy Carter (Atlanta); boxing great Muhammad Ali (Louisville); two network newscasters—CBS anchor Dan Rather (Austin) and ABC anchor Hugh Downs (Phoenix); NBC sportscaster Bob Costas (St. Louis); record-breaking quarterback Steve Young (San Francisco); best-selling mystery author Robert B. Parker (Boston); American Movie Classics host Nick Clooney (Cincinnati); former Texas first lady Nellie Connally (Houston); and former New York City Mayor Ed Koch (New York).

While the books have been enor-

TOWERY PUBLISHING PRESIDENT AND CEO J. ROBERT TOWERY HAS EXPANDED THE BUSINESS HIS PARENTS STARTED IN THE 1930S TO INCLUDE A GROWING ARRAY OF TRADITIONAL AND ELECTRONIC PUBLISHED MATERIALS, AS WELL AS INTERNET AND MULTIMEDIA SERVICES, THAT ARE MARKETED LOCALLY, NATIONALLY, AND INTERNATIONALLY.

mously successful, the company continues to improve and redefine the role the series plays in the marketplace. "Currently, the Urban Tapestry Series works beautifully as a tool for enhancing the image of the communities it portrays," says Towery. "As the series continues to mature, we want it to become a reference source that businesses and executives turn to when evaluating the quality of life in cities where they may be considering moving or expanding."

CHAMBERS OF COMMERCE TURN TO TOWERY

In addition to its Urban Tapestry Series, Towery Publishing has become the largest producer of published and Internet materials for North American chambers of commerce. From published membership directories and Internet listings that enhance business-to-business communication, to visitor and relocation guides tailored to reflect the unique qualities of the communities they cover, the company's chamber-oriented materials offer comprehensive information on dozens of topics, including housing, education, leisure activities, health care, and local government.

The company's primary Internet product consists of its introCity™ sites. Much like its published materials, Towery's introCity sites introduce newcomers, visitors, and longtime residents to every facet of a particular community, while simultaneously placing the local chamber of commerce at the forefront of the city's Internet activity. The sites provide newcomer information including calendars, photos, citywide business listings with everything from nightlife to shopping to family fun, and online maps pinpointing the exact location of businesses, schools, attractions, and much more.

SUSTAINED CREATIVITY

The driving forces behind Towery Publishing have always been the company's employees and its state-of-the-art industry technology. Many of its employees have worked with the Towery family of companies for more than 20 years. Today's staff of seasoned innovators totals around 100 at the Memphis headquarters, and more than 40 sales, marketing, and editorial staff traveling to and working in an ever growing list of cities.

Supporting the staff's endeavors is state-of-the-art prepress publishing software and equipment. Towery Publishing was the first production environment in the United States to combine desktop publishing with color separations and image scanning to produce finished film suit-

able for burning plates for four-color printing. Today, the company relies on its digital prepress services to produce more than 8,000 pages each year, containing more than 30,000 high-quality color images.

Through decades of business and technological change, one aspect of Towery Publishing has remained constant. "The creative energies of our staff drive us toward innovation and invention," Towery says. "Our people make the highest possible demands on themselves, so I know that our future is secure if the ingredients for success remain a focus on service and quality."

TOWERY PUBLISHING WAS THE FIRST PRODUCTION ENVIRONMENT IN THE UNITED STATES TO COMBINE DESKTOP PUBLISHING WITH COLOR SEPARATIONS AND IMAGE SCANNING TO PRODUCE FINISHED FILM SUITABLE FOR BURNING PLATES FOR FOUR-COLOR PRINTING. TODAY, THE COMPANY'S STATE-OF-THE-ART NETWORK OF MACINTOSH AND WINDOWS WORKSTATIONS ALLOWS IT TO PRODUCE MORE THAN 8,000 PAGES EACH YEAR, CONTAINING MORE THAN 30,000 HIGH-QUALITY COLOR IMAGES.

THE TOWERY FAMILY'S PUBLISHING ROOTS CAN BE TRACED TO 1935, WHEN R.W. TOWERY (FAR LEFT) BEGAN PRODUCING A SERIES OF COMMUNITY HISTORIES IN TENNESSEE, MISSISSIPPI, AND TEXAS. THROUGHOUT THE COMPANY'S HISTORY, THE FOUNDING FAMILY HAS CONSISTENTLY EXHIBITED A COMMITMENT TO CLARITY, PRECISION, INNOVATION, AND VISION.

PHOTOGRAPHERS

A Columbus, Ohio, native, **Rod Berry** owns and operates Rod Berry Photography, a stock agency covering a range of subjects from landscape to recreational activities. He works on freelance assignments and fine art photography, and his images have appeared in several galleries throughout the Midwest.

Self-employed at InCamera Studio in Perrysburg, **David M. Bewley** specializes in advertising, editorial, people, portrait, and forensic photography. His clients include FirstEnergy Corp., Toledo Edison Company, Venzel Communications, Techneglas Corp., Koontz-Wagner Electric Co., and McHugh & McCarthy, and he has received fine arts awards from the Toledo Area Artists' Show.

Roger Bickel is a Bingham Farms, Michigan, photographer who specializes in travel and nature stock photography. His images have appeared in *National Geographic Traveler, Better Homes and Gardens, Yankee* magazine, *Woman's World*, and Delta Airlines' *Sky*, as well as in books produced by Houghton Mifflin, Harcourt Brace, Barnes & Noble, Insight Guides, Children's Press, and Towery Publishing.

Employed by Shoot For The Moon and specializing in corporate and commercial photography, **Karen Bowers** has won numerous Crystal Awards from Women in Communication; an Award of Excellence from Consolidated Papers, Inc.; an Excellence in Media Award from the Toledo Press Club; and a Citation of Excellence from Advertising Club of Toledo. Her clients include the Toledo Symphony Orchestra, Figg Engineering Group, ProMedica, Swan Creek Candle Co., Toledo Public Schools, Toledo Community Foundation, and Toledo Museum of Art.

Originally from Toledo, **Jinnie Corthell** works for Moto Photo and specializes in scenic and children photography. Several of her photos appear in the 1995 directory of Holy Angels Church in Sandusky, and one client redecorated an entire room to complement one of her images.

Originally from Chicago, **Brad Crooks** specializes in travel pho-

tography and owns B. W. Crooks Photographics.

The Image Finders, founded by Jim Baron in 1986, is a stock photography company located in Cleveland, Ohio. Its files cover a broad range of subjects, including agriculture, animals, butterflies, families, food, sports, transportation, travel, trees, and the western United States.

A 12-year-old visual communications firm, **Image Source, Inc.** has local, national, and international clients such as General Motors, Dana Corporation, Toledo Hospital, and the Toledo Museum of Art. With a 6,000-square-foot studio complete with conventional and digital photographic capabilities, the firm allows clients to use its images for brochures, displays, newsletters, Web sites, multimedia projects, and annual reports.

Megan Jankowski, a Toledo native, is currently enrolled at Ohio University, studying photojournalism.

An award-winning amateur photographer from Grimes, Iowa, **John Jentsch** specializes in city, people, and travel photography. His most recent assignments have taken him from the Indiana Sand Caves of northeast Iowa to the Badlands of South Dakota.

Dave Lehman, owner of Lehman & Co., specializes in corporate, commercial, and advertising photography. His images have earned local and regional ADDY awards and various national print awards, and have appeared in print design publications.

A photographer for the Toledo Zoo and the Greater Toledo Convention and Visitors Bureau, **Linda S. Milks** also photographs for charity organizations. Her images have appeared on the covers of several visitors'

and zoo guides, as well as *Talk of the Town.*

Laurie Mullen, a student at the University of Northern Iowa, has had images published in magazines and several Towery publications. A recipient of the photography award from Finest in the Nation for Education Foundation, she has photographed in the boundary waters of Canada, Mexico, Costa Rica, and France.

Photographer, filmmaker, designer, and owner of Filmwerks Studio, **Mark Packo** studied graphic design at Pratt Institute in Brooklyn and taught typographic design at Parson's School of Design in New York City. His print and still photography has been featured in numerous publications, and his PBS documentary *Air Force One: The Planes & the Presidents* earned an Emmy nomination.

Judi Parks is an award-winning photojournalist living and working in the San Francisco Bay Area. Her work has been collected by museums and public collections in the United States and Europe, and her documentary series, *Home Sweet Home: Caring for America's Elderly*, was recently honored with the *Communication Arts-Design Annual 1999* Award of Excellence for an unpublished series. Her images have appeared in numerous Towery publications.

A fine art photographer working primarily in black and white, **Mary Pencheff** has exhibited her work extensively in galleries throughout the United States and in solo and group exhibitions. Both her corporate and fine art photographs have received numerous awards locally as well as nationally, and have appeared in books, journals, calendars, magazines, and greeting cards, as well as in dozens of corporate publications.

A student at the University of Toledo, **Ralph Ramirez III** owns Breaking the Mold Photography and also teaches music and kung fu.

Specializing in color and black-and-white portrait, wedding, and family photography, **Melanie Reichart** owns Melanie Reichart Photography and has had images published in several magazines. Her awards include the International Award of Merit with the Professional Photographers of America and a Court of Honor award from the Professional Photographers of Ohio for portrait prints.

Curtis B. Stahr has photographed the migration of the American eagle from Alaska to Florida, as well as nearly 20 national parks and monuments and all 99 Iowa courthouses. He has walked with his camera across Canada from ocean to ocean and photographed life in each of the contiguous United States. He has exhibited in 32 juried/invitational art shows and 16 one-man shows, received 11 purchase awards, and is listed in *American Artists of Renown.*

Focusing on people and still-life color photography, **Lori Wozniak** has won several awards throughout her career, and has participated in art exhibitions around the country.

Originally from Wisconsin, **Eric Wunrow** specializes in photography, graphic design, landscapes, and wilderness sports. His images have sold worldwide in publishing and advertising media, often including text and graphics or illustrations of his own design, and he has explored 80 of the United States' highest mountains. His first coffee-table book, *Mountains of Colorado*, documents 150,000 vertical feet of his trekking.

Other contributing photographers and organizations include **Craig Bell/Bowling Green State University, Dean Hoard, Jamie Farr Kroger Classic**, and **Toledo Mud Hens Baseball**. For further information about the photographers appearing in *Toledo: Treasures and Traditions*, please contact Towery Publishing.

LIBRARY OF CONGRESS CATALOGING-IN-PUBLICATION DATA

Toledo : treasures and traditions / introduction by Jamie Farr ; art direction by Karen Geary.
    p. cm. — (Urban tapestry series)
  Includes index.
  ISBN 1-881096-99-8 (alk. paper)
   1. Toledo (Ohio)—Civilization. 2. Toledo (Ohio)—Pictorial works. 3. Toledo
(Ohio)—Economic conditions. 4. Business enterprises—Ohio—Toledo. I. Farr, Jamie,
1934– II. Geary, Karen, 1953– III. Series.

F499.T6 T625 2001
977.1'13—dc21

                                                                    2001043077

Printed in Mexico

Copyright © 2001 by Towery Publishing, Inc.

TOWERY PUBLISHING, INC.

THE TOWERY BUILDING , 1835 UNION AVENUE, MEMPHIS, TN 38104

WWW.TOWERY.COM

Publisher: J. Robert Towery **Executive Publisher:** Jenny McDowell
Marketing Director: Carol Culpepper **Sales Manager:** Dawn Park-
Donegan **Project Directors:** Carl Orban, Jeanne Schedel, Jim Tomlinson
Executive Editor: David B. Dawson **Managing Editor:** Lynn Conlee
Senior Editors: Carlisle Hacker, Brian L. Johnston **Project Editor/
Caption Writer:** Stephen M. Deusner **Editor/Profile Manager:** Ginny
Reeves **Editors:** Jay Adkins, Rebecca E. Farabough, Danna M. Greenfield,
Sabrina Schroeder **Profile Writer:** Amy E. Rowe **Creative Director:**
Brian Groppe **Photography Editor:** Jonathan Postal **Photographic
Consultant:** Kim NaVarre **Production Manager:** Laurie Beck **Profile
Designers:** Rebekah Barnhardt, Glen Marshall **Photography Coordi-
nator:** Robin Lankford **Production Assistants:** Robert Parrish **Digital
Color Supervisor:** Darin Ipema **Digital Color Technicians:** Eric
Friedl, Mark Svetz **Digital Scanning Technician:** Brad Long **Print
Coordinator:** Beverly Timmons

INDEX OF PROFILES